RONALD REAGAN'S CRUSADE

Norman Wymbs

VYTIS Publishing Company, Inc.
Ft. Lauderdale, FL

RONALD REAGAN'S CRUSADE

LCCC 95-061103
ISBN 0-9645786-1-1

VYTIS Publishing Company, Inc.
Ft. Lauderdale, FL
(954) 772-1236

Printed in the United States of America

First Edition - March 1996
2 3 4 5 6 7 8 9 10

(Ordering information at the back of the book)

TO HARRIET,
WITHOUT WHOM
THERE IS NOTHING

RONALD REAGAN'S CRUSADE

CONTENTS

----

* * * * *

PREFACE

History, the art and profession as practiced by historians, is the recounting of events past with an attempt at gaining insight on events present. Hopefully, this enlightens us as to why we are where we are and what we are.

News, as practiced by reporters, both print and electronic, is the art of documenting events present so we and future historians will understand where we think we are going.

Growing out of the great body of news reporting is the sometimes clairvoyant, but often hokey, art of commentary. The media stars of our world, televised or syndicated in writing, are the chroniclers who combine history and news to project the future. Unfortunately, many of these modern day commentators have their own agenda that warps their projections to fit desired goals.

Future students of our times will draw their conclusions based upon their talent at sifting through frequently-varying news accounts and heavily opinionated commentary to arrive at a factual history. Fortunately those future historians will have the advantage of being able to pursue their task without the burden of being emotionally involved with the subjects of the times they are studying.

History, as chronicled fifty or one hundred years from now, will be able to clear away much of the distortion we experience today. Just as today's researchers give us a less-biased picture of Lincoln and Washington, latter-day historians will give a clearer view of Ronald Reagan and other contemporary figures.

Just as today's students of history have far more material to study on Lincoln than they have on the more distant Washington, tomorrow's analysts will have an even greater trove to pour over concerning Ronald Reagan. The final judgement on Reagan, the President and world leader, will come well beyond these years. That is not to say, however, that we are not now to be subjected to volume after volume of analytical "history" of the Reagan years.

Our free enterprise system, focused as it is on every conceivable commercial opportunity, cannot ignore the potential presented by even a quietly-retired Ronald Reagan. Arguably one of the most popular United States Presidents in our history, few will question that he was certainly the most media-friendly of all time. Whether supportive or non-supportive, the media never tired of picturing, writing and talking about Ronald Reagan. With his retirement, many of those who had made a good living pounding their word processors in passion over every Reagan move suddenly found themselves struggling to maintain the flow with far less interesting subject matter. What would be more natural than these commentators' capitalizing on the residual popularity of the man and becoming instant historians and couch psychoanalysts to let us all see the "real" Ronald Reagan?

Unfortunately, for the task of future scholars pouring through all this material, much of what appears at this stage will range from innovative fiction to misguided speculation. I remember, several years ago, talking with a world renowned Lincoln scholar about this problem. He pointed out that, at that time, he knew of over 12,000 individual volumes of biography on Abraham Lincoln. Each of those authors, of course, stoutly maintained they had been factual and dispassionate in their chronicles. Lincoln would have had to lead an active life of over 750 years to have done all the things attributed to him in those volumes! A tedious task awaits historians of the future who wish to pluck from the thousands of accumulated pages of print a picture of the real Ronald Reagan!

Already this phenomenon is manifesting itself as writers rush to get on paper their insight on Reagan. As is to be expected, just as in prior publications on prominent public figures, the earliest to hit the commercial markets come from those who, for one reason or another, were in personal contact with the individual. It also follows that these writers approach their tasks with already strongly-formed opinions about their subject. Such biographies can seldom be accepted as factual historical accounts because of the bias of the philosophy of the chronicler.

It appears to be the nature of the public to be drawn more to the sensational claptrap poured out by the supermarket tabloids than to the more staid and factual reporting common to most news journals. Although learned minds keep probing this tendency, seeking deep meaning in the public thirst for sensationalism with little success, we need only note that it seemingly always exists. It is not unexpected, therefore, that a second-rate work of fiction masquerading as biography, such as produced by a Kitty Kelly, would attract more readers than a scholarly study by a legitimate biographer. Most readers, being reasonable people, after the initial titillation, brush off these fish wrappers for the cheap fiction they truly are. For current readers, as well as future serious historians, the problem lies more with writers who hide their fiction amidst a torrent of apparently irrefutable facts, making it doubly difficult to glean the truth.

Ronald Reagan, who most would agree is one of the most personally likeable individuals you could ever meet, presents a most difficult problem for many writers. While disagreeing strongly with his philosophy of life and governing, they find it hard to attack those beliefs without letting their personal affection for the man be distorted. This sometimes causes commentators to use unusual extremes to find explanations for their strong differences in philosophy.

In a recent volume, Lou Cannon, a former White House correspondent for the *Washington Post*, resorts to some far-out psychological analysis in an attempt to justify his critique of Ronald Reagan. Obviously torn by his personal liking for the former President and his own lifelong indoctrination into a liberal political philosophy contrary to Reagan's, Cannon ends up falling off his couch. Using a theme common to other writers about Reagan, he dwells heavily on the supposed alcoholism of Reagan's father. Expounding upon this theory, he quotes lengthily from obscure "experts" to justify his conclusion that all of Ronald Reagan's "wrong" political philosophy is common to disturbed children of alcoholics! His reasoning falls apart, however, when he justifies his expertise on children of alcoholic parents by proudly proclaiming that he is the son of an alcoholic! Unexplained in this murky venture into analysis is how his alcoholic background leads him into a "correct" political philosophy, while Reagan's supposedly similar background leads him astray!

In a similar vein, other writers find outside influences of an even more bizarre nature to explain Ronald Reagan's deviation from what they consider a "normal" or proper approach to governing.

Author Gary Wills, in an early biography on Ronald Reagan, avoids the creative fiction exhibited by Lou Cannon by resorting to that master story teller, Mark Twain. In his convoluted attempt to explain Reagan's improper stand on matters of world import, he blames it on the influence of Huckleberry Finn! Somehow, in his book he manages to leave us with the impression that Ronald Reagan is as fictitious a creation as one of Twain's characters. In his rambling analysis, the Mississippi River somehow comes into play (although that mighty river flows a long way away from where Reagan grew up) leaving the reader floundering in the shallows after wading through his dissertation!

Is it really necessary to reach so far out to understand Ronald Reagan? Everyone who has had any contact with the former President recognizes his strong and appealing personality. The strength of will and singleness of purpose in the man do frequently seem alien to the warmth and compassion he radiates. But, are these characteristics necessarily incompatible? Having delved into Ronald Reagan's roots for the past ten years, particularly his parents and their community life, the picture makes sense. Emerging from this study is a remarkably complex, but uncomplicated, individual. If you were to take all the average American citizens, mold them into one individual, and then give that person the remarkable talent to express himself so we all clearly understand his message, you would have Ronald Reagan!

INTRODUCTION

In 1980, when Ronald Reagan won the nomination for the U.S. Presidency from the Republican Party, his enthusiastic partisans showed little doubt they really understood their charismatic candidate. His campaign speeches, and every other public expression, struck them as clear and understandable, leaving no question as to his position on every political issue. His opposition, every bit as fervent and positive as his supporters, were just as sure there was nothing there, and they showed real puzzlement over his appeal. Reagan, in the opinion of both sides, was not a complex man. He appeared so uncomplicated, in fact, that few who met or heard him could retain any pretense of neutrality. With Ronald Reagan, the American people did not have to strain their intellects; it was an instant love or hate reaction!

Although he had served two reasonably successful terms as governor of California, little was known nationally of his accomplishments or failures in leading that giant state government. In addition, his strong support of the unsuccessful Goldwater campaign for the Presidency, as well as his own personal losing effort to wrest the GOP Presidential nomination from Gerald Ford in 1976, left no lasting impression as to his qualifications to lead the country.

Politically murky though he may have been to most observers before his later successful campaigns, there was one facet of his background which everyone felt fully qualified to evaluate: his career in Hollywood. Even casual followers of the glamorous motion picture industry were well aware of the handsome young man who appeared in so many glitzy, if unremarkable, offerings of the movie capital of the world. Of the dozens of eminently forgettable motion pictures featuring Ronald Reagan, a few did stand out sufficiently to etch an image of the star on the public consciousness.

One of those performances, his portrayal of the dying University of Notre Dame football hero, George Gipp, had such an impact on his audiences that it created a public persona that has lasted through Ronald Reagan's life. Even though his detractors have tried for years to tie him to less-sympathetic characters in his old movies, the public still retains the positive image of young Ronald in that Notre Dame classic. Long outlasting that old movie or its maudlin story line is Reagan's fondly used nickname, the "Gipper". From the make-believe role came a full-blown American hero!

In 1965, when Reagan published a biography of sorts entitled "Where's the Rest of Me?", the political movers and shakers guiding him towards the national scene knew the motion picture mystique was his most telling asset. Even the title, taken from one of his more memorable pictures, was calculated to attract readers who normally would not stretch their intellects beyond the weekend movie reviews. The book, taking advantage of this attraction, dwelt heavily on reviews of many of Ronald Reagan's Hollywood productions. In a work obviously produced to promote a public political career heretofore limited to parochial battles in the Screen Actor's Guild, why all the emphasis on the make-believe world of moviedom?

For today's generation too young to remember the heyday of the motion picture industry, it's probably hard to understand the deep and pervasive influence that the entertainment medium had on the country. Although today's generation shows some of the same influence through its adulation of current rock music and television sitcom stars, it doesn't compare with the fanatical devotion its elders showed for earlier movie kings and queens. Latter-day performers have not had the durability of those darlings of the older generation. Today, a media star is lucky to last in the limelight for a year or two, seldom for more than three years. Certainly, none of today's crop can show the lasting ability of a John Wayne or a Greta Garbo!

Ronald Reagan, with impossibly handsome "boy next door" good looks, hit the Hollywood movie scene at the right time. In the 1930's and '40's the major motion picture studios developed "stables" of stars. With the public exhibiting a nearly insatiable appetite for their productions, the popular stars were literally worth their weight in gold. Anyone with talent or good looks who photographed well was locked into a studio performance contract stronger than any document since the early bills of sale for the African slaves shipped to our shores centuries ago. These indentures not only limited public performances by their glamorous employees, but also dictated their private lives.

Ronald Reagan, young, handsome and personable, fit the mold and was quickly taken into studio bondage.

The contracting studios determined the type of character each star was suited to and closely limited stars on the roles they were allowed to play. No performer was ever allowed to appear in a role the studio had not first determined was in the company's best interests. To enhance and reinforce the desired image, the studio promotion departments cranked out volumes of publicity concerning the "private" lives of their stars. Although largely fictional, the public consumed every little detail poured out by the studio flacks. During those heady years, movie magazines and newspaper gossip columns concerning the stars were among the country's most popular publications. Fan clubs devoted to the following and adoration of their members' favorite motion picture performers sprang up around the country. The popular stars and premium money makers for their studios, like John Wayne, always the good guy hero in his movies, received reams of publicity about his real life good-guy(ism).

Swashbucklers like Errol Flynn got their share of raucous "real life" stories. A Marilyn Monroe, always the seductress on celluloid, was not allowed to look anything but sexy in public. Ronald Reagan got his share of star worship; his very active fan club flooded the movie magazines' regular popularity ballots with votes for their hero. The devotion of these thousands of ardent fans kept him on the list of the top ten most popular movie stars in the nation!

We, the public, wanted what the movie publicity departments fed us. We insisted our fictional heroes be real-life heroes as well. We couldn't have survived the shock if steely-eyed "Duke" Wayne, facing down those unkempt vicious cattle rustlers on the giant screen, had turned out to be a meek wimp in real life! Think of how many male fantasies would have been destroyed had we learned that Marilyn was really a simple girl-next-door type, instead of the vampy seductress we had been sold! Woe be it to anyone under contract to a studio who attempted to display a public life not in keeping with the story line laid down by the purveyors of our fantasies!

Ronald Reagan was a motion picture publicity department's dream. When they stereotyped him into the "All-American Boy" category, he slipped neatly into place. With his forever-boyish good looks, manly body and charming smile, they did not have to think twice about his place in the scheme of things Hollywood. Never did Reagan's personal life or public appearances outside the studio in those early days deviate in the slightest from the ordained image.

Although he was not a world class performer in the narrow range permitted by the studio, his physical presence and quickness in memorizing and understanding a part moved him well up the ladder in a motion picture industry loaded with outstanding stars. It wasn't until Ronald Reagan had become thoroughly established in his performing niche and, most importantly, had a lucrative employment contract, that his real character began to shine through the shallow studio publicity image.

Possessed of a fierce patriotism typical of his small town schooling and family life, Reagan was anxious to move into the thick of the World War II fight for his country. He was to be thwarted to a degree in that area, however, when his miserable eyesight kept him from active military duty. The armed services were just as happy, though, since they needed and used actors and performers to promote recruiting, training and War Bond sales. Ronald served well in this capacity, not only helping the war effort, but also expanding his already well-established sense of the "righteousness" of his country.

Back from the military after the war was over, Ronald Reagan, like most veterans, was primarily interested in getting on with his interrupted civil life. In this respect he was in better shape than most, since he was still under a lucrative contract with the Hollywood movie studio that built his career before the war. He was relieved of the burden many veterans had in finding a career after the war, and another fortunate happenstance gave him more room to branch out. The studios, although anxious to plunge back into production after the restrictions and lack of personnel during wartime, found themselves suffering from a surplus of performers to merchandise. Many of their returning stars, like Reagan, found themselves with time on their hands as they waited in line for the studios to schedule them into a new production.

Ronald Reagan, at his physical and mental peak, with a substantial income and lots of free time, launched himself into "causes". Later in this narrative we'll see how this characteristic was a carry-over from an extremely socially active mother and a politically aware father. Still carrying the concern, shared by many fellow returnees, that his country not make the same mistakes again, he became active in veterans' affairs. A natural at public speaking, with a sometimes quirky sense of humor, he quickly became a popular speaker at many veterans' meetings. Although at first he hit heavily on the theme of protecting the country against further attacks from fascist aggressors, he didn't begin to gain widespread attention until he expanded his scope to preaching the evils of communism.

Already somewhat active in motion picture union activities, he still didn't create much of a stir until he launched his public attacks on the far left threat to Americanism. This tack triggered a prompt and violent reaction among many of his Hollywood brethren. The motion picture industry had long been a hotbed of communist cells and sympathizers. When the Soviet Union, due to a classic double cross by Hitler, found itself on the same side as the United States in the war, the communist sympathizers in the U.S. suddenly found themselves respectable. Unfortunately, the entertainment industry had never been noted for producing deep thinkers, and many of the movie people were becoming active proponents of a political system and set of values that Ronald Reagan and most citizens saw as a critical danger to their country. Now, almost overnight, this pleasant, witty young star was propelled into the highly politicized area of national policy. His speeches were gaining notice beyond the confines of Hollywood, and he was developing personal contacts with powerful political figures behind the scenes in California, as well as nationally.

Ronald Reagan, while beginning to make sizeable ripples beyond the narrow field of moviedom politics, was not yet drawing broad public notice from his strong denunciation of the communist threat. As he delved deeper into the political arena, however, his personal life was collapsing with the dissolution of his short marriage to fellow motion picture performer Jane Wyman.

His increasing attention to causes outside the actual making of motion pictures appeared to be the final blow to an already weak marriage. Wyman was thoroughly indoctrinated into the movie studio's make-believe world of glamour. She devoted herself to playing, for a lifetime, the part her studio publicists scripted for her. She could see nothing outside the glamorous world they provided; each new movie part became the current

Mrs. Reagan. Ronald, without a scripted part in her performances, became less and less relevant to her life. To Ronald, the make-believe world of the performing arts represented by Hollywood was more a means to an end than a pattern for real life.

An important factor in the development of Ronald Reagan, little noticed by the public, was his devotion to and reliance on home and family. The Reagans were a close-knit family unit. While never ones to put on public displays of family affection, each of them was there when another needed help. As we move along, we'll see this strong internal support carrying the whole family forward at critical points in their lives. Ronald was looking for the same sort of unity when he ventured into forming his own family. Although he came a cropper in his first effort with Wyman, he hit the jackpot on his second try!

Nancy Davis, also a motion picture performer at the less-than-blockbuster level, proved to be the perfect match for the assured personality that Reagan had now become. She too, while enjoying the fruits and rewards of public performance as an actress, had larger and more serious goals in mind. Their marriage in 1952 was the start of a love affair and partnership of a quality seldom seen in public or private life. The combination they created was destined to have a profound effect on American history.

Events were now rapidly drawing together to project Ronald Reagan into the awareness of the American people. His eloquent expression of a vision for his country gained the attention of the public during a stint hosting a dramatic anthology program on the rapidly-growing medium of television. Here, no longer hampered by the movie studio's fictional image, he gave free reign to the real Ronald Reagan. To his still relatively small following he came through as an

"All-American Patriot", easily spelling out what so many felt but had never heard so clearly projected.

Public awareness of this dramatic spokesman for Americanism took a quantum leap when he undertook open support for the doomed candidacy of Barry Goldwater for President of the United States. Goldwater, himself an eloquent exponent of conservative patriotism, was totally unable to project beyond an antagonistic news media. No matter what he said or how well he said it, the press and newly-influential television commentators depicted him as a near-demented kook and radical. With his campaign on a downhill run with the brakes failing, most of the best-known politicians in the Republican Party were scrambling to distance themselves from their own candidate. Into this vacuum of support appeared Ronald Reagan!

The supposedly knowledgeable commentators and politicians looked upon Ronald Reagan's agreement to lend his public support to Goldwater as the kiss of death for this brash newcomer on the political scene. The insiders running the Republican Party, never ones to take kindly to someone outside their country club circles, rubbed their hands in glee over Reagan's move. They and the always-liberal TV moguls viewed his action as one of self destruction. What better way to get rid of this threat to the closed club than to watch him be consumed in the flames taking Goldwater out of the picture! Seemingly unaware of the experts and their "conventional" wisdom, Reagan plunged into the fray, giving a nationwide television address on behalf of the Goldwater campaign.

Ronald Reagan, on that occasion, as he has so many times in his life, proved that the inside experts in the area of public service were woefully deficient in their understanding of the American public. Reagan, while heroically supporting a candidate he believed in, more importantly gave an eloquent exposition of what Ronald Reagan believed in! Although his speech that evening was little changed from those he had been repeating many times before local groups and small meetings, television on this occasion gave him his first national audience in a purely political stance. That audience found what only a few people had known before . . . Ronald Reagan close up projected an air of intimate sincerity that was perfect for the merciless glare of the television camera. Although his audience liked what they heard and saw in Ronald Reagan, his speech was to have no discernible positive effect on the election which Goldwater lost by record numbers. Ronald Reagan emerged, however, as a national political figure not to be taken lightly. Independent, and this time truly knowledgeable powers, took serious note of Ronald Reagan after the Goldwater campaign. They were quick to sense the responsive chord he had struck with the American public. While GOP bean counters could not see beyond the dismaying electoral count, wiser heads recognized that Ronald Reagan had pulled a rabbit out of an empty political hat! Fighting for a losing cause, his sincere exposition of straightforward conservatism had achieved a significant personal victory!

Ronald Reagan's personal charisma and the inherent popularity of his message, were responsible for his election victories twice as governor of California. It is revealing of the political system that the inside powers of the Republican Party still did not recognize the emotional attraction he generated among voters. National political party leaders have always tended to write off anyone outside the eastern states as outside the mainstream.

Reagan and his backers were forced to form their own independent committee to support and run his campaign for governor. Even after two outstanding terms in California, his own party continued to discount him as a national political force and withheld insider support. This firm refusal of real support forced Reagan to use his independent committee from California in later runs for the Presidency. Typically, those same hardnosed insiders were later to be the loudest critics of the "California cabal" who helped him run the White House!

Why his own political party and the spokesmen for the news media did not support Ronald Reagan, despite his obvious popular appeal, becomes more understandable as we move along. More important to our narrative is how Ronald Reagan developed such appeal for the majority and such revulsion from a minority. How did Ronald Reagan get to be Ronald Reagan?

Nothing appears in his career prior to public office to indicate where his ideas came from. Although Hollywood and its make-believe life provided a fertile testing ground for his philosophy, they certainly had nothing to do with the formulation of his fundamental beliefs, nor did these provide many allies in the cause. By the time he arrived on the acting scene, his personal character and standards were well cast. The kookie mindset of Hollywood's neon intellectuals wasn't about to deflect him from his course! Ronald Reagan was already Ronald Reagan when the first cameras began to roll on the handsome young man from the Midwest. The roots were there and firmly attached, but how were they nurtured?

Ronald Reagan's foundation was solidly cast in the Midwestern heartland of his country. It is only there that we can even begin to understand what made Ronald Reagan, Ronald Reagan!

CHAPTER 1

THE YOUTH OF MYSTERY

Shortly after Ronald Reagan won election as President of the United States, I was asked to help a group of local citizens and national supporters in acquiring and restoring Reagan's boyhood home in Dixon, Illinois. Since the President acknowledged the comfortable little prairie town as his home, having lived there from early youth until graduating from Eureka College not far away, many of us felt this was a natural place to establish an historic landmark honoring the new President. The first home occupied by the Reagan family and the one most fondly remembered by both Ronald and his older brother, Neil, was duly restored and is now a popular visitors' stop for citizens and serious students of Americana.

During the historical detective work and research necessary to the restoration, the private, nonprofit Reagan Home Foundation accumulated a wealth of information about the early life and times of Ronald Reagan. Neil Reagan, two years older than his famous brother, joined with the President to provide a gold mine of interesting anecdotes concerning their early life in that typical Midwestern hometown. Possessed of natural story-telling ability and the good memories that marked all the Reagans, the two of them were able to recreate for us the sense and pace of life in the 1920's Midwest.

Aiding our studies were two unexpected factors, interesting enough to merit serious scholarly attention on their own. People in Dixon never seem to leave their home town, and more importantly for what we were doing, they seem to live forever! Accustomed to doddering geriatrics in my home state of Florida, I found it a difficult struggle to keep up with the many contemporaries of Ronald Reagan we found in Dixon. Ronald's vigorous lifestyle as our oldest President appeared to be one of those Midwestern roots we were looking for!

Research on the early life of Ronald Reagan looked as though it was going to be a cinch; everyone wanted to talk to us and relate their own favorite stories of his youth. With such a rich source of chronological contemporaries of the President, it looked as though we might have more detail than we really needed! Happily, we set to work accumulating and recording all those intimate first-person accounts of life with young Ronnie.

Stories of the youngster, some day to be President, growing up in Dixon flowed from everyone we interviewed. All of the narratives were positive, giving a pleasantly typical view of an all-American boyhood. With bulging notebooks and files, the subject of a book on Reagan's early life arose as a matter of course. The resulting publication, "A Place To Go Back To", was modestly acceptable and, to date, the only publication on the President's early years.

The ease with which the material for that early book was accumulated, aided immeasurably by the obvious affection everyone held for "Ronnie", caused this reporter to wonder why others considered historical research so difficult. With so many people bursting at the seams to tell their stories about the community's leading citizen, the only mystery was why there were not more books on the subject. Even the President, in his always gracious manner, was fully cooperative, agreeing to meet with me and review the preliminary manuscript on "A Place To Go Back To".

The President read the manuscript of that modest effort, scribbled a few clarifying notes on the margins and quickly mailed it back to me. Now you talk about "seventh heaven"! In my first crack out of the box as a serious writer, I had the President of the United States as a proofreader, and I was in orbit.

As the Reagan Home restoration grew into a major historic center and popular visitor's stop, it became apparent that the first book was not adequate. The American public simply could not see and hear enough about this world leader, the most popular President since Franklin Roosevelt. Since our concern was only with his early years, leaving the Hollywood and

Washington years for others to chronicle, we began considering the publication of a broader treatise.

The enthusiastic interest young children showed while visiting the old home particularly attracted our attention. Guides at the home and visitors' center could not seem to tell them enough about how President Reagan lived and learned as a youngster. Every new group of students came up with more questions we could not answer. There was no doubt we needed another book which would go into considerably more detail concerning Ronnie's young friends, home life and schooling.

President Reagan, now retired to California, was contacted with the plans for a book essentially about his boyhood, and he agreed to cooperate in every way. Preliminary work began on the proposed literary effort, involving frequent contact with the President's California staff and an early, relaxed, private meeting with him on a visit to our hometown in Florida. Later he was to spend a full day in our company on a nostalgic visit to his old hometown, Dixon.

Our files were now really bursting their bindings. We had not only reams of personal notes, but also dozens of personal video interviews. Everyone who grew up with, and around, young Ronald Reagan was on record with "first-hand" memories. If there can be a state beyond "seventh heaven", this aspiring author was there!

By this time, my wife (Harriet) and I were so deeply involved that it became necessary to spend more and more time near the source of our research. We were developing a stronger appreciation of the deep affection Ronald Reagan has for his hometown. It was growing on us as well. In July 1990, we decided to adopt Dixon as our own hometown, and we bought a home overlooking the beautiful Rock River. As residents, we began to absorb the aura that had so captivated Ronald Reagan and other distinguished sons of Dixon, such as Charles Walgreen and John Deere.

Now able to pursue details of the Reagan family life without the constraints of time and travel, we were absorbed into the quiet lifestyle of the small town by the river. Amazingly, that ambience is not too unlike what it had been in the 1920's when the young Reagan family arrived!

Everything was moving swiftly and smoothly toward putting the proposed book together. It was so easy, in fact, that a more- seasoned researcher would have known instantly there was something wrong.

Finally, with all material in hand, bright and early one morning I parked in front of my word processor ready to share our wonders with the world! With the cursor blinking insistently at me to get going, I tried to launch a coherent narrative. To my horror, after all the preliminaries, I felt a nagging doubt concerning the validity of all those impressive notes and interviews! Having heard about this sort of thing before, I concluded I was just suffering from a classic case of "writer's block". Turning the unsympathetic electronic prompter off, I leaned back, thinking what an ego booster it was to think of myself as a "writer"!

After what seemed a respectable period of time for a real "writer", there was still no magic inspiration. I had to conclude that my trouble was in not knowing how to put my thoughts into words and phrases interesting to a teenage reader. That lame excuse did not hold for long. Who in the world can claim the deep wisdom and ability necessary to penetrate the psyche of a teenager? Clearly there was something else causing the roadblock. My well-inflated ego would not allow that it was simply because I was not up to the task! OK, Norm, back to the drawing board .

Combing through the copious written and video notes accumulated to this point was a frustrating experience. The information was so clear and unequivocal! How could I fail? Matching all the notes and interviews, a pattern finally began to appear. Every time I had managed to slip what I thought was an astute question concerning his boyhood to the affable President, my files ended up with another of the oft-told and thoroughly familiar stories he had used all through his life in public appearances. When I had attempted to persist in a particular line of inquiry, the response was always another enigmatic smile followed by a dissertation completely off the subject!

I was beginning to understand how persistent and quick-tempered reporters, like Sam Donaldson of ABC News, got so frustrated and angry as they questioned the President. Ronald Reagan never answered a question or talked about a subject in any way other than the way he wanted it presented. His pleasant diversion of my inquiries, rather than being irritating, was an intriguing clue to a personality and character far more complex than most analysts would let us believe.

Unable to touch the core of the mystery through my own notes, I turned back to the many taped interviews we had accumulated. These were the people who had been there, I thought. Their answers should clear the problem. Gradually my stubborn insistence on ferreting out his childhood was being replaced by a growing awareness that there would be no simple childhood book in this line of inquiry. Instead, it appeared I should be writing a mystery! The elements were certainly there: a powerful public figure, an idol whose every word and action were dissected and analyzed in minute detail, but whose early years seemed to be shrouded in an impenetrable fog!

Approaching the subject from the mystery angle meant looking at the evidence the way those super sleuths by Agatha Christie or a Sherlock Holmes would.

When a professional investigator finds that his witnesses are relating stories that are too smooth and too much alike, he knows the facts so imparted cannot be relied upon. Everyone is familiar with those experiments in which a phony violent event is staged before an unsuspecting audience, such as a school classroom or theater patrons. After the episode, the eyewitnesses are asked to relate what they have just seen. Its always amazing to the uninitiated to read those accounts and to wonder how so many people could see the same thing so differently! Amusing though it seems, to professional investigators it is always a frustrating part of their jobs. Seldom will two people remember an event in their lives in exactly the same detail. We all recall past events in a context that matches our own experiences or prejudices. Our country, a mecca for the legal profession, is providing lucrative living for lawyers who wrangle over the differing accounts given by eyewitnesses to an event!

Reviewing all the stories "remembered" by contemporaries of Ronald Reagan revealed an almost word-for-word recounting of virtually every incident. How could they all have interpreted what they saw in exactly the same detail? Considering that we were asking them to remember events that took place fifty to sixty years ago, the sameness of their responses made our vast files of notes suspect. The only conclusion to be drawn from what we had was that our story tellers were not really eye witnesses, but were relating events they had picked up from another source. None was consciously trying to be misleading. To the contrary, most of them sincerely believed what they were relating was really a part of their own personal history!

This is not an unusual circumstance. Most of us have similar situations embedded in our own memories. In my own case, as I tell my grandchildren stories of the great war, I find myself recalling events as a participant, when in actual fact, I couldn't have been there. I vividly recall, for example, hearing President Roosevelt deliver his angry attack against the country of Japan right after their sneak attack on Pearl Harbor. Logically I know I could not have heard that speech to Congress directly, since on that day I was in the process of enlisting at an Army recruiting office. Since the war became an intimate part of my past, many of its events have been implanted in my memory as personal experiences!

Ronald Reagan, over the years, has used many first-person anecdotes to illustrate points in his speeches. These little stories have become an integral part of his history, and have been repeated as well in books and articles about his life. Early in my study of the Reagans I picked up all those personal anecdotes and probably contributed to the mystery by repeating most of them in "A Place To Go Back To".

With a somewhat different approach, continuing study of the stories concerning Ronald Reagans boyhood revealed another interesting fact. Virtually every story, such as the President's own favorite concerning his misadventure with fireworks and the local police department, involved only Ronald Reagan! There are no other youngsters in these narratives of his youth. All the incidents occurred as solo performances by Ronald Reagan! Now I could see why all the notes and interviews we had were so similar. They were second-hand repeats of stories heard, but not seen.

There could be some question raised about whether these were true stories or merely fictional anecdotes used only to prove a particular point at a given time. It really was not critical that these little stories be proven truth or fiction, since they were all innocuous incidents with no real bearing on our study. What is more important is that they open up a whole new insight and a somewhat different line of inquiry into the early life and character development of one of our most popular Presidents.

This new understanding and the revelations from our records were revealing Ronald Reagan to have been a "loner" as a youngster. There were no close boyhood pals in his life; there was no special friend to turn to with the usual childhood worries and trauma. Every avenue of research was revealing a youngster who maintained his own counsel, whose life seemed to be on a steady course from birth and who never let anything divert him from whatever he set out to do!

The inescapable conclusion from all the study of the boyhood of Ronald Reagan was that there was no young "Ronnie" there!

Ronald Reagan was born grown up!

CHAPTER 2

WHO DID IT?

Ronald Reagan is a product of the life and culture of the broad prairies of Northwestern Illinois, little changed by exposure to the make-believe of Hollywood or the never-never land of Washington. In the heart of the agricultural plenty that feeds a good part of the free world, life moves at a different pace and with simpler, more-easily defined values than in the more urban areas of the country. The Reagan ancestors had settled into the region early and, with varying degrees of success, had lived and prospered there. All of the family history revolved around a cluster of small communities just over a hundred miles west of Chicago.

John Edward (Jack) Reagan was born in Fulton, Illinois, on July 13, 1883, the third of four children from the union of John Michael Reagan and Jennie Cusick, Jack's father, born in London, England, had migrated with his family to Illinois at an early age. Jack's mother, in one of those interesting details showing the limited territory of the President's ancestors, was born in Dixon, Illinois in 1855. Many years later, her grandson Ronald would grow to maturity in her hometown. Jack Reagan's parents died within days of each other when he was only six, leaving four small orphans to be raised by relatives. Of his two sisters and one brother, one sister and the brother died without offspring, and the remaining sister has not been traced.

Ronald's mother, Nellie, (later in life she was to change the spelling to Nelle, feeling it more sophisticated for a grown woman) was born in Fulton on July 24, 1883. Her father, Thomas Wilson, was born in Whiteside County, Illinois, a first generation Scotsman. Her mother, Mary Ann Elsey, was from Epsom, Surrey, England. Nellie, part of a larger, more long-lived family, had four sisters and three brothers.

Jack and Nellie, both of whom worked as clerks in Broadhead's dry-goods store in Fulton, on the surface, at least, seemed an unlikely pair for mating. Jack, of solid Irish background, was raised a Roman Catholic. Nellie, from Scotch ancestry, was raised a Protestant in the Methodist Episcopal Church. Religion was not to be a factor, however, as Jack was not very Roman in his Catholicism, and Nellie was far from a protesting Protestant!

12

While Jack was a prototype of the happy-go-lucky Irishman with a raucous sense of humor, Nellie was far from a dour Scotsman. Breaking the stereotype, she too had an active sense of humor with a flair for the dramatic. Jack showed signs of musical talent and was quite an accomplished singer, leaning naturally toward Irish ballads. Not to be outdone in that area, Nellie was known as an enthusiastic and talented dancer. Although later we learn that her musical inclination stretched to singing and playing the ukulele, her dramatic abilities overshadowed the musical talent.

Thrown together in the little dry-goods store, he as a popular and successful shoe salesperson, and she as a personable counter clerk, their chemistry clicked. They were married on November 4, 1904 in the rectory of the Immaculate Conception Church in Fulton by the local priest. At that time, Catholics were not allowed to marry Protestants in church — it had to be done in the rectory. Jack's Catholicism, at the time, presented no problems to Nellie.

Two years later, they were to move to the tiny community of Tampico, Illinois, some fifty miles from Fulton. There is no record as to how Jack came to make this change, going to work for Mr. H. C. Pitney in his general store, but the association was to be a lasting one. The strong business and personal bond between Jack and Pitney, which developed on initial contact, was to play a major part in the future of the Reagan family. It's not hard to speculate the move to Tampico came about through family contacts, since the young couple had relatives scattered throughout the area.

The Jack Reagans settled into domestic life in their small upstairs apartment in Tampico. Now well-established in the compact community, they soon produced their first offspring, son Neil, born on September 16, 1908.

The Reagans' second child, Ronald, was born in Tampico on February 6, 1911. Young Ronnie, arriving in the snowbound apartment, gave his mother a hard time, checking in at a robust ten pounds!

The family was to continue their relatively stable life in Tampico for another four years before Jack went through a series of job changes that moved them rapidly around the prairie country for four more years. After holding retail sales positions in Chicago, Galesburg and Monmouth, Jack was to return to work for his old boss in Tampico. Always well-liked and good at handling the public in retail sales in the small towns, Jack was extremely unhappy and a "fish out of water" in his short-lived position in Chicago. At first thinking the bustling metropolitan area of Chicago would present more opportunity, he soon found that he and his family did not fit well into that congested, urban life.

The return to Tampico was triggered by one of those quirks of fate that so frequently alter our lives. H.C. Pitney, his old employer, now in failing health, had contracted to sell his store in Tampico. Before the deal could be closed, the buyer died, forcing Pitney to take the store back. The Reagans, who always kept in touch with old friends no matter how often they moved, were contacted by Jack's former boss with a plea to return and

14

run his store. With little debate, the Reagans enthusiastically returned to the community where they had started their family.

Even though, on their second sojourn in Tampico, the Reagans became more deeply involved in the community, from the onset it was considered to be a temporary stopover. Pitney was still determined to sell his store and retire from his active business life. As part of the enticement to get Jack back to Tampico to mind the place until he found another buyer, Pitney agreed to finance Jack as a partner in a new venture. While the older man was seeking a buyer for the Tampico general store, Jack was busy considering the type and location of their new business.

When a firm sale was finally set on the old store, Jack Reagan was ready. The new venture was to be a shoe store in Dixon, about 30 miles northeast of Tampico. That Dixon was not a casual choice for the location of the "Fashion Boot Shop", as it was to be called, becomes apparent as we move deeper into the Reagan family history.

Jack, Nellie, Neil and Ronald Reagan moved into a rented two-story home on Hennepin Avenue in Dixon, Illinois, during a cold December in 1920. The opening of the new business was heralded, after a fashion, in the February 28, 1921 edition of the *Dixon Telegraph* newspaper: "H.C. Pitney and J.E. Reagan will open an exclusive shoe store in this city in the building formerly occupied by O.H. Brown & Co. All new fixtures have been installed, and the store will be stocked with all new spring styles. The new establishment will be known as the 'Fashion Boot Shop'. Mr. Reagan, who will act as manager, is an

15

experienced shoe man and also a graduate *practipedist* and understands all foot troubles and the correct methods of relief for all foot discomforts, having had years of experience in this line in many of the larger cities throughout the state."

The new firm extends a cordial invitation to all the people of Dixon and vicinity to visit them in their new store on their opening day, which will be announced later."

The Reagans had arrived in Dixon! Although there may not have been much public notice of the arrival of this new family and their new business, in some areas the impact was already considerable. Nellie Reagan had already served notice on the quiet little community astride the Rock River that here are some folks you cannot ignore for long!

CHAPTER 3

SHE DID!

You will seldom get an argument on the old truism that few individuals achieve lofty goals in life without much of the credit going to their mothers. Despite the modern trend to play down, and even denigrate, the role of motherhood, it is still the pillar of the family structure and the single most important influence on any developing child. Ronald Reagan was no exception; he had a truly remarkable mother! Mrs. Jack Reagan, "Nellie" as she arrived in this world, was a woman who, while sophisticated in worldly matters beyond her time, was as old-fashioned and fundamental in her personal faith and devotion to family as any all-American "Mom" you could find!

Nellie, as the young, soon-to-be bride of Jack Reagan, was an unusual combination of sparkling good humor and vigorous approach to life, combined with a deep sense of compassion and understanding for humanity. Jack, on the surface a happy-go-lucky, live-it-up sort of guy, but with a deep sense of social justice, related perfectly to Nellie, and their union was a natural. Although Jack has not fared well in the recording of Ronald Reagan's background so far, in fact there were more similarities than dissimilarities between Mom and Dad. Jack will get his turn at bat later; for now let us take a long look at Nellie.

Although her early religious training was unimportant when she married Jack, after her children arrived, Nellie's faith was to become the most pervasive force in her life. That their marriage was performed by a Roman Catholic priest in a Catholic Church gives every reason to believe, at that stage in her life, Nellie was ambivalent on the subject of personal faith. Born and raised a Protestant, her Methodist background did not appear to cause any hesitation in going along with Jack's church. Even later in Tampico after her first son Neil was born, she showed only perfunctory concern about religious training for her child.

After Neil's arrival, Nellie was approached by the local Catholic priest on the matter of baptizing and raising her son in the Roman faith. When the cleric informed her she had agreed to raise her children in the church as part of the marriage agreement, she vehemently denied ever having made such a promise. Jack backed up his wife, taking some of the pressure off when he admitted he had not followed through before the marriage in getting Nellie to sign the agreement. Despite this apparently heated confrontation, it did not appear that Nellie was too adamant in her rejection, as Neil, in fact, was baptized by the priest!

Two years later, however, after the birth of her second child, Ronald, she would have no part in going along with the priest's admonition and would not allow her younger son to be baptized a Roman Catholic! Something profound had happened to Nellie Reagan in the short period between the arrival of her two sons!

Although detailed records do not exist, it appears that Nellie joined the Christian Church in Tampico sometime after the arrival of Neil and before Ronald. This union with the small community church was not a simple matter. The Christian Church was a member of the Disciples of Christ denomination, and church rules required a strong commitment to the standards of their faith. Her name on the Tampico church's membership role (although undated, it appears to be around 1910) means she pledged herself to their creed. Before acceptance, she had to make a public profession before the full congregation of her faith in Jesus Christ as her personal savior and submit to the ceremony of baptism of the saved through full immersion in water. This was no small or insignificant act on the part of the young mother who only a few short years earlier had quietly gone along with her husband's Roman Catholic faith! The act becomes even more profound when considering that the Disciples of Christ denomination at that time was quite militant in its denunciation of the Roman Catholic faith and the perceived rule of a foreign pope!

Unfortunately, there is no record indicating who or what influenced Nellie into making this major decision during her life. We can surmise, however, that her propensity toward doing good in the community had a lot to do with the decision. The Disciples, as a church group, were far ahead of their time when it came to social activism. As a congregation, wherever located, they were "do-gooders" of the first order! Church members were constantly exhorted to press into the community and minister to the poor and less-advantaged among them. So whether Nellie chose that church because of its social activism, or she became an activist because of the church is a moot point. Her community impact has been well recorded.

More intriguing, and even more important in our study of the influences molding Ronald Reagan, was the emerging of Nellie's strong and decidedly fundamental Christian faith.

From all the research and interviews concerning the Disciples of Christ, particularly the churches in Tampico and later in Dixon, their theology would best be described as "liberal". In the context of the Protestant Christian faith, "conservative" believers are those who hew to a strict interpretation of the bible and rely upon Jesus Christ as their personal savior. Their faith rests securely in the belief that eternal salvation comes only through the basic act of accepting the gift of Christ's sacrifice on the believer's behalf. Although many Protestant denominations follow the form of personal salvation, liberal interpretation has tended to obscure the

20

original profession of faith, replacing it with the sort of secular social activism the Disciples were noted for.

Here we encounter the first of several anomalies in Nellie Reagan. Throughout her life she remained an outspoken advocate for reform in the handling of prison inmates, for equal treatment and acceptance of all minorities, and for strict prohibition of alcohol in all forms. She did not just talk the good fight; she plunged into the battle with a missionary zeal that left her contemporaries breathless. While sweeping through the community, sword in hand, often treading where angels would fear to go, she continued to exhibit a simple, straightforward and gentle faith in her personal savior that presented an unusual combination with her social activism. She was not only a fervent and effective spokesperson for her principles, she also exhibited an unusual organizational ability that thrust her to the forefront in her church congregation.

In Tampico, on their second residency, with an admittedly small congregation, Ronald's mother quickly emerged as the leader and the glue that held the organization together. About this time in her life, well-aware of her leadership position in the church and the impact her frequent public appearances were having on the community, the young Mrs. Jack Reagan decided her name was too unsophisticated. No longer would she use "Nellie", her given name. From now on the more dignified "Nelle" would be the preferred appellation!

While husband Jack was busy helping Pitney sell his old

general store and plan the new joint enterprise, Nelle was running her church and expanding her community activities. By this time in 1919, during a prolonged period when the Tampico Christian Church was without a pastor, Nelle was preparing the weekly services and writing the church bulletin. To all practical purposes, Nelle was the Tampico Christian Church.

Until this second stay in Tampico, the Reagan family had bounced around from town to town seemingly without a unified purpose in life. Now, however, there were some profound things taking place in the life and character development of Nelle which would begin to lay the foundation for the development of a future President.

Although they had left little mark on any of the communities they had called home up to this time, Nelle and her youngest son were rapidly emerging as individuals with clearly-defined missions in life. Nelle, after her conversion and union with the Disciples of Christ, not only threw herself wholeheartedly into the internal operations of the church, but also found time to take to the road as a roving missionary. Hers was not a bible-thumping type of evangelism. She leaned more heavily on community good works to make her point.

Despite her frenetic activity in the community, she in no way neglected her family or her deeply-felt responsibility to raise her children in the "Lord's way".

Young Ronald, unable, or more likely not inclined to relate to other youngsters his age during their many moves in those early years, was rapidly developing as his mother's son. While both parents spent many hours with their children during those early formative years, making their home life a closed and satisfying union, Nelle was the leader in their education.

Nelle read to her youngsters every evening, patiently answering all their questions and leading discussions on those subjects that tickled the boys' curiosity. With her deep devotion to her recently-activated Christianity, much of her reading and subsequent discussions centered on the bible. It was during this early period in Ronnie's life that one of his more outstanding abilities surfaced.

The President likes to relate an episode in his preschool life that startled his family. Jack, noting his youngest son lying on the floor one evening, head propped in his hands and the daily paper spread before him, asked,

"Whatcha' doing, son, reading?"

"Yup," came the laconic answer.

Jack, who would not accept any indication his boys were being untruthful, sternly ordered,

"OK, read to me then."

He was quite prepared to give Ronnie a severe lecture on truth in communication!

The youngster promptly startled both parents by reading aloud the news story he had been studying on the floor! Excited discussion revealed that he had learned to read on his own by closely following the written words as his mother read to him every night! That fascination with the written word has never left him. Ronald Reagan has always been an avid reader.

Learning to read at such an early age was the manifestation of an inherent ability that has served the President well throughout his life. He has always had what is popularly called a "photographic memory". That talent served him well in his early schooling and later was to be a major factor in his success in the field of acting and public performances.

Nelle, at this stage in her life, was revealing a great talent for drama and a very poised stage presence. Her missionary activities were propelling her into many dramatic presentations outside her church. She quickly recognized kindred talents in her youngest son, and Ronald, at the tender age of six, was taking an important part in her little plays and readings. That the youngster's charm and acting ability were drawing public attention is attested in local newspaper stories referring to their "well received" performances. As time went on, these public presentations were to expand into a virtual road company starring the whole family!

Meanwhile, Jack and his boss (soon-to-be partner) were about ready to move to Dixon to launch their new venture.

We could find no concrete indication as to why Jack Reagan and Pitney chose Dixon for the site of their new retail establishment. Tampico was only a few short miles from the thriving and more densely populated areas of Rock Falls and Sterling, which would seem to have been an easier move on their part. Locating in one of those nearby communities would have meant it would not be necessary to uproot his family for yet another move. Although Jack's mother had been born in Dixon, she had died so early in his life that he probably had no memories of that bit of family background and certainly no affinity for the community.

There are some intriguing clues indicating Nelle might have been the causative factor behind this important move. In any event, Dixon, some thirty miles distant, was their destiny.

In that last year, 1919, in Tampico, the Christian Church went for a long period without a pastor. At the same time, coincidentally, the First Christian Church (also a Disciples member) in Dixon was desperately struggling without a leader. The much older church congregation in Dixon did not even have a building, and services, such as they were, had to be held at off hours in the local Baptist Church. This awkward arrangement only aggravated the already sad state of the organization. The home base for the Disciples of Christ denomination, located in Eureka, Illinois, took note of the desperate plight and in September, 1919 dispatched Reverend H. G. Waggoner to take over the Dixon church. We take particular note of Rev. Waggoner, for he was to have an important influence on Ronald Reagan and is part of a small mystery in Nelle's and her children's lives!

Norman Wymbs

CHAPTER 4

ACT ONE

The Reagan road company was now ready for a permanent theater and a long stand! The small, closely-knit company had honed its skills on the road playing the small towns of Tampico, Galesburg and Monmouth. Except for a premature and ill-planned short run in Chicago, they had played well. To use the sort of show business metaphor so dear to Ronald Reagan, they had seen how it played in Peoria and were now ready for the big time!

Perhaps it is too easy, given Ronald Reagan's Hollywood background, to use the show business analogy, but in retrospect it seems to fit and does make it easier to understand what impelled the future President.

Nelle Reagan put the road company together and certainly deserves the lion's share of credit for its success. She was not only the producer and director, but also during the early struggling years, the star. Ronald, although the juvenile in the cast, quickly stood out as the second lead and in a few short years was to show that he was fully capable of taking the starring slot.

Jack, while playing a supporting role in the performances, proved his worth with an outstanding job as business manager and booking agent for the road company. The oldest son, Neil, while still playing juvenile bits, was critically important for his lighthearted support for his younger sibling. Later he would become even more important as a stable link to the outside world.

Nelle wrote the script with a sure knowledge of her family's abilities and shortcomings. The picture that emerges from those early formative years in the Reagan family is not so much of her as a matriarch, but rather as a benevolent dictator. From the start, she seemed to have a clear-cut mission in her life. With the advantage of looking back, it is obvious that she was not going to let anything in this world deter her from what she knew was the real destiny of her family.

That the mother of the Reagan boys was an activist seems an inadequate term to apply to such dogged determination. She approached life with little personal doubt that she had the right master plan and with an unshakable confidence it would be fulfilled just as she planned it!

Through all of her drive and social activism, she displayed a simple, but solid, faith in God and His Divine plan. Ronald Reagan, throughout his life, has made frequent reference to his mother's constant admonition that no matter how discouraging things may look at the moment, God will work it out for the best in his own way. In this respect, Nelle exhibited the basic faith of a fundamental Presbyterian in predestination!

Nelle's enthusiastic charge into battle against the forces of evil on behalf of the forces of good was not to be a lonesome fight. While she was well-supported by her husband and eldest son in her crusade, it soon became apparent that young Ronald was her true soul mate in the cause!

When asked by a reporter whether he was surprised by the outcome when his younger brother was elected President, Neil replied in his usual direct and pithy way, "Surprised, hell no! After all, my mother spent her whole life training him for the position."

Norman Wymbs

CHAPTER 5

THE MYSTIQUE OF DIXON

Probably no public figure has ever shown the love and reverence for his hometown that Ronald Reagan has for Dixon, Illinois. Seldom does he let an opportunity to reminisce about the good old days at home pass by without a few heartfelt remarks about his prairie town upbringing. This is not just the usual political public relations act on his part. To the contrary, most of the self-important political handlers around him over the years have done their best to shut off his frequent nostalgic ruminations. It is apparent that, early in his political career, the experts decided that his hometown background did not have enough political pizzazz to play it up in his resume. Even Nancy Reagan, herself a product of the posh North Shore area of Chicago, has had difficulty concealing her disdain for the humble small town of Ronald's early years.

Despite the distinct lack of sympathy around him, Ronald has never lost his deep love for the locale of his roots. I recall one meeting with the President in the Oval Office during a busy period in his administration with a group of old friends from Dixon. What was supposed to be a short "photo-op" visit began to stretch out as the President launched into enthusiastic discussions with his visitors about the old hometown. As time moved on, officious young staffers kept popping into the meeting, tugging at Reagan's sleeve and warning him he was running late. Shaking them off as absent-mindedly as you would a playful puppy, he continued his relaxed visit with the hometown folks, forcing the timetable for national affairs to be set back. When the reunion was finally broken up and we left the President's office, The Secretary of State and the President's Chief of Staff were seen anxiously pacing in the outer office waiting for their late appointment.

This was not an isolated or an unusual incident. Over the years I've frequently heard staff people admonish visitors, "Don't get him started on Dixon, or we will never be able to keep to our schedule."

What is there about little old Dixon, Illinois, that has maintained this strong hold on Ronald Reagan? It is not just that this was his family home, although like most of us, he does tend to overly romanticize that part of his past. Most of us usually hold such strong emotions for our roots only when there are family members or close personal friends still in the area. When Ronald became successful in California, he bought a home there and moved his mother and father out to spend their remaining years nearby. His brother, Neil, left Dixon after graduating from college, just as he did, so there were no relatives left in the old town. It is not a family attraction, and since Ronald has never been one to form strong personal friendships, the only conclusion to be drawn is that Dixon itself is the bond!

In studying the life and times of Ronald Reagan in Illinois, little doubt is left that his hometown and its physical presence had much to do with the formation of his character and the goals he set in his life. We do not discount the importance of family and other associations in that molding, but it is inescapable that Dixon's influence on them, as well, had much to do with the making of Ronald Reagan!

So what is it about this quiet little town in Mid-America that creates such a lock on the heart of this well-traveled President and world leader? A casual visit to Dixon will probably leave you just as perplexed as you now are in reading this. More time is needed to begin to understand how a small community on a little-known river can so thoroughly penetrate an individual's personality.

Although little noted by the outside world or history books over the past century, Dixon came about as a key strategic stop along the path of the westward migration that developed our country. A critical crossing point for migrants heading west was the crude ferry started by Father Dixon over the treacherous Rock River. As aggressive and ambitious explorer/settlers funneled through the little settlement at Dixon's Ferry, a number of things critical to its future character took place. Enterprising Yankee entrepreneurs set up shop to supply the wagon trains passing through. Simultaneously, many westward-bound settlers, tired of the difficult travel, took note of the potential in the local area. Many gave up their wanderlust and started farming what is now commonly referred to as the breadbasket of the world. This old-fashioned independence and "can do" attitude continued through the years as descendants of these early pioneers continue to be the mainstay of the community.

One of the enterprising early settlers of the area was young John Deere who, recognizing the importance of the region's farming community, established his first plow-making shop. That early vision was to evolve into making Deere one of the world's leading farm equipment manufacturers. Showing that the Dixon influence was not totally oriented towards farming, another local resident, Charles Walgreen, was to launch the world's preeminent drugstore chain from his Dixon roots! To indicate the stability of this quiet little Midwestern hometown: until recently the Mayor of Dixon, still carrying the family name, was a direct descendant of Father Dixon, the founder of Dixon's Ferry. This town was later to become known as Dixon.

Today, as you visit Dixon's main residential area where Ronald grew up, it is like stepping into a time warp. Under towering oak trees, the immaculate homes and tidy yards remain unchanged since young Ronnie made the short trek from his home to the neighborhood school. In fact, when the Reagans arrived in 1920, the neighborhood looked much as it had for the prior 30 years! Dixon has grown older over the years, but it has not aged!

Despite explosive growth throughout most of the country over the past half century, Ronald Reagan's hometown is much the same size and continues at the same confident pace as it did in his "good old days"!

So, OK, Dixon is a nice quiet "hometowny" place, but does that explain its unusual hold on Ronald Reagan? Surely that is not enough to attribute any special influence on the development of his character . . . or is it? Much of President Reagan's popularity stemmed directly from his appeal to our desire to return to old-fashioned community and family values. Quietly walking the streets of Dixon and visiting the friendly neighbors, you can see these basic American standards shining through. Family units are intact, churches are active, the library is full every day and parents enthusiastically participate in school activities with their children. But still, is that enough to explain its influence?

Despite prime-time news emphasis on street gangs, non-functioning schools and rampant crime in the large urban centers, there are thousands of small communities around the country where the old values still survive. Is Dixon unique, or is it that we have come to think of what once was normal as now being odd or even unattainable?

Ronald Reagan still looks upon his life in Dixon as normal and certainly attainable, even today. It is that unshakable faith that has so endeared him to the American people, who deep down still hold the same faith. Even granting all this, there is still something special about Dixon and its pervasive influence on Ronald Reagan. It is probably impossible to quantify this element, but its effect is readily apparent, and much of his nostalgic love for his hometown is the result.

This writer has never been one for mystical meandering, but it is hard to deny that certain places hold profound meaning in our history. You cannot gaze over the hallowed grounds of Gettysburg without being struck by the awesome change in the world wrought by those who clashed on that battleground. Closer to personal experience, the same wonder is engendered as you visit Omaha Beach on the coast of France. These places, forever etched in the permanent history of humankind, do take on a mystical aura as you contemplate what might have been without them! Dixon cannot raise the deep awareness of Gettysburg or Omaha Beach, but in its own way, it had a profound effect on the course of history.

As the bottleneck crossing of the Rock River, Dixon had great importance in its early days. The difficult Chief Blackhawk and his Indian tribe saw this as a place to halt the steady advancement of the white invaders. Fort Dixon was built by the fledgling U.S. Army to protect that vital transportation point. Periodically, as Blackhawk flexed his muscles, the Army was forced to beef up its defenses at the fort. During one of those recruiting periods, a young Abraham Lincoln volunteered for Army service at Fort Dixon.

In those days, Army volunteers signed up only for the time necessary to accomplish the specific campaign planned. Thus it was that Lincoln's third enlistment in the U.S. Army was to take place at Fort Dixon as the fervently patriotic young man rushed to help his country in need. Arriving at the fort, anxious to do his part against the rumbling Blackhawk, Private Lincoln was sworn in. The 41st Company Adjutant, an equally young and ambitious Lieutenant, Jefferson Davis, administered the oath. Overseeing the assembly of this small fighting force was their commanding officer, Colonel Zachary Taylor!

So, here, generally unnoted in history, on the shore of the Rock River were gathered two future Presidents of the United States and the soon-to-be President of the insurgent southern Confederacy, united to serve a common cause. Although deliberately ignored by most historians because of the deep scars and animosities left from the Civil War, this brief association of three key men in the history of the United States was later noted by Abraham Lincoln himself as he pondered the fate that guided their lives.

Dixon's brush with the political history of Abraham Lincoln ran deeper than that short Army association (Lincoln's third enlistment in the military lasted less than two months, as the "Blackhawk" problem was quickly resolved).

Another of the early leaders of Dixon was Ben Shaw, Editor/Publisher of the *Telegraph* newspaper. (That paper continues today, still being run by fifth-generation Shaws).

Shaw, along with a handful of community leaders from around Illinois, saw in young Abe Lincoln a potential state and national leader for an increasingly troubled country. On his way to debate Douglas in the famous senatorial campaign, Lincoln's train stopped in Dixon to pick up Ben Shaw. On the way to his historic confrontation, Shaw and his other advisors discussed with the lanky young lawyer the pros and cons of bringing up the slavery question with regard to the imminent statehood of the Kansas and Nebraska territories. Lincoln, strongly anti-slavery, debated on the side of admitting the territories as "free states". Douglas, with strong support from pro-slavery forces in Illinois, took the opposite position and went on to defeat Lincoln in the senatorial election. Later, Lincoln was to confide to Shaw and other close advisors that he knew his anti-slavery position would hurt him in that Illinois race, but he said, "I knew his (Douglas') position would kill once and for all any chance he had to be elected President!"

Shaw and the other insiders were to later pull some masterful inside maneuvering to secure Lincoln's nomination as the first presidential candidate of the newly-formed Republican Party.

The early entrepreneurs and the close association of Dixon to the emerging new political leadership of the country in the mid-nineteenth century does lend this old community a certain majestic air. It was into this tradition that Jack and Nelle Reagan brought their small family in 1920. Who is to argue that this mystique of Dixon did not start the youngest Reagan on his way in the footsteps of Lincoln and Taylor?

CHAPTER 6

THE FIRST DISCIPLES

The paper trail of the Reagans was hard to follow for those years, as the young family of four jumped from town to town before their return to Tampico. All indications are they made little impact on the earlier communities. In Tampico the second time, with the boys now well into their schooling and active in the community, the Reagans began to be noticed. Here, as in most small towns with limited outside distractions, the social fabric was held together by the churches. Social leadership and its resulting community impact were determined very much by the strength of personalities within the church congregations. For the most part, there was simply no other organized society group. In Tampico, the Christian Church was probably the most dominant group in town.

For most of those last months the Reagans lived in Tampico, Nelle's church, without a minister, still dominated in the community. This strength was due in large part to its parent denomination, the Disciples of Christ. The Disciples, for years a rapidly-growing and powerful influence in the Midwest, was probably at its peak in the state of Illinois at this time. It was not particularly unusual for the denomination's churches to go for long periods without ordained ministers. This shortage seemed to be a penalty of their outstanding success; they simply outgrew their own ability to train new leaders. An important factor as our story unfolds was that Dixon's Christian Church during this same period was also going through a long pastorless ordeal.

In those last months before the family moved to Dixon, Nelle was running the Tampico church virtually single-handed. She prepared the Sunday programs, wrote the church bulletins and exhorted the faithful to render their full support to the struggling church. There is every reason to believe that Nelle also did much of the preaching at that time. It was not unusual for laymen to fill in at the pulpits, as the parent body was hard-pressed to provide substitutes everywhere needed. It is interesting to note that, at the same time, the Dixon church was also being lead by an aggressive layman, Ward Hall, who later was to become close to Nelle and her family when they arrived in Dixon. At Nelle's side, participating with the same enthusiasm as his personable mother, was young Ronald.

The Disciples of Christ, headquartered in the little town of Eureka, was not unaware of the importance of church activists like Nelle Reagan in keeping the machinery running. The leaders of the denomination, unwilling to see any congregation fail and lose the church's grip on the community, were providing whatever help was in their power to keep the small groups of faithful in the fold. Knowing Nelle's forceful personality and dedication to the cause, you can bet she was not shy in demanding assistance for her flock.

Meanwhile, up in Dixon, the Christian Church was in the same desperate condition. Without a minister for many months, and without a regular meeting place (they met for some months on Sunday afternoons in the local Baptist church), the Dixon congregation was a special problem for the leaders in Eureka. A larger and older church than Tampico, the Dixon group was too important to allow to slide into oblivion. The Ward Halls, like Nelle in Tampico, were the strength holding the Dixon church together. Not surprisingly, they were to become close allies of Nelle and an important influence on young Ronald when the Reagans arrived.

The Disciples, in 1919, came up with one of their biggest guns to move in as pastor of the Dixon church. Reverend H.G. Waggoner not only injected needed new life into the organization, but also, with critical financial and business support from Eureka, set about acquiring a church building. His strong leadership was to result in the Dixon Christian Church's moving into an imposing landmark in 1922. Unfortunately, he was to die shortly before the dedication.

There is strong indication that Nelle had some meaningful contact with the Dixon Church and its new minister, Waggoner, some time before the decision was made by Jack and his partner on where to establish their new business.

The mother of Ronald Reagan, always meticulous in her writing and record keeping, chronicled the family's vital statistics on the flyleafs of her well-used bible. The same bible, incidentally, which President Reagan carried with him through both terms as Governor of California and throughout his Presidency. Here she faithfully recorded all births, deaths, marriages and baptisms of her family. Such entries in family bibles are not taken lightly by Christians, and, in fact, have frequently been accepted in courts of law as legal documents.

The significance of Nelle's bible will become apparent several times during our ongoing narrative, but for the moment we are concerned with her entries under "Family History" where she recorded the baptisms. Nelle, herself, she lists as having been baptized a "Christian" in Fulton, Illinois in 1900 by "R. Tibets Massey" and John (Jack) Reagan, a "Catholic", with no date or priest shown. Our interest is drawn to the next two entries where she shows Neil Reagan and Ronald Reagan baptized "Christian" in Dixon, Illinois, the year 1919, by "H.G.Waggoner"!

These entries are intriguing, since she shows both boys being baptized in Dixon in 1919 when the family did not move permanently to Dixon until December, 1920! The mystery becomes more interesting since the Dixon Church has officially adopted June 21,1922 as the baptismal date for both the Reagan boys. The official church records are somewhat suspect, however, since researchers have been able neither to corroborate the date nor to determine who was the officiating pastor (the church, at that time, was again without a leader). Since Reverend Waggoner died on June 2,1922, it seems rather unlikely the local church would have conducted the highly formalized baptism of the believer so soon after his passing and with the local group in disarray without a minister.

The subject of the boys' baptisms is of no great importance other than the implication the mystery has for the way the decision to move to Dixon was reached. If Nelle was already actively assisting the new minister in Dixon a year before the family move, as seems to be the case, it would appear she was the one who determined where Jack and Pitney should establish their new business! Nelle's assertive nature had already been well-established by this time, and what Nelle wanted, Nelle got!

Old newspaper reports, along with personal recollections and letters, attest to the immediate impact Nelle Reagan had on the Dixon Christian Church. Virtually as soon as she arrived on the scene, she assumed important positions within the church leadership as head of the major women's group and teacher of the lead Sunday School class. This instant prominence lends further credence to the evidence she had established an earlier contact with Reverend Waggoner. All indications are that he was the type of forceful church leader who would take advantage of the abilities of someone like Nelle Reagan without concern for her seniority in the congregation. In view of the very tight social organization usual to the Disciples churches at that time, it is questionable that the minister would have given her such prominence without some prior knowledge of her abilities and character.

True to her empathetic character, Nelle did not forget her old struggling church in Tampico. Newspaper reports indicate she made frequent trips back to her prior home town to assist her old friends with their still pastorless congregation. She regularly took Ronald with her on these missionary forays as a full-fledged participant in her programs from the pulpit.

The Reagan family's association with the Dixon Christian Church for the next decade was to be a crucial factor in the shaping of Ronald Reagan's character and his journey towards the Presidency!

CHAPTER 7

THE FEMALE LEAD

As pointed out earlier, the Disciples of Christ were as much dedicated to social activism as they were to spreading the news of the Holy Gospel. Church members were exhorted to venture forth into their communities doing good works. An article in the local newspaper shortly after Waggoner arrived as the new minister of the Dixon Christian Church is revealing of where the primary emphasis was placed. The report consisted mainly of interviews with people in Macomb, Illinois, concerning their former minister. He was remembered and highly praised for his work in that community's Red Cross chapter. Officials there reported, "He will be hard to replace!" There were no comments concerning his pastorate, nor any indication his preaching from the pulpit would be as sorely missed!

A prominent member of the Disciples of Christ at that time was the famous (or infamous) Carrie Nation. For you younger readers, Carrie had gained international fame as the militant leader of the Women's Christian Temperance Union. The term "militant" here carries the strongest connotation possible. Carrie regularly marched upon taverns and other purveyors of strong drink, axe in hand, and literally destroyed the premises of those suppliers of "demon rum". Today's militants in the women's movement are the mildest of pussycats compared to Ms. Nation!

Nelle Reagan, although never taking axe in hand, took Carrie Nation to heart as one of her personal heroines. With a real writing talent and a flair for dramatics, Ronald's mother devoted much of that ability to public preaching against the evils Carrie attacked more directly with her axe! Nelle became something of a celebrity as the local newspaper carried many accounts of her diligent activities in the cause of alcohol abstinence. Not only was she reported as giving spirited "readings" and dramatic performances in her church on the subject, but also she was becoming much in demand for her lectures at non-church community groups as well. Nelle was right in sync with official policy of the Disciples of Christ. The local church reported regularly in its public bulletins, "We take pleasure in cooperating with WCTU activities."

Time was devoted at most church meetings to exhortations against the ingestion of alcohol, and spots during the regular Sunday services were regularly made available to speakers on the subject. Nelle Reagan, never one to hide her light under a bushel, enthusiastically took advantage of the license provided to preach against the "demon" at every opportunity. Now joining her as a regular in these spirited (or should we say "spiritless") performances was nine-year-old Ronald. The paper took special note of the precocious youngster, reporting his recitations in the church as early as May and June, 1920, only a few months after arriving in town!

There can be little doubt of the influence Nelle's WCTU activities had on the young and impressionable Ronald. As a full partner in her public mission to rid the world of the scourge of alcohol, he played an important role in her dramatic productions which she wrote and cast with her family and friends. Her approach was simplistic and unequivocal, with such sterling prose as this line she put in a pitiful crying waif's mouth in one play, "I love you, Daddy, except when you have that old bottle."

That this training and stern guidance from his mother were lasting is attested by later events in Ronald's life. His lifelong near abstinence from alcohol is well-known and was not an easy position to have maintained, considering his profession. The glitzy movie world of Hollywood and the never-never land of politics are largely kept afloat on a flood tide of scotch and martinis.

Even with the serious intent of Nelle's strident campaigning, the Reagan's irrepressible sense of humor could not be squelched, as the "old bottle" line from Nelle's play became something of a favorite inside family joke. Unfortunately, the good-humored and sensible approach of the family was lost in later years as the political image molders got into the act. More on that later.

Nelle Reagan's fanatical devotion to the doctrine of the Women's Christian Temperance Union at this time in her life is especially surprising, considering her early years. As a young lady being courted by the handsome man-about-town, Jack Reagan, she was remembered as an accomplished dancer and very popular at social gatherings. Having been raised a member of the Methodist faith, her social proclivities would seem to indicate her early church training had been ineffective. The Methodists were adamantly opposed to dancing and the social customs usual to that activity.

Jack, raised a Roman Catholic, had no hang-ups in these areas and was acknowledged to derive joy and satisfaction not only from the social custom of dancing, but also from the soothing effects of occasional alcoholic beverages. At that time, it would seem a mutual interest in these mainstays of social relationships was one of the major attractions drawing the young couple together.

During the first two decades of this century, the subject of alcohol's good or bad effects on society was a hot topic. There was little room for ambivalence in the debate, which raged mostly over moral, rather than health, issues. You were either for or against its use, unless you were among the affluent smugglers and bootleggers who were publicly against, but private suppliers of, booze. The temperance movement grew primarily among the women of the country. Sociologists have studied and written many learned volumes on this period and the formation of the militant Women's Christian Temperance Union, but for our purposes it is sufficient just to know they were there. Nelle's aggressive personality and active mind were such that she could hardly have avoided getting involved with the WCTU.

Had she been born at a different time, she would have been just as militantly involved in women's suffrage or our later generation's "Women's Lib" movement! Nelle was a natural activist looking for a cause!

Later, as Ronald grew into his teens, Nelle began to broaden her views and expand her activities with her youngest son. It is almost as though she early on saw in him the tremendous potential he held, and she wanted to expand his horizons.

Despite her activism outside the home, Nelle, unlike many modern feminists, insisted on maintaining a close and intimate family life with her husband and two sons. Woe be unto anyone who presumed to place any obstacle in the path of Nelle's boys!

Nelle's conversion to a strict form of Christian fundamentalism and prohibitionism is interesting in light of her marriage to Jack. Throughout their marriage, the fun-loving Irishman continued to enjoy his occasional union with "spiritus fermenti" and participated frequently in those social activities where it was a standard. Later, we will note how Nelle's growing awareness of the potential in her youngest son tended to moderate her militancy on demon rum, and how, in turn, Jack eventually moderated from the other direction.

Nelle Reagan's constant public attacks on the evils of strong drink and her condemnation of those who succumbed to its lure had profound, but opposite, effects upon her children. Her oldest son, Neil, as the first born, always close to his father and more sympathetic toward Dad's broader views of social relationships, chafed under her standards. Finally, as he neared completion of high school, Neil made the break away from the Disciples of Christ denomination and reunited with his father's Roman Catholic faith.

The younger sibling, Ronald, more attuned to his mother and an enthusiastic student of her dramatic training, hewed closely to the WCTU line she preached. Unfortunately, the narrowness of her position on this subject during those early years was to cause her favorite offspring to develop something of a guilt complex concerning his father. As we move along, we will see how that complex has had a tendency to warp the family history and even to affect later editorial analysis of President Reagan's psyche.

CHAPTER 8

THE JUVENILE LEAD

That the arrival of the Reagan family in Dixon had a special impact on that sleepy community is understood, as far as most of the family was concerned. Nelles' civic and church activities could hardly go unnoticed, nor could the outgoing and handsome manager of the town's latest and most modern shoe store, Jack Reagan. Even Neil, possessed of all the bubbling personality of his father with an ample dose of his mother's aggressiveness, became an instant leader among his contemporaries. With Ronald, though, there was no discernible impact. The best thing that could be said for the youngest offspring of the Reagan clan was that he did not disturb the normal orderly flow of life in the prairie town!

Although fully possessed of the same dramatic flair as his mother and with a sense of humor chipped right off his Irish father's block, Ronnie broke the family pattern with his thoroughly self-contained reserve. Despite all else that has happened to him over the years, even his outstanding accomplishments in public life, that inward containment has been the most frustrating characteristic to those trying to analyze and explain his success. What many writers and would-be biographers have chosen to see as a flaw in his character is really one of the major sources of his strength and success in leading the country.

When the family first arrived in Dixon, it was the middle of the boys' school year. Neil was enrolled in the neighborhood grade school with no difficulty. At that time, despite its small size, Dixon had two separate school systems (Northside and Southside), each with its own administration and locations. The fifth grade class that Ronald should have attended in the school a few blocks down the street from their home was full and could not accept another student. The quiet youngster was forced to attend a school in the other district, removing him from the day-to-day contact he would normally have enjoyed with the other kids in his own neighborhood.

Already exhibiting little desire to form close associations with his young contemporaries and now tossed midterm into a school far from his home, Ronnie was not destined to make much of a mark in the system. Although, as in all of his associations throughout life, his experience in that first school made an indelible impression on him, the reverse was not true.

I had the pleasure, some years ago, to meet and interview Esther Barton, retired principal and fifth grade teacher of the old E. C. Smith Grade School Ronald was thrust into that December of 1920. A dynamic and vital little woman, Esther talked with enthusiasm about her experiences in those early years. In her modest little home, a living museum of her lifelong interest in American Indian lore, she painted a vivid picture of the classroom environment Ronald moved into those many years ago. We know her impact on the youngster was substantial, for a number of reasons, not the least of which was the warm personal contact and correspondence he maintained with her after he became President.

Esther, as a young teacher, developed a consuming interest in the history of early Arizona and California and the life and times of their native Indian tribes. Each year, after summers spent in study of that western culture, she came back loaded with interesting stories and artifacts to share with her young students at the Smith School. Young Ronnie, deeply impressed with the colorful word pictures she painted of the old west, began a lifelong love of the western life. True to another of his enduring characteristics, wanting to always be a participant rather than an observer, the youngest Reagan decided to live the authentic Indian life at home. Nelle had to call a halt to his attempt at realism, however, as he tried to build a full-size tepee in his bedroom! Although thwarted in that early attempt, stubborn Ronnie eventually got his way. Later in life, he acquired a much-loved ranch and horses to authentically enjoy the western life. Esther's lectures had hit the mark!

The important part of this little story, however, is not the teacher's impact on the student, but the student's lack of impact on the teacher. One of the problems mentioned earlier in digging for information on Ronald Reagan was the tendency of people to create memories of him at that young age. Esther Barton, with a quick and snappy mind, made no pretenses in that area. She readily admitted not being able to remember anything about young Ronald in her school, even though many other students of those days stood out quite sharply in her mind. She did make one remark about Ronnie that fit the picture we were building. As principal of the little school, she was chief enforcer of discipline and known to be a strict taskmaster. "He must have been a good boy," she remarked with an impish smile, "because he never had to come to my office, or I would have remembered him!"

Esther, a small and slightly built woman, had always kept a large razor strap in her office as an instrument of punishment for students who got out of line. She sheepishly admitted never having used it, claiming its ominous presence was sufficient deterrence to cause instant reform on the part of those unfortunate enough to be called to her office. The fact that Ronnie had never deviated far enough from the path of righteousness to be required to appear before the high judge is an early indication of his compliant nature and desire to follow proper procedures of conduct.

Contributing to his naturally introspective nature was the fact he was born with extremely poor eyesight. Unable to see much of the world beyond his nose, he learned to develop and enlarge upon his phenomenal memory to get by in school. What he could not see on the classroom blackboards, he committed to memory from the teacher's lectures and the class's responses.

A naturally good memory, through necessity, was honed into a major asset in his life.

Ronald's eyesight disability was discovered accidentally by his family in much the same manner as they had earlier learned of his self-taught reading ability. One day, while riding in the family auto, he playfully picked up his mother's glasses and tried them on. When he suddenly discovered he could read roadside signs that had been only blurs before, he excitedly told his parents. They wasted little time in getting him to an eye doctor who quickly tested him and fitted him for eyeglasses. Like most youngsters at that age, although happy about the world opened up by the glasses, he was resentful of the need to wear them and unhappy over the teasing from his classmates. As he became older and prominent in public life, the advent of contact lenses resolved that problem.

Those early years in the life of the future President of the United States present something of a contradiction. While appearing to be shy and retiring in the classroom and in his personal association with schoolmates, he showed quite a forceful nature in activities in which he wanted to make a mark. We have noted his early and increasingly frequent appearances with his mother in public performances of her readings and playlets. Quiet and apparently shy in school and among friends, he exhibited the ultimate in public extroversion when he had to perform!

The YMCA was an important civic and social influence in Dixon during those early years. Ronald's interest and participation in the Y activities sprang naturally from the fact his church was holding their Sunday services and other meetings in the association's facilities. Reverend Waggoner had quickly made arrangements for his church to meet in the Y in order to expand congregation functions beyond their severely-limited arrangement with the local Baptist Church.

Neil was taken by the YMCA's boys' marching band and lost no time in joining. The band, in those days, was an important and popular participant in all civic affairs and an important symbol of status to those fortunate enough to make the grade. Neil, possessed of the same natural musical ability exhibited by both his mother and his father, had no difficulty making the grade as an accomplished tooter of the french horn. Ronald, however, seemingly with a misplaced gene, exhibited a total lack of talent with any of the instruments critical to a marching band.

The younger Reagan, with a dogged determination now familiar to the world, was not to be denied his place on that beautifully-uniformed performing body. Unable to blow a tune or beat a rhythm, the youngster gave an early demonstration of his persuasive ability when he convinced the Y leaders that he was a natural to lead the marching group as their drum major! Given the chance, he embarked upon a crash course in self-instruction to learn all the moves necessary to prove he could do what he had bluffed his way into! After many off-school hours of practice using a broomstick with a brass knob from his parents' bed attached, he became so proficient at his craft that the Drum Major's position at the head of the parade became one of his early trademarks!

Here, as it appears again and again in his early life, we see a strange combination of characteristics in the young man. Nothing could be more extroverted than the cavorting, brightly-attired drum major of a marching band. His natural flair for leadership and showmanship would seem to thrust him into the forefront of his contemporaries. That was not the case, however, in his personal relationships with the other members of the band while not marching. He showed no signs of seeking or wanting a leadership role. Although not elected to any of the high-profile officers' positions on the band, such as president or vice president, his compatriots did recognize his devotion to maintaining the proper order of things, and he was the unanimous choice to be sergeant-at-arms for the group. This characteristic of towing the line on proper performance in all things was something the adults around young Ronald quickly recognized, and they frequently chose him to lead his peers in many school and social functions.

His desire for conformity and order was to lead to some unkind charges by fellow students that he was "teacher's pet". Such childish epithets didn't hold for long, as Ronald, from the start, showed a natural ability to get things organized and moving. In those youthful years, it wasn't until after the fact that his contemporaries realized how well things ran after he stepped in and took charge! In many of our interviews, that characteristic kept showing up. Everyone remembered that Ronald was a whiz at running organizations and school functions. He demonstrated an early knack of knowing how to pick the right person for a particular task and not only getting maximum performance from the individual, but also creating in him or her the same enthusiasm he held for the project.

Strangely enough, for one with such a natural leadership ability, Ronald showed no interest in arousing adulation or approval to bolster his personal ego. At no time in his early life, or later for that matter, could anyone say Ronald Reagan was

57

possessed of an overpowering ego driving him to do what he did. Once he adopted a mission, all his drive and abilities were focused on accomplishing the goal, with little regard as to how he personally might appear in the process. Coupled with this desire to accomplish was a strong feeling that there was a proper way to perform in every situation and no need to deviate from what he saw as the "right" way to do things.

Older brother Neil represented an opposite bookend from Ronald. His ego was ever-present, and he showed little patience for the "proper" order of things. An episode in those early years accents this difference in the two offspring of Jack and Nelle Reagan. Neil, always a rule bender if not outright breaker, and some of his neighborhood friends concocted the ultimate Halloween prank. Their elaborate plan was to swipe a wagon (normally horse-drawn) from a local coal company and place it atop the portico entrance of Dixon's South Central School. This rather substantial caper involved the partial disassembly of the wagon into manageable parts and its reassembly on the roof some twenty feet over the school's main entrance. On Halloween, the perpetrators gained eternal local fame for their rather prodigious feat. Local folks still speak in awe of the never-topped prank and the fame and acclamation it brought Neil and his cohorts. Young Ronald, much to the disgust of his brother and friends, refused to participate in the venture. He expressed his concern that he felt it was just the wrong thing to do, primarily because of the distress and anguish it would cause the owner of the wagon. This deep and consistent concern for the feelings of others has been a natural part of his reluctance to deviate from the normal and proper way of doing things. In later public life, Ronald Reagan himself was to be frequently hurt by those who didn't share his faith in proper human relationships. Even in the face of devious and often reprehensible behavior from those around him, he has clung to his principles.

In my years of working for and with Ronald Reagan, I have had some first-hand opportunities to observe this enduring and sometimes frustrating characteristic of the President. His deep respect and reverence for his country extend beyond the normal bounds of patriotism. To this man, who cannot hide his emotions while listening to the national anthem or while paying tribute to the men and women who serve their country in the armed forces, his country's traditions and institutions are a sacred trust.

Nowhere did this deep feeling show more markedly than during two very key points in his political career. During one, he reached the heights of personal triumph, and in the other he scraped near the bottom of political purgatory.

Reagan's quest for the Republican presidential nomination in 1976 was the most emotionally-charged campaign of his career and the one, from the outset, least likely to succeed. With the resignation of President Nixon and the resulting elevation of the lackluster Gerald Ford to the Presidency, the Republican Party had hit rock bottom. Not even during the futility of the Roosevelt years had that political organization attained such a low level of public esteem and morale. With little real support being evidenced for the election chances of Ford in 1976, conservative leaders outside the Republican inner circle persuaded Ronald Reagan to run for his party's nomination that year.

Reagan's announcement of his candidacy was greeted with heartfelt enthusiasm and optimism by most rank and file Republican Party members. Although they had already written off the Party's chances for that year and many more to come, Reagan presented hope for the future. As a columnist for a small weekly newspaper in 1975, I had interviewed Reagan concerning the possibility he would lead a third political party into the 1976 campaign. He indicated then that his loyalty was with the Republican Party, and under no circumstances would he consider associating with another political movement. His decision to run was, again, based upon a sincere belief that this was the proper way to do things. His Party was in trouble, and he felt duty bound to pitch in and help where he was needed.

The insiders controlling the GOP did not greet Reagan's announcement with the same enthusiasm as the rank and file members. The Republican National Committee, then under the firm control of the eastern liberal wing of the party and lead by Nelson Rockefeller, quickly mustered all its heavy artillery to blow Reagan out of the water.

Rockefeller, who had been appointed Vice President to Gerald Ford when he took Nixon's place, was so unpopular within the party that he was incapable of winning nomination or election in his own right. Like Teddy Kennedy on the Democrat side, however, he had acquired an iron-fisted control over the insider party machinery. He was able to dictate party direction and anoint party candidates at will. Aside from the fact that Gerald Ford was his personally hand-picked candidate, Rockefeller held a deep personal hatred for Ronald Reagan.

Reagan did well in the popular vote primaries leading up to the 1976 Convention, but Ford came to the gathering with a safe lead. The archaic way the Republican Party picks its delegates assured Rockefeller of having full control when the meeting convened. Although the inner Republican powers could control the votes, they could not engender any real enthusiasm for the unappealing Ford. The wild affection and personal support exhibited at that convention for Ronald Reagan was a severe irritant for the testy Rockefeller.

Wearing two hats, as a delegate from Florida and as a certified correspondent, I had the opportunity to observe much of what went on behind the scenes in Kansas City that year. In all my years of writing about and participating in politics, I have never witnessed politics at a dirtier level than that practiced up to and during that meeting. The Rockefeller machine was not content just to defeat Ronald Reagan for the nomination, which they easily had the votes to accomplish. They wanted to destroy him both politically and personally. Fearful that some of their delegates might be caught up in the excitement and break ranks by switching support to Reagan, the Rockefeller/Ford combine resorted to political blackmail like I had never witnessed before.

Some delegates, themselves candidates for local and national offices, were openly threatened with active opposition from within their own party if they switched their votes from Ford. One Congressman I knew quite well was told they would leak some damaging information collected by the Justice Department if he did not tow the line. It made no difference that they knew and admitted the personal information was unproved. The mere airing of the charges would doom his candidacy. Others, who had relatives or close friends in good government jobs, were privately advised those jobs could be eliminated and the individuals either discharged or transferred to untenable positions. When the time came to vote on the convention nominee, even though a majority of delegates personally supported Reagan, Rockefeller had their votes solidly in hand for Gerald Ford.

After the convention went through the motions and Ford had the nomination, the Florida delegation quickly went into private session to discuss a move to draft Ronald Reagan as the vice presidential nominee. Lead by then Florida Congressman, Lou Frey and former Florida GOP Chairman Tommy Thomas, the delegation unanimously voted to endorse Reagan for vice president. A reluctant state Chairman, Bill Taylor (a solid Rockefeller follower), was dispatched to the Ford headquarters to inform him of the activity on behalf of Ronald Reagan. Gerald Ford sent his personal word back that he would hold off his announcement on a vice presidential choice the next day until afternoon. Ford advised that, if the convention showed solid support for a draft of Reagan, he would go along with Reagan as his running mate.

The Florida delegation jumped to the phones and started contact with all the other delegations scattered around Kansas City. By 2:00 AM the following morning, thirty-three state delegations had held formal caucuses and voted overwhelmingly to support a draft of Ronald Reagan for vice president. That morning, at 9:00 AM, a group of us was scheduled to meet with Ronald Reagan at his hotel to present the result of the caucuses and secure his formal agreement to go with the wishes of the convention. As we pulled into the hotel parking garage around 8:30 AM after a wild ride across town, a news bulletin came over the car radio announcing Gerald Ford had just held a press conference and declared that his choice for vice president was Senator Bob Dole of Kansas! No mention of Ronald Reagan came up during Ford's presentation, with a smug Nelson Rockefeller standing by.

Stunned at the unabashed double cross, we trooped up to the hotel ballroom where Reagan was waiting with his campaign team to receive our delegation with its announcement of the draft movement. Our meeting with Ronald Reagan behind closed doors that morning was an emotional one. No one was more shocked than Reagan to think that a President of the United States would so callously go back on his word as had Gerald Ford. With tears in his eyes, Reagan, in response to the Rockefeller/Ford public assertion that he did not want the vice presidential nomination, advised that he never had even been asked the question by anyone from that cabal. He told us, "Of course I would accept the nomination. If my party felt it was for the good of the party and our country, I'd be proud to be on the ticket!"

Later, I learned that, prior to Ford's press conference, in a private meeting with Rockefeller and one of his top aides, the frustrated former Governor of New York had killed the deal. Ford, realizing that it would make the ticket nearly unbeatable, wanted to offer the position to Reagan. Rockefeller angrily pounded the table and shouted, "I will not have that SOB on my ticket!" Ford meekly gave in to the man in control and guaranteed that Jimmy Carter, the Democrat nominee, would become the next President of the United States.

Although urged by angry supporters to disavow Ford and the Republican ticket, Ronald Reagan, as he has done so often, rose above the fray and announced he would loyally support his party despite what it had done to him. Congressman Lou Frey, although trying several times afterward for elected office with the Republican Party insiders allied against him, was never again elected to office. Tommy Thomas, himself scorned by the GOP elite, continued as a loyal supporter and Florida campaign manager for Ronald Reagan in subsequent elections. The national campaign for Ford, still under the control of Rockefeller, meted punishment on the Florida instigators of the draft movement by virtually cutting off the state from any financial campaign support. William Taylor, Florida GOP Chairman who was openly opposed to the Reagan draft, was rewarded by the National GOP with lucrative inside lobbying connections.

Ironically, as so frequently happens in history, this Reagan/ Ford matter was to come back in a bizarre manner at the 1980 Republican convention in Detroit. This time, despite the old line Republican insiders who were riding the George Bush horse after the miserable failure of Gerald Ford in 1976, Ronald Reagan came into the meeting with a solid majority of delegate votes for the nomination. Although Rockefeller was no longer a factor in the GOP, having gone down with the Ford ship, the old line core of the party was still opposing Reagan.

With the nomination a foregone conclusion, the convention, as is usually the case, had little to excite interest as the delegates convened. The only matter to be considered even remotely newsworthy was speculation over whom Reagan would chose as a running mate. Most of us delegates had already concluded that he would chose George Bush as his running mate, since that would force the old line party insiders into his campaign camp.

Things were to liven up, however, as one of the many rumors usually circulating at these political bashes took on a soap opera type of life.

Apparently concocted, or at least adopted early in its life by CBS Television, was the story that former President Gerald Ford was to be Reagan's choice as a running mate. With no political intrigue to discuss and nothing but the usual endless boring speeches by the has-beens and would-bes to occupy them, the conventioneers picked up the CBS story, and it became an instant topic of private debates. To most of us, particularly those who had been through the 1976 execution, the story made no sense at all. We knew Reagan, who finds it difficult to dislike anyone, still had no special love for Ford after the Kansas City double-cross. It was hard to imagine his even listening to such a proposal. Despite the general skepticism within the convention, CBS News anchorman Walter Cronkite persisted in hyping the idea and acting generally like a Ford campaign manager.

Cronkite, puffed with his own importance as TV's most-watched "talking head", apparently considered himself to be a premier king maker. The story became more and more ludicrous as "Uncle Walter" exploited every rumor (most of which were manufactured by his own staff flaks) advancing his plan of conquest. The compliant Ford, himself possessed of an ego that had long ago consumed any rational thought processes, was drawn along by the TV king into a vaudevillian exchange on prime-time television. With a serious mein, Ford bumbled into the Cronkite plan, expounding upon the confused idea he would be a "co-president" with Ronald Reagan!

It is sad testimony to the make-believe world of television that these two would even get on the air with such nonsense, but even worse that many supposedly knowledgeable political leaders would go along with the fantasy. It boggles the mind to consider they were apparently seriously proposing the Presidency be put in the hands of a committee.

Think of the potential fireworks when Betty Ford and Nancy Reagan had to decide how to divide the White House living quarters to accommodate their respective families! How about the Oval Office? Would Gerald and Ronald work out a time sharing plan? There is hardly enough room for one desk in the Oval Office now. How do you decide which co-president uses it? Maybe a divided day would have been best. Ronald could take the 9 to 12 shift, and Gerald, after a fun morning on the golf course, could move in for the 1 to 4 tour of duty. Think of the problem with the official music. There would have to be a "Hail to the Chiefs" march when both were present, with a "Hail to One of the Chiefs" when they made solo appearances.

Of course the whole affair was silly, but the crazy scramble by TV Networks to find something for their talking heads to fill air time with at these political conventions spawns silliness. Even the weird imagination of "Geraldo" or "Oprah" could not top that performance. In the murky atmosphere of politics, when the media moguls pontificate, nary a cool head dares raise the obvious questions, such as, "What possible help could Gerald Ford be in a campaign, or in the White House?" After a totally undistinguished short career as the appointed replacement for Richard Nixon and a dismal performance as a candidate in his own right, Ford's resume did not look promising. Such questions did not slow progress of the fantasy, as the bureaucratic news media rushed to feed their own creation.

During the Detroit convention, while visiting in the hotel lobby with one of my fellow delegates, we were approached by a "stringer" for CBS News. These were the foot soldiers sent out by all the TV news people to gather the tidbits that their writers turned into the learned pronouncements put out by the talking heads on prime time. The stringer, with notebook in hand, in a confidential tone, asked me what I thought of the plan to nominate Gerald Ford for the vice presidency. My response was that I did not believe there was such a "plan". As far as I could see, George Bush was the frontrunner and logical choice for vice president.

Clearly disappointed by my answer and pointedly not taking any notes, the young fellow turned to my friend with the same question. Even having known this delegate for some years and knowing he was something of a practical jokester, I was unprepared for the audacity of his answer.

With his arm over the stringer's shoulder, he drew him confidentially towards a quiet corner of the lobby. In a low, but authoritative, voice, he confided, "You understand this is confidential?" The excited stringer, eyes popping, held his pencil poised. "We don't want it spreading until Ron makes the formal announcement. I just came from Ron's headquarters, where we put the deal together. Gerry has agreed to run!" The CBS stringer, hardly able to contain himself, hurriedly thanked us and rushed out of the lobby.

As I stood there shaking my head, my friend with a broad grin said, "Wait until you see Walter tonight." Sure enough, Cronkite, in his patented pompous manner which brooked no argument, announced the deal was set!

Ronald Reagan did go on, of course, to pick George Bush as his running mate, as had been his intention from the start. Reagan, with his deep respect and reverence for the United States institution of the presidency, felt that he had to respect ex-President Ford to the extent of giving the appearance of serious consideration to the preposterous plan. It was not in his character to dismiss it out of hand for the foolishness it was, any more than he could have publicly denounced the shabby treatment he had received from Ford earlier at Kansas City.

The Cronkite ploy in this two-day story became more understandable a few years later after he had retired from active TV appearances. In an interview, he admitted to having been a lifelong liberal Democrat with little, if no, sympathy for the Republican Party or any of its candidates. His special contempt for any conservative political viewpoints had always been obvious. Ronald Reagan was definitely not his kind of guy. What better way for him to advance the cause of his Democrat favorite than to help the Republicans put together a laughing stock of a presidential ticket! Like most of his contemporaries in the media, he continually underrated Ronald Reagan's inherent good sense.

Reagan, while exhibiting this devotion to proper procedure or protocol, if you wish, was not unmindful of the political alliance against him within the Republican Party National Committee. He had run his election campaigns from outside the party, bucking their inside dirty tricks all the way. When he entered the presidency, he quickly took steps to neutralize that cancer. His old friend, Senator Paul Laxalt from Nevada, was appointed by the President to assume the position of President of the Republican Party. There was no provision in party rules for such a position, but Reagan's tremendous personal popularity squelched any attempt by the insiders to complain. He, thus, effectively by-passed the Chairman of the GOP, rendering him a mere figurehead for the duration of Reagan's term in office. All political activity and appointment plums normally channeled through the GOP Committee were now handled directly through the White House and Laxalt. Ronald Reagan continued to give public lip service to the National GOP, but he had his final revenge against the gang that had done him in during 1976 and had tried again in 1980.

The Republican diehards in the national organization never gave up, however. During Reagan's whole first term as president, they provided a rumor mill, feeding the press cockeyed stories predicting the President's eminent resignation. I listened to National Committee members in closed party meetings frequently expounding upon that theme. Reagan would resign in time for Bush to take over prior to the 1984 election. It was one of the ploys they used to keep the faithful in line, making sure they understood Reagan was only temporary.

During Ronald's years in Dixon, particularly during high school, his stubborn insistence on following the proper form and procedure was to endear him to his teachers and community leaders. Even though he made little effort to win personal popularity with his schoolmates, his reputation as a straight shooter, along with the obvious approval of the adults in his life, brought him many leadership positions. Those positions, as president or chairman of many school organizations, he earned by quickly developing a reputation as a youngster who got things done. Not only did he get them done, but also his contemporaries, sold on his clear-cut, even-handed way of doing it, gave him unflagging support.

CHAPTER 9

THE EXECUTIVE DIRECTOR

Through all the probing into the life and times of the Reagan family, Jack Reagan was the most difficult to bring into focus. Understandably, since Ronald was so close to his mother, Nelle easily developed into an almost larger-than-life figure. Unfortunately, some early decisions in the political life of Ronald Reagan were to distort the picture, generally accepted as the portrait, albeit sketchy, of Jack Reagan, father, family provider and role model.

The negative image of Ronald's father and the bum rap he continually receives from Reagan biographers in all honesty must be laid directly at the feet of his youngest son. It is important to note that this occurred because of one of Ronald Reagan's most enduring characteristics. This trait, contributing in large measure to his political successes, became the root cause of the apparent trashing of his father.

Early in his youth, school, church and civic officials recognized and capitalized on Ronald's willingness to take direction. Much akin to the earlier-mentioned desire to follow proper form in personal and governmental relationships at almost any cost, was his willingness to blindly follow the advice of political "experts" or image makers during, and even after, his campaigns. While maintaining a stubborn "damn the torpedoes" attitude on major domestic and international issues dear to his heart, he was always compliant on the political methods of image building. This, of course, was the same trait that had made him so popular with his movie studio. He easily accepted, without quarrel, the image that they decreed was best for his career.

When Reagan's book, "Where's the Rest of Me?", was being prepared, the image makers pulled out all the stops to portray him in the most saleable manner to the potential voters. One of their "politically correct" approaches misfired, and one of them seriously smudged the memory of his father. Sadly, although the political experts would never admit to this, neither of their ploys was at all necessary in the selling of Ronald Reagan.

Much has been written recently on the subject of "political

correctness", particularly as a result of the academic world's attempt to rewrite history to suit current fashions in human relations. Shortened by the media to simply "PC", we are lead to believe that this is a new phenomenon foisted on an always gullible public. Political correctness has been part of the standard operating procedure for the political image makers ever since the birth of politics itself. Professionals in the art of selling candidates for public office have always known the value of certain personal characteristics in their subjects and concurrently have been well aware of the need to avoid the "no-no's". Physically, "PC" is easy enough to understand — tall candidates are more saleable than short ones, a full head of hair beats a bald one and firm square jaws have always been in. It's in the personal background of the candidate, however, in which "PC" begins to come into major play.

The American dream that anyone can overcome an adverse background and achieve success has long been established in our folklore. This dogma is so well-fixed in our collective consciousness, that we find it hard to accept successful people who were born with silver spoons in their mouths. Political candidate managers, well aware of this quirk in our thinking, go to extraordinary lengths to create "proper" backgrounds for those they would promote into our major leadership positions. If they can create a background of poverty, or at least a more-than-average disadvantage in the early youth of their charge, the game is already half won. The old "Horatio Alger" image of the poor, but honest, hero rising against nearly impossible odds to achieve success and wealth in later life is still the American standard we like to use to define our leaders. Well-versed in this peculiarly American lore, the image makers always attempt to create poverty in their candidate's background, or at the very least, obscure any indication the potential officeholder had an affluent family.

In an interesting study, Baltzeil and Schneiderman of Rutgers University did much to dissolve the reality of the Horatio Alger myth. Briefly, they showed that of the thirty-six United States Presidents from Washington to Nixon, thirty-one came from well-to-do upper or upper-middle class backgrounds. Even the five they concede as from less-than-affluent families are suspect. Lincoln, for example, did not have anywhere near the poor background attributed to him. Despite the contrary facts, it is still considered politically correct to create poverty in your candidate's early life.

The attempt at the "poor beginnings" gambit with Ronald Reagan was a bust. Anyone who visits Reagan's hometown in Dixon will quickly note that Ronald did not grow up on the wrong side of the tracks! The President's own assertion, repeated many times, while speaking of his youth — "It was a good life. I couldn't have asked for anything more, then or now!" — has pretty well stifled the "rags to riches" story.

Although intellectually accepting Reagan's solid middle-class early life, most commentators have twisted statements in that early book to give him a decidedly lower-class father. In this approach, the image makers salvaged at least a bone. Now they could depict him as rising above a failed parent.

Next to the "rising from poverty" bit, in modern politics it has become quite fashionable and right in line with current "PC" to have had an alcoholic, preferably abusive parent. It is in this area that Jack Reagan has taken an unfair beating from writers too slipshod to delve into the facts. It all started in that early book by Reagan, right up front on page twelve. Here he recounts an episode, as an eleven-year-old, finding his father passed out drunk on the floor. Thus the die was cast! Forevermore, Jack Reagan was to be known as a fall-down drunk!

One of the troubling little details nagging us as we compiled our research notes was this matter of Jack Reagan's drinking. The people that we talked to who could still remember Jack simply did not recall him as a man with a drinking problem. Several of them expressed real concern as to why both Ronald and his brother Neil perpetuated the stories of Jack's "alcoholism". They all remembered Jack as a pleasant, sociable man who was unfailingly courteous and friendly in all his public dealings, in and out of his store. One of the oldest family friends and staunchest supporters of the President wistfully told us that she hoped the boys (Ronald and Neil) would some day make it right about their father. One old friend of the family pointed out that Jack was a regular golfing partner of one of the town's leading doctors. She indicated, from her friendship with the doctor's wife, that such a relationship would not have lasted had Jack really been an uncontrolled drunk!

So how did this all come about, and what was the father of the President really like? More important to our study, what was the real contribution of Jack to the raising and molding of a future President? Did Ronald Reagan, as the image makers would have us believe, through sheer grit, rise above the handicap of a wastrel of a father? Was Jack just an irksome burden to the family and a drag on their progress through life? Was he, as one harsh writer reported, just an "itinerant, drunken shoe salesman"?

The truth of the story is far different from that painted so far. Much of what the public came to admire and love in his son are characteristics that he inherited and learned from his father.

That Jack was a compassionate and easy going member of the family group goes almost without saying. Consider first his marriage to Nelle. Presented in her early years as a fun-loving, outgoing young wife, well-suited to Jack's gregarious personality, she underwent radical changes throughout their marriage. Her conversion to a strict religion and becoming a near fanatic in the fight to ban alcohol did not cause Jack to waver in his love and devotion to his Nelle. Not only did he stick with her, but also, as we will see later, he became very much a participant in her activism and public life. This closeness and unquestioned devotion between his parents were extremely important factors in the development of young Ronald. His blossoming from a painfully shy youth into a fantastically popular, mature personality was due in large part to the compassion and understanding of his father.

Writers who have brushed casually through Reagan's early life tend to dwell upon the frequent moves made by the family in those beginning years. This is usually cited as evidence that Jack was footloose and incapable of holding a steady job. The truth is that Jack had a driving ambition to be his own boss. He wanted to do things his way and had enough confidence in his own ability to keep driving until he got to the head of the pack. In that respect, Ronald is certainly a chip off the old block. He strove for the front of the parade all his life as well!

Since Jack and Nelle were both oriented to and preferred small town life, Jack's thriving ambition was confined to narrow choices. His natural ability at retail sales, especially shoes, limited the opportunities to move ahead in those little communities. Usually the local market was dominated by only one or two general stores, with the top positions held by the owners or their families. To Jack's credit, he never gave up striving to get ahead and to make things better for his family. In Tampico he finally hit the jackpot, convincing his boss, H.C. Pitney, to finance him in his own shoe store in Dixon. Finally, he was his own man, leading his own parade and a highly respected business leader in his community.

The Fashion Boot Shop in Dixon flourished for ten years before the Great Depression and business crash of 1929 took it down. That the Reagan business failed in those dark days is no disgrace. Tens of thousands of others folded during those bleak years. By 1932, virtually none of the many small-to-medium businesses that had thrived during the '20's were still in existence. If Jack Reagan had truly suffered from a major drinking problem, the Great Depression would have driven him right into the gutter. Many of his contemporaries did give up, and the back streets and alleys were crowded with broken, aimless men drifting without hope.

Jack Reagan, a feisty Irishman, was not about to surrender to the hard times. During that stretch of four or five years, with the country dominated by breadlines and charity soup kitchens for the unemployed, Jack continued to scrape out a living for his family. He hit the road selling shoes, he worked in seedy little stores, he even served a stint as a menial office clerk, but most importantly, he managed to continue working. Considering that general unemployment topped one-third of the work force, and that most of the out-of-work had given up, Jack's performance was pretty remarkable.

During those traumatic years for Jack and Nelle Reagan, one important fact is overlooked in most narratives. During the worst economic crunch this country, or the world for that matter, has ever seen, with all around them reduced to abject charity, Mr. and Mrs. Jack Reagan were still able to maintain both sons in college. Granted, both Ronald and Neil worked to support their education, but any parent can tell you there are not enough scholarships and student jobs to relieve the parents of the whole burden. That Jack and Nelle not only survived, but also saw their sons through to graduation from Eureka College during those years is eloquent testimony of their success as parents.

Back to Jack Reagan and those persistent stories of his "problem". The first hint that the story was more to bolster a political game plan, rather than to chronicle real history, came in that early Reagan book. Ronald is purported to remember his mother's counseling him and his brother to forgive Jack's drinking problem because it was a sickness he could not control. The book goes on from there, permanently labeling his father as an "alcoholic". It is highly unlikely that Nelle would have so characterized her husband. The concept of alcoholism, as a disease, was not generally accepted and received little discussion in those days. The WCTU, Nelle's guiding light in the crusade for the Eighteenth Amendment to the Constitution, preached that the consumption of alcohol was purely and simply a sin. WCTU was unequivocal in its condemnation of alcohol as being of the Devil; therefore, its use was a mortal sin. Had the concept of alcoholism as an illness had any broad following then, it's doubtful that Nelle would have bought it. Her fanatic following of the legions of Carrie Nation, along with her firmly-held religious convictions, would have prohibited her budging from the basic concept of sin. It is far more likely she would have counseled her children to help seek the forgiveness of God for the sins of their father, if they were that serious. That she herself found no reason to permanently condemn her husband will be borne out as we follow the story of this rather remarkable couple.

To have reported the facts concerning this personal matter would have flown in the face of the ritual "PC" promoted by the political image makers. Later we will see how that sort of political counseling has presented a continuing problem with Ronald Reagan and his strong Christian faith.

Jack's influence on his youngest son was deeper and more long lasting than most narratives of his past would lead us to believe. Dad was there at many critical points in Ronald's youth, bolstering and promoting his shy son. Later we will see how Jack's strong political convictions and activism shaped Ronald's standards throughout his life. What the United States got in political guidance from President Reagan bore the strong imprint of Jack Reagan!

Norman Wymbs

CHAPTER 10

SCRIPT CHANGES

Today's strong public interest in the environment and personal health habits, even while changing many long-established life habits, cannot be compared to the fanatic fervor of the "ban the bottle" forces early in the century. None of the modern environmental terrorists or nuclear ban activists can hold a candle to the singleness of purpose and the militant aggression of the alcohol temperance gang prior to 1920!

In our world of continuous sales promotion, especially through television, it is impossible to imagine a world without alcoholic beverages. Today's attitude, conditioned as we are to constant scenes of fun-filled sports and outdoor activities served up by beautiful people at carefree beer parties, simply does not relate to the history of the turn-of-the-century prohibition movement. Never in this information-saturated world could the mind conceive of public opinion's reaching such a fever pitch that a nationwide popular vote would turn off the national alcohol spigot. Although the more subtle forces gradually closing down the tobacco industry may accomplish the same end, a direct Constitutional assault is unthinkable. Yet, in 1920, with the final passage of the Eighteenth Amendment to the U.S. Constitution, an aroused public did just that to the drinkers of America!

Looking back from our present, supposedly more enlightened, position, it is easy to believe that the influence of the Christian church denominations reached their peak during this period in our history. Certainly it would be hard to imagine their exerting such persuasive powers today. This era's split in the formerly monolithic Roman Catholic Church over the issue of abortion best illustrates the decline of church influence on everyday life. Abortion, as a moral issue, easily fit into church dogma until a few generations ago, and such was the Church's power that few of the faithful would dare espouse an opposing position. Matters considered to be moral issues were decided by religious leaders and usually were given, at least publicly, unquestioned compliance by the faithful. Such was the case for alcoholic abstinence after World War I.

Physical and medical considerations were not paramount in the booze war. This was to be, purely and simply, a moral battleground. God was brought down foursquare on the side of the "drys", leaving the "wets" with only the Devil to support their pleasures. Given the times and the status of the church, a direct squaring off between the God Squad and the Devil's

Followers left little doubt as to the ultimate outcome. The issue was considered truly heaven-sent by the relatively obscure, mostly middle-American, Protestant church denomination, the Disciples of Christ.

With small, generally poor churches scattered among modest communities throughout the central and southern states, the Disciples could not be considered in the same big hitter class of such mega-denominations as the Baptists and the Presbyterians. Their relatively short period of glory, as a matter of interest, coincided with their whole-hearted adoption of the issue of "Prohibition". Already strongly inclined towards social activism in their home communities, the Disciples were forever seeking worthy "causes". With active and motivated congregation troops at the ready, the temperance movement was truly heaven-sent. With their membership dominated by actively organized women's groups, not especially unusual in any church denomination, the temperance movement became the cause to end all causes. Forming a close alliance with the national "Women's Christian Temperance Union", the Disciples of Christ boomed in popularity during the ensuing all-out war. In most communities, the Disciples and the WCTU were indistinguishable.

There is no indication how Nelle Reagan became so fervent a champion of the temperance movement, but there is ample evidence she was marching in the front ranks from the first call to battle. Among liberated women, Nelle easily put to shame most of her contemporaries and, in today's world, would be miles ahead of most feminists in her activism. While a constant lecturer on the subject of temperance in her own and other churches in the area, she hardly expended all her energies preaching to the saved. Her tireless campaign carried her into the local community of business and civic organizations, in effect bearding the lion in his own den. Jack Reagan was no small factor in her mission, although he generally maintained a low profile on the subject. An active local business owner, Nelle's husband used his professional and business contacts to guide and promote her into a lucrative public opinion territory much beyond the scope of her small church.

Nelle held her audiences with more than the force of her considerable personality. She had the facts and experience to back up her lectures. From the early days of her marriage to Jack, she spent many hours visiting and ministering to the unfortunate residents of the local jails and public institutions. She believed firmly that most of the souls she tried to help were in poor straits through circumstances that could be remedied with a little loving care and a helping hand. Many of the destitute inmates she visited were victims of excessive consumption of alcoholic beverages. Using her well-worn bible freely, she preached love for the Lord, coupled with temperance, to solve their personal problems. Her unquestioned sincerity and upbeat personality proved very effective in this ministry.

Although Jack Reagan may not have held fully concurrent views with his hyperactive wife on the subject of alcohol, he did share her deep concern for less fortunate members of humanity. He was as outspoken on the subject of discrimination and lack of opportunities for the forgotten little man as she was on the matter of drinking. Later, we will see how this strong sense of fair play was to propel Jack into an activist political role and attract the attention of the first Roosevelt Administration. That role, in turn, was to have a powerful lifelong effect on Jack's younger son and his political path.

Both Ronald and his brother Neil recall in those early years how many times their parents provided shelter and care for one of Nelle's "boys", as she called the unfortunates she befriended. It was not uncommon for Nelle and Jack to provide temporary food and shelter in their home for one of Nelle's charges just released from jail or some other institution. While Nelle ministered to their spiritual needs and saw that they filled up on good home cooking, Jack helped them find jobs so they could become self-sufficient members of society once again. Later, during the first Roosevelt Administration, Jack's experience and compassion were to be put to good use for his country.

The elder Reagans never made any effort to draw attention to their tireless efforts to help the less fortunate. Even today, President Reagan refuses to capitalize on the family's compassionate work in their community. Nelle quietly accepted that God would provide whatever approval was warranted, while Jack gruffly maintained, "They would do it for me if they could."

This deep sense of responsibility toward those whom fate had dealt with unkindly has always been an integral part of the Reagan character. Like their parents before them, the two boys have always shunned any public notice of their efforts. The President still quietly makes phone calls, scribbles off notes and offers financial help to many individuals who have been treated poorly by circumstances beyond their control. Older brother Neil, a financially successful businessman in later life, usually brushes off any comment on his generous support of worthy causes with a patented Reagan quip.

While Nelle continued her ministry to the forgotten throughout her life, much of the militancy left her activities when the Eighteenth Amendment became law. Suddenly, the war against the evils of alcohol had been won, and the army had to be demobilized. The WCTU, deprived of the impetus for its battle flag, gradually faded into a shadow of its former might. The more raucous, such as the Carrie Nation clones in the organized cadres, had to discard their axes and seek a more normal function in society. It was impossible for many of the activists to adapt to their victory, and the psychological consequences strained many families. Nelle Reagan, however, hardly missed a beat as, even without the flashing banners of the prohibition wars, she had enough inner drive and sufficient goals to march firmly onward. For several years after the WCTU victory, Ronald's mother threw herself vigorously into the activities of her church. As always, her youngest son was at her side all the way.

The Dixon Christian Church, as well as the whole Disciples denomination, like their soul mates of the WCTU, lost much of their activist steam with the advent of legal prohibition. Reverend Waggoner of the local church had his hands full acquiring and developing a new church property during these difficult years. Nelle and her young son Ronnie were two of the firmest rocks in the foundation of his struggling congregation. Nelle's considerable abilities were now concentrated on her church and her strong personal Christian faith.

While doing her part to help acquire and develop the new physical facilities for the church, she did not neglect the spiritual side. She became a standout leader in congregational activities, as well as one of its most knowledgeable Christian teachers. The bible was her text, and she taught her faith with every bit of the fervor she had been expending in the war against alcohol. These were particularly important years for young Ronald, now in his most vulnerable, formative period. Not only was he a quick learner with an instinctive leaning toward the dramatic, but also, from the first, he exhibited an evangelical spirit. Quickly absorbing the biblical teaching, he continually surprised his elders with a mature grasp of complex theological concepts.

Although never one to form strong friendships, Ronald Reagan did have some heroes in his life that were instrumental in guiding him toward his ultimate goal. Given the closeness of his mother to their church and the strong personal influence exerted by Reverend Waggoner on the family, it is not surprising that one of Ronnie's early heroes would be the son of the minister. Garland Waggoner, six years older than his youthful admirer, was already a standout student athlete in high school when the Reagans arrived in Dixon. To the well-traveled youngster, finally settling down in one community gave him his first opportunities to form close associations outside the family. With the church and his personal faith becoming such important parts of his life, it was natural that young Waggoner would attract his attention.

Garland Waggoner was to prove a worthy hero to this future President of the United States. A good scholar, devout Christian and, very importantly, an outstanding football player, he fit every criterion young Ronald held important. Naturally enough, the son of the popular minister soon moved on to college at his father's old school, Eureka College.

Ronald, just approaching high school age himself, vowed to emulate his hero, making clear to all concerned that he too, would ultimately attend Eureka College. At that age, already exhibiting the stubborn purposefulness that was to be his hallmark throughout life, he began tucking away his meager earnings from odd jobs toward a "Eureka College Fund". Although handicapped by his poor eyesight, he not only was determined to go to the college, but also he firmly announced that he would star in football like his hero, Garland.

Always intellectually more mature than his peers, Ronald generally formed his attachments to those older than he. While attending South Central School in Dixon where the facilities housed both grade school and high school, the sixth grader formed a strong friendship with Gladys Shippert, a high school student and an active member of his Christian Church. When her family moved away from Dixon, Ronald corresponded regularly for several years with his friend. One of those letters, written in 1922 (reproduced in full in "A Place To Go Back To"), revealed much about the depth of feeling the young man had for those he looked up to as role models. That letter, in atrocious handwriting (not much improved since) and impossible spelling (much improved with the advent of glasses), indicated his continued attention to young Waggoner. Referring to his mother's regular correspondence with the Waggoner family, he advised Miss Shippert that Garland had made the football team at Eureka and had even played in a game against the University of Illinois. In his schoolboy scrawl, he went on to report about the local high school football team's progress, mentioning in passing that he was now drum major of the boys' band.

Jumping ahead four years later, we find Ronald and Garland crossing paths once again. The Dixon Christian Church's Easter week services of 1926 included "John Garland Waggoner, Jr., Eureka College, '26 — preaching the Good Friday service at the church". Ronald Reagan is listed in the same bulletin, along with Frances Smice, as leading the church's annual sunrise prayer meeting on Easter Sunday.

Nelle's important position as teacher of the leading adult Sunday School class and her continuing lectures before the congregation on social issues as well as church doctrine inevitably drew her inquisitive younger son into a deeper awareness of his Christian heritage. Never one to meekly accept as rote fact what was dished up by his elders, Ronald sometimes drove them to distraction with his constant insistence that the facts back up the theory. This unceasing thirst for knowledge and understanding propelled him deeply into the bible and the foundations of Christian doctrine. Much later, after entering the Presidency, he gave his political staff ulcers with frequent applications of his religious faith to political and governmental problems. The White House spin doctors nearly went bananas as the media pundits zeroed in on his early references to the Soviet Union as the "Evil Empire" so prominent in biblical prophecy. After the Soviet Union crumbled in 1991, one of its former leaders was to remark, "Reagan was right; we were an 'Evil Empire'." Even though his political staffers were generally successful in tempering some of his stronger public statements, we'll note as we go along how the deep faith of his mother continued to guide his every major move in public life.

When the Reverend B. H. Cleaver took over the Dixon Christian Church after the death of Reverend Waggoner, it had a decided effect on the Reagans, both mother and son. Cleaver was less inclined to leave church operations to his flock, as had been the policy of his predecessor. His "hands on" approach to his ministry and the church organization left the congregation's activists with less to do, bringing on another script change for Nelle Reagan. At the same time, a rapidly-maturing Ronald was drawn more into the functioning of the church, as the new minister and his family took a quick liking to the intense, but quiet, youngster.

Nelle, meanwhile, blossomed out into community activities beyond anything seen before, and, as always, drew her younger son with her. Some of these new directions were to become among the most important factors in developing the Ronald Reagan personality that captivated the world decades later!

CHAPTER 11

SIBLING SUPPORT

The worst nightmares of political candidate managers arise from the actions of close family members of their charges. By the time an individual office seeker advances through the system and is ready to run for one of the highest offices, the campaign and personal staff members generally have a very good handle on how he or she will react under every possible condition. Unfortunately for the peace of mind of the spin doctors, this does not necessarily hold true for the candidate's immediate family.

Being the spouse, brother, sister or even the parent of a congressman or governor is not so big a deal as to cause much difficulty for the officeholder. Generally, the public, or even the ever-watchful media, find little of interest in the wives or husbands of this level of officeholder. It is a whole new ball game, however, when the family of the President of the United States is concerned. Our President and his family traditionally have been our country's *de facto royalty* and, therefore, fair game for almost any form of public inquisitiveness. The personal probing and rude scrutiny of the President's family has gone far beyond what any individual in a lesser position would tolerate in his or her own life.

Historically, presidential families have seemed to be special targets of the hungry press — and, more recently, the leering eye of television. No matter how exemplary the behavior of these generally unwilling targets, the pictures usually painted are not flattering. Few past Presidents have escaped the poison pens or insulting cameras of the "royal family" chroniclers. It has taken years for the unpleasant memories of the sharp attacks on Roosevelt's family, Eisenhower's driver and Nixon's brother to begin to fade. More currently, who can forget the field day the media had with President Carter's brother, Billy?

Some of this hunger to attack those surrounding our national leaders probably is brought upon them by the slick, and usually totally phony, image our presidential candidates try to project to the voters. During our quadrennial circus we call the presidential campaign, those aspiring to lead our country can be counted upon to perform a ritualized dance for the benefit of the public. The media largely goes along with the performances, finding it easier to insert them into their three-inch columns or twenty-second sound bites. But, even while taking the easy route, the reporters resent the way they are being "had" and frequently resort to the attack in other areas. During these campaigns the presidential wanna-bes can always be found in prominent view on Sundays, attending church with the slavish media trooping along behind. Aside from campaign time, most of these candidates and, one suspects, the media probably could not find the building without a guide. Similarly, it is obligatory in this ritual opera to march in St. Patrick's Day parades and attend Labor Day picnics, while not forgetting the all-important wreath-laying on soldiers graves' on Memorial Day. Mandatory at these carefully-staged performances is the spouse who shows intensely devoted support without projecting too obtrusively into the spotlight. If the candidate has children, they are expected to be in prominent attendance and, if young, properly tranquilized for the occasion.

Generally, most candidates and their families know the basic manual of operation so that the wholesome image of the loyal all-American family is properly projected. Within this same category of performance falls the act of kissing babies and hugging little old ladies (being sure they are truly old). All of these acts of image control, dictated by the candidate's handlers, are basic to the campaign and present little more difficulty than choosing the proper necktie color or hair styling.

When it gets to family members beyond immediate spouse and children, the problems get stickier. It is not difficult to have an alert staff member nearby to yank the stimulating beverage from the candidate's hand just before the photographers snap pictures, but what do you do if a relative insists on giving television interviews while sipping from a can of beer? Your candidate can be photographed every Sunday in church, but what do you do when a tabloid interviews the spouse's astrologer? That's why the image makers develop ulcers and heart problems early in life, as they rush around trying to camouflage the story.

President Reagan, throughout his time in office (and even since retiring), has suffered through multiple wolf pack attacks on his wife, Nancy. Remarkably absent from the media gorilla attacks has been Reagan's brother, Neil. There are good reasons for the media's lack of negative reporting on Neil, reasons that speak eloquently to the character of the President's older brother as well as the unusual closeness and mutual support between these two Reagans.

If ever there was a strong-willed, highly capable, media-enticing personality in a President's family, Neil Reagan fills the bill. Two years older than his famous brother, extremely successful in his own right and every bit as articulate as Ronald, it is a real tribute to his good character and common sense that he has maintained such a low profile. The unobtrusive public image, however, belies a strongly supportive relationship between the two throughout their lives. While apparently so different in public personalities, they are uncannily alike underneath and, in many ways, as similar as fraternal twins!

As mentioned earlier, while Ronald exhibited a quiet, self-contained personality during his early years, Neil could best be described as a scamp. In later years, the older brother enjoyed relating, "When we were kids, he was the quiet one, and I had all the personality. When we got older, I became shy and retiring, and look what he turned into!"

During those early years together, Ronnie could always be counted upon to follow established rules and traditional behavior, while Neil always appeared to be exploiting every avenue to shake up the established order of life. Neil was wildly popular with his contemporaries and always able to draw a crowd eager to participate in whatever outlandish escapade he concocted. The younger brother, while outwardly expressing dismay at some of his antics, deeply admired his brother and reveled in Neil's most notorious accomplishments. Ronald particularly admired Neil's superior abilities in sports, one of the young fellow's early and lifelong passions, and seldom missed the opportunity to graphically relate dramatic accounts of his brother's spectacular performances as an end on the high school football team.

Even though he was the envy of his younger brother because of his natural physical abilities, Neil's "devil-may-care" attitude toward life precluded his concentrating hard enough to become a true star at anything in those early years. Although just as lackadaisical toward academics, he had the brightness and quick wit natural to all the Reagans and slipped through school with little visible effort.

The youthful personality traits of these two closely- bound brothers were quite effectively revealed in their nicknames. There have already been many stories as to the origin of the affectionate names these two carried through much of their lives, but the story related in later life by Neil seems to best fit the actual personality traits of the boys.

Neil, in his youth, with a real penchant for music and public performing (as a teenager he performed in local stage productions of minstrel shows), was much taken by the street dandies of the times. He and some of his friends liked nothing better than slipping downtown on a Saturday night to observe the dashing Lothario of the time putting on a show at the local pool hall for the young ladies. He could hardly wait to get old enough to earn his own living and afford the fancy duds those role models wore.

As Neil relates, about this time in their lives came a day when their father, revolting at their long, unkempt hair, marched them down to the local barber shop and ordered the locks shorn. Laughing derisively at his younger brother's closely-cropped head, Neil offered, "You look like a Dutchman!" Stung by the attack, Ronnie retaliated with, "Oh yeah, well you look like Moon Mullins." Moon Mullins, at the time a popular cartoon character, was a caricature of the derby-hatted dandies that Neil and his friends so admired down at the pool hall.

For a time these two brothers used the nicknames "Dutch" and "Moon" to tease each other, but eventually they came to be terms of affection. To this day, they use the old nicknames.

As is so frequently true with nicknames, they really fit the character of their owners. Ronald, considered stodgy and fixed in his ways by many of his contemporaries, certainly gave the impression of a stubborn "Dutchman". Neil, on the other hand, with all his leanings towards the sophisticates of the day, truly played the part of the derby-wearing, cane-swinging "Moon Mullins" of comic strip fame.

One of the reasons Neil and Ronald have remained so close over the years has been Neil's ability to accept his younger brother's differing roles in their lives. In intimate talks with Neil, he slips easily into different reference planes for his younger brother. Whenever he speaks of their early years together growing up in Dixon, he recalls "Dutch". On those rare occasions when he lets down his flippant barriers to reveal his true affection for his younger brother, he refers to him as "Ronnie". Possessed of strong positions and opinions of his own that don't always coincide with those of his President brother, Neil, usually cryptically, refers to that persona as simply "Reagan"!

During the many months of piecing together the early years of Ronald Reagan, the closeness of the two brothers showed at every turn. As history evidenced the fact that the youngster had not developed a closeness to any of his contemporaries, the Neil factor loomed ever more importantly. When the President reminisces about his past, the few individuals he specifically recalls were mostly friends and contemporaries of his older brother. The fondly-remembered and often-recounted football skirmishes in the back yard and the corner lot were with Neil and his classmates. The much-told story of the firecrackers on the Rock River Bridge in Dixon (now called the Ronald Reagan Bridge) was a put-up job that Neil and his cohorts conned the youngster into. Never, in any of these reports, has there been any indication that Neil showed any irritation over his younger brother's always tagging along. To the contrary, all signs indicate that he actively and enthusiastically drew Ronnie into all his activities. The younger one, born big and always ahead of his age in size, was also quick-witted and mature enough to keep pace with the older gang. That "old beyond his years" characteristic probably had much to do with his apparent inability to relate to boys his own age, while drawing him closer to Neil and the older group.

When the boys grew older and ready to leave Mom and Dad to face the world on their own, their unique closeness took on greater significance in their lives. As we have noted, from an early age Ronald had mapped out a clear-cut path for his future. As far back as he or his family could remember, he was single-minded in his determination to acquire a college education. This resolve was somewhat unusual, since no one in his immediate family had ever reached so far. There was, in fact, little indication that the elders in the clan particularly encouraged such ambition. Even before he reached high school, the thrifty youngster was salting away his meager earnings from odd jobs toward his "college fund". Neil, a full year ahead of Ronnie in school, openly expressed contempt for higher education. Expressing disdain for the fancy-pants college sissies, his ambition was to get through high school as quickly and easily as possible, get a paying job and get on with the real joy of life. True to his aims, after shaking the dust of high school, he got a job at the local cement plant. Now, with money in pocket, he became a free-spending member of what passed for the swinging younger set in Dixon during those depressed years.

Enjoying his new affluence as a paycheck earner, Neil unmercifully ragged his brother about wanting to join those "stuck up" kids at college, but he never budged the determined Ronnie from his goal. True to his ambition, when Ronnie graduated from Dixon High a year later, he went on to enroll as a freshman at Eureka College. Later we will see how he was aided in his move on to that citadel of higher learning by the Dixon Christian Church, Reverend Cleaver and the Hall family.

When the young man left for college, the Reagan family, like most in the country, was struggling against the cruel early blows of the great economic depression of the late 1920's and '30's. Although, his family was unable to provide an auspicious sendoff, the eager student left with a prized new steamer trunk carrying his possessions. That first separation was to accentuate, rather than diminish, the already close bonding of the two brothers.

Ronald lost little opportunity during that first year at Eureka to remind his brother how the older boy was wasting his potential at the cement plant. With his now-legendary communication skills beginning to blossom, he pulled out all the stops to excite Neil over what he was missing by not being in college. Neil likes to recall this campaign and its end result.

One night, when Neil arrived home from work on a day that marked the end of summer vacation and Ronald's return to Eureka, he found his brother's prized steamer trunk sitting right in the middle of his bedroom. When he went downstairs to ask his mother about it, she turned to him with tears in her eyes and said, "He left it there for you, praying you would change your mind about going to college."

Neil recalled the reaction of his boss at the cement plant when he heard how Ronald had offered to help his older brother. "Hell, he up and fired me. (He) said anybody stupid enough to turn down encouragement like that was too stupid to work for him!" As Neil grinned with a tear in his eye, remembering the episode, he said, "So, what the heck, I went to college!"

Continuing to recall that time years ago, Neil went on, "Ronnie found me a job, a cheap room — everything!" Pausing, he gruffly cleared his throat, "Proud of him? (The newly-elected President of the United States) We don't talk that way. We're not that kind of stock." Now, unable to hide the emotion in his voice or the glistening in his eyes, "So we don't talk about being proud of each other — but we care all right!"

The college episode, like so many similar events later in life, speaks most eloquently of the genuine closeness of the

Reagan boys to each other and to their parents. Eureka College, an adjunct of the Disciples of Christ church denomination, hewed closely to the strictures and discipline of that conservative group. The college, itself, was a primary source of future ministers for the denomination, and, with the high-level church support he enjoyed, there is reason to believe administrators had high hopes of leading the articulate Ronald into the calling. While Eureka College in every way appeared a natural for Ronald Reagan, the same was not true for his brother, Neil.

Neil, who had openly chafed under what he considered the overly strict and stuffy attitude toward life exhibited by the Disciples, broke from the church of his mother while he was in high school and joined his father's Roman Catholic Church. His decision to join Ronald at Eureka College was a major concession, which only the unusual closeness of the two boys could bring about. As characteristic of all the Reagans, he threw himself into the college life and became an outstanding graduate of the small church institution. The discipline and relatively narrow teaching of the college did not bother him at all, and even to this day, he is a loyal supporter of his old alma mater.

When Ronald got out of college and went on to the radio job at a small station in Clinton, Iowa, he did not forget his older brother, still back in Eureka. Neil, graduating in the depths of the depression, faced a tough row to hoe when he struck out on his own. Although he obtained a very good position with the Federal Government through the efforts of his father (which we will examine later), his interests were aimed toward the private sector. His brother, having attained a high level of popularity in the broadcasting business, was now poised to move on to a larger station in Des Moines, Iowa. In the Reagan tradition, Ronald used his influence and was instrumental in Neil's being offered the station manager's job at the small broadcast outlet in Clinton.

Having found his niche in show business management and promotion at the radio station, it didn't take Neil long to find a way to move on to the more lucrative show biz hunting grounds in Hollywood, California. Attaining almost instant success in the advertising and promotion business, Neil soon followed the Reagan clan pattern and summoned brother Ronald to come on out and have a shot at the golden jackpot. Neil got him the interviews and screen tests that triggered the almost meteoric success of the handsome younger Reagan. Although the story of Ronald's success in Hollywood is now history, his maturing and movement toward politics and national statesmanship required one more helping hand from brother Neil.

During the post-World War II years, Neil was so closely linked behind the scenes to the glamorous world of show business that he became a real power who was highly respected in his profession. As Ronald's motion picture career began a downturn due to declining motion picture industry fortunes and his maturing beyond the "pretty boy" parts at which he had excelled, Neil did the "Reagan bit" once again. As an executive close to the giant General Electric Corporation advertising account, Neil arranged for Ronald to have a shot at the position of master of ceremonies for a theater program the company was planning for the growing medium of television. Ronald got the position and not only regained his slipping popularity with movie (now TV) audiences, but also, through his new position, became an important spokesman for old-fashioned American standards. More than anything else in his life, this connection with television and the giant corporation, made possible by the ever-present Neil, was to propel Ronald towards the Presidency of the United States.

The Reagan brothers, both of whom were born with abundant doses of the family sense of humor which was often irreverent and self deprecating, refuse any public display of their close affection for each other. Although still remaining close through all the public years, their family intimacy is well-shielded from the public.

While working on the book, "A Place To Go Back To", during the early years of Ronald Reagan's Presidency, I relied heavily on interviews and information about the family from Neil. When the President invited me to bring a copy of the manuscript to the White House for him to review, while assuring me he had no intention of censoring anything, he explained, "That brother of mine seems to remember a lot of things I never heard of before." When I assured him all Neil's memories of their life together were positive, even though his stories seemed to change on each telling, the President flashed his famous grin and said, "Yeah, I know. Moon really is a devil sometimes!" He offered no changes in the text, providing only a few statistical notes in the margins.

Neil's public attempt to treat his brother's exalted position casually created some consternation among the President's Secret Service contingent before they finally adjusted to his quirky sense of humor. At the Republican Convention in 1984, when Ronald Reagan was nominated for a second term, Neil reached his zenith as the President's big brother. With a room next to the President, where the top floors were sealed off to all but his closest advisors, Neil took special delight in twisting the tails of the security force. Having been provided with a special pass bearing a photograph and numerous signatures and seals of importance, Neil adamantly refused to wear the thing around his neck, as did all the other important and pompous officials. Cheerfully maintaining that he was "the older brother", he barged into all the restricted areas, including his own room, without the all-important pass.

I was with him one day as he attempted to board the elevator to the restricted floor and was temporarily barred by the guards. He insisted, "I'm paying an exorbitant rent for that room. If you don't let me up there, I'm calling my Congressman!" By this time, all the security personnel knew him, and with broad grins they waived him through, explaining to the uninitiated, "That's the President's crazy brother." When I asked Neil why he did not wear his pass and stop all the hassles, he grinned and said, "It's a matter of principle. I've been his brother longer than he's been a big wheel. They should remember me!" Sometime later, when I mentioned I had a friend who needed a pass to get into the convention, he reached into his coat pocket and pulled out a handful of official passes, including delegate passes to the convention floor. "Here, have one of these. I don't need them." When I asked how he got so many highly prized and limited sets of credentials he laughed, "When these big shots around here see me hassling with the security folks, they all feel sorry for this poor neglected brother of the

President, and they give me their passes!" Neil left little doubt he was having fun being the President's older brother!

Since Ronald Reagan ascended to the presidency, every attempt by media reporters to interview Neil about his brother has been turned away with, usually, a quick one-liner. Although a man of strong personal opinions, Neil has never allowed himself to be drawn into anything that might sound like serious criticism of his younger brother. Through it all, the remarkable similarity of the two Reagans is evident.

In July 1985, when doctors detected that Ronald Reagan had cancer and operated to remove a large portion of his colon, reporters descended on Neil, seeking comments. Asking such stupid questions as whether he had been in touch with his brother since the operation, Neil responded that he had not contacted him or sent a card or gift since the operation! He went on to tell one reporter that, "If I did send a card, Ronnie would probably say I've been drinking again!"

In actual truth, if the reporters had done their homework, they would have learned that Neil had undergone the same cancer operation as Ronald the week before the President went to the hospital. Continuing their closeness, this well-matched pair even had the same physical problems!

The truth of the matter was that Neil and Ronald had been in constant phone contact prior to and after both operations. Neil had even asked his doctor to contact the President's doctor to compare notes before the second operation.

Prying writers have never been able to get the two Reagan brothers to admit of any sentimentality or affection for each other, but the bond since their youth has been unbreakable. Old friends of the family recall that closeness, remembering the two boys as being, in many ways, like two peas in a pod. Many of them expressed surprise early on, when it was Ronald that made his mark in the movies and later in politics. Most felt that, as youngsters, Neil exhibited more of the personality and good looks they would have expected for that type of career.

Ronald Reagan may have suffered the slings and arrows of the media and some second rate writers, but big brother Neil was never a catalyst for any of the cheap shots!

Norman Wymbs

The Reagan Family, 1915
l–r: Jack, Moon, Ron and Nellie

Portrait of Nellie Reagan in Ronald's California office. Ronald's mother suffered from Alzheimer's Disease in her later years.

Nellie Reagan's well-used bible—carried and used by Ronald Reagan through California Governorship and U.S. Presidency—each term, taking the Oath of Office on Nellie's precious volume.

Besides running "Fashion Boot Shop," Jack Reagan restored and resold automobiles in the barn behind the family home in Dixon, Illinois. Here, a vintage Model "T", his specialty.

108

Reagan Home kitchen, Dixon, Illinois.

Nellie Reagan, an excellent cook, turned out
popular meals for frequent guests.

Reagan Home family dining room, Dixon, Illinois.

Nellie collected a full set of Chinaware from the
Jewel Tea Grocery Vendor who called every week.

Women's Section
Northern Illinois Golf Tournament
Aug. 10-11, 1921.   Dixon, Ill.

Ronald Reagan, golf caddy; above, far left, wearing "beanie," August 1921 and below front and center.

110

Dixon Boy's Marching Band, Ronald Reagan, Drum Major,
front row, far left Brother Neil, back row, second from right.

Ronald, age 12,
dressed for church.

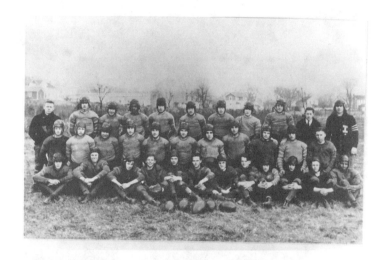

Ronald Reagan, footballer; front row, fourth from the left.

South Central School, Dixon, Illinois

Ronald Reagan attended sixth and seventh grade here.
Building now serves as the Dixon Historic Center, owned by the
Non-Profit Ronald Reagan Home Foundation.

Dixon's favorite lifeguard clowning with a high school admirer.

Ronald served as Chief Lifeguard at Lowell Park, Dixon, summers through high school and college.

Unable to adequately participate in baseball or football, the teen-aged Reagan took to swimming at the "Y," later to become City's lifeguard.

Here, left, posing, at Eureka College where he became the swim team coach.

113

Ronald Reagan, 1930, sophomore, Eureka College; back row, far left.

Ronald Reagan, college student, Eureka College; back row, far right.

Ronald Reagan, pre-"Gipper" days at Eureka College; second from left.

Ronald Reagan, Eureka College; far right.

Ronald, 1932; Senior, Eureka College

At Eureka College, Ronald's acting career took root.
Here, at far left, he poses with fellow performers
including "Mugs" Cleaver, seated at left.

Publicity still from *Knute Rockne—All American*
Ronald Reagan played tragic Notre Dame football hero, George Gipp.
Thus began the enduring legend of "The Gipper."

Ronald, Nancy and Neil Reagan testing bed

As a youngster, Ronald hid pennies under a loose tile on the hearth.
Here, President Reagan hides some more, February, 1984

118

Neil, Nancy and Ronald Reagan at dedication of restored
Reagan Home in Dixon, Illinois, February, 1984.

Ronald Reagan, Harriet
and Norman Wymbs,
Dixon, Illinois, 1991.

Ronald Reagan receiving
rough draft of *Crusade*
from the author, Norman
Wymbs, California, 1993.

120

Ronald Reagan at Camp David

Norman Wymbs

CHAPTER 12

FORMATIVE YEARS

Two factors were converging toward having a major effect on young Ronald Reagan within a few years after the family moved to Dixon, Illinois. Finally settling down in one community, after almost constant moves over the prior eight years, gave all the Reagans an opportunity to sink real roots in a hometown. As the youngest of the clan, Ronnie was the most affected by the trauma of constant shifts and the lack of a stable community life. Whether those early years contributed to his shyness and self-contained personality or were the major causes of those traits is unimportant in this narrative. What is important is that, after a few years of regular school and home life, Ronald Reagan began exhibiting some of the strong personal characteristics that were to turn him into a world leader many years later.

Just as important in the development of the youngster was the changing role of his mother in their church and the outside community. With the temperance movement concluded and the Dixon Church becoming more settled under the leadership of Reverend Cleaver, much of the need for Nelle Reagan's aggressive activism seemed to have dissipated. Not yet ready for retirement from her vigorous life style, Nelle redirected her "hyper" personality toward the community at large. She did not lessen her intense Christian faith and church teaching activities, but free of her more secular church work, she, in effect, became something of a domestic missionary. Her flair for the dramatic, no longer needed on the WCTU campaign trail, was refocused and broadened into the general community. In short order, Nelle Reagan became an entertainment producer unmatched in the local area. As was always her wont, she included her youngest offspring in her activities, effectively molding the personality and talent that were to pay off so well in his future.

Nelle, while giving little outward appearance of a forceful personality, was an active, outgoing woman who would rank high today as a truly liberated feminist. The most outstanding feature of her accomplishments was that they were achieved without ever jeopardizing the close family relationship she had with her husband and children. We found many little clues in old newspaper records that underscored her high level of independence and self confidence.

From early in their marriage, through even the tough depression years, the Reagans always had a family automobile. At a time when most considered the auto a luxury, Jack and Nelle found it an important adjunct to their way of life. Jack showed a natural ability with the mechanical marvels of the time and always had the latest gadgets to aid sales in his shoe store. As a sideline, he acquired well-used automobiles and spent his spare time rebuilding them for resale. Nelle was no passive observer in this, becoming quite adept at handling automobiles.

After moving to Dixon, Nelle, for several years, maintained a close association with old friends in Tampico, visiting them frequently and helping in her old church. She regularly drove the family auto (one of Jack's reconditioned Model T's) back for weekends in her old hometown. Sometimes she was alone, but usually she had her two small sons at her side. Considering the car's frequent need for mechanical attention and especially the hand-cranked starts, the slim little woman with the snap-brimmed hats showed unusual self reliance for her time. Even more remarkable was the fact she often made these long drives alone over unpaved, unlighted country roads at night. With that kind of free spirit, her ventures into public dramatic performances seem rather natural, if not tame!

Nelle's early efforts at dramatic readings in her church and with small social groups were so well received that she was encouraged to expand her horizons. From the start, she detected a kindred spirit in her youngest son, and he became a regular partner in her histrionic efforts. While shy and almost painfully retiring in contemporary groups, Ronnie blossomed when given a part to play before a strange audience. All Ronie's latent personality and natural quick wit seemed to flow without effort when given the little dramatic parts in his mother's productions.

As the Reagans became more firmly established in the community, with Ronald growing into a tall, handsome teenager, Nelle's productions became more elaborate. From simple dramatic readings, which she usually wrote herself, she now had expanded to more varied programs, including short playlets. As she wrote and planned production for her little skits, she recruited many of her friends to supplement her family cast members. In interviews with old friends of Jack and Nelle, they recalled for us how she was so persuasive that her designated stars seldom refused invitations to perform in her shows.

The following article from the *Dixon Telegraph* newspaper of June 10, 1925 is typical of many accounts of Nelle's productions.

"Mrs. J. E. Reagan to Give Recital"

"Mrs. J.E. Reagan of Dixon, will give an entertainment of readings at the Christian Church in Grand Detour next Friday evening, June 12th, at 8 o'clock, under the auspices of the Ladies Aid Society of the church.

The program is as follows:

Poem: 'Twinkling Light', composed by Mrs. Reagan.

Chapter 12

Reading, 'Loves Labours Lost', Negro dialect.
Dramatic, 'Face to Face', the story of a young girl disillusioned, weary of life, spends the night with a former servant whose son is sentenced to die at dawn: the girl learns that one who has not known sorrow, as well as joy, has never lived. The dawn brings happiness to the mother, girl and rejected suitor.

Solo by Miss Margaret Cleaver, Louis Leydig, accompanist.

Reading, 'The Hoosier and the Minister', humorous.

Impersonating three characters in a one act drama, 'The Lie'
Ruth Nolan — The daughter
Connie — The Jazz girl
John Nolan — The prisoner

'The officer of the Law', a musical number.
Impersonating a small boy in 'George Has a Grouch on Sister's.'

'The Italian's Story of the Rose' in dialect - pathetic.

'Livinsky at the Wedding', Jewish dialect. Very funny.

'From a Far Country', reading with song and music. Sublime.

Song duet to the old but well-loved song, 'Annie Laurie', performed by J. E. Reagan and sister Mrs. L. H. Hunt."

Most of the skits and readings were written by Nelle, with one or more parts for her young son. Ronnie had proven quite adept at memorizing the lines and repeating them with all the flair and emotion his mother had written into them. As the young man grew older, he was also to play a major part in writing the skits.

In this and many other reports of the activities of the Reagan road company, Nelle's penchant for preaching and presenting strong moral lessons is apparent. Although always keeping her eye on what she considered the major moral issues of the day, she made them palatable with liberal doses of sometimes irreverent humor. This family characteristic was to become quite familiar to the American public when President Ronald Reagan later presented his programs and policies.

It is interesting to note that the humor of those days would have a hard time passing muster in today's uptight world where every possible minor constituency seems to devote much of their time to taking offense at other groups. Much of the humor of that time revolved around light-hearted emphasis on ethnic differences. If you think Nancy Reagan has had a hard time with the sniping media, consider what would happen to Nelle Reagan with the items on the program just related.

A reading in Negro dialect? I can think of at least fourteen major interest groups that would march, protest or bring suit on that one.

A young girl commiserating with a servant? What is a servant, anyway?

A bumbling "Hoosier" confronting a minister in ignorance? Indiana might secede from the Union!

We won't even attempt to explain to the women's movement group what a "Jazz Girl" was!

George's trouble with his sisters, of course, was just another manifestation of male chauvinism.

An Italian story in dialect? Lucky she didn't mention the Mafia!

One of the more interesting items on the program, one which was extremely popular and much used by Nelle in her shows, was the story, "Livinsky at the Wedding", done in heavy Jewish dialect. This was a skit reminiscent of the sort of thing that Bob Newhart used to do when he was at the height of his popularity. The narrator, a recent Jewish immigrant, relates his impression of an elaborate Jewish wedding, with the humor coming from a wild confusion of words and impressions of the ceremony. This skit, which runs to six closely-typed pages, became almost a trademark of the Reagans, not only in their shows, but also in a social context as well. In recent years, President Reagan, in a note to an old family friend, mentioned the "Livinsky" skit, advising that he still remembered the whole routine with the exception of the final paragraph. He was quite pleased when the friend was able to provide him with a full copy of the bit, which many old timers in the area still recalled with amusement.

Nelle, while exerting her strong persuasive powers to recruit friends as participants in her shows, always enjoyed whole-hearted volunteer support from her family. Records indicate particularly that her husband Jack was a regular performer, often doing humorous bits in Irish dialect, and as in the aforementioned, frequently singing Irish ballads in a strong singing voice. Mrs. L.H. Hunt, in the duet with Jack, was Nelle's sister Lavinia, who maintained a close relationship with Nelle and her nephews. In passing, it is interesting to note that Miss Margaret Cleaver, daughter of the Christian Church Pastor, was also a regular in Nelle's shows. Later we'll look into the often-reported romance between "Mugs" Cleaver and Ronald Reagan.

To note the humor in Nelle's writing and the family performances is not, in any way, to diminish the serious undertone and strong moral positions taken in all the Reagan efforts. Nelle's deep Christian faith and Jack's strong sympathies for the world's underdogs came through in everything they did. Nelle's name appears frequently in the newspapers of the day, as she held regular meetings in her home with the Women's Missionary Society of her church (which group she lead as president for a number of years). She was active in researching the history of her church denomination and regularly presented learned papers before the congregation on key church leaders and their contribution to society. One of her deeper studies, unfortunately lost with other old church records, was a report on the important role of Negroes in the early formation and growth of the denomination. She still seemed to find time for more secular activities as well, serving as president of the local Parent Teachers Association and as an active promoter of the Dixon Symphony orchestra. You would think, with all this peripatetic activity outside the home, there would be no time for any social life. The Reagans, however, were active socially and frequently entertained at dinner and housed out-of-town guests for weekends in their home. With all the outgoing activity on the part of the elder Reagans, there was no way that Ronald could remain shyly isolated from the outer world.

Ronald's inability to excel at the team sports of football or baseball because of his poor eyesight turned him toward an active interest in swimming, which he could quietly pursue on his own. With his church, in the early years, meeting in the local YMCA building, he was naturally drawn into its membership and use of the Y's facilities. The indoor swimming pool provided an excellent outlet for growing physical abilities he was unable to hone on his school's athletic fields. His determination and natural grace not only turned him into an accomplished swimmer, but also he advanced into life saving and became an expert in the art. Growing into a lithe, muscular teenager, his routine at the Y was to determine a major pattern in his life.

Supremely confident of his swimming ability while still a high school freshman, he announced to his father that he wanted to apply for the lifeguard position at the public swimming beach in Dixon's Lowell Park. Although his son was considerably younger than anyone previously holding that responsible position, Jack was impressed by his ability and determination. The proud father, with Ronnie at his side, eloquently convinced the operators of the park that the young man not only had the physical ability and training to handle the job, but also had the maturity to cope with the adult responsibility. With some skepticism, the officials agreed to give Ronald a try for a few weeks. In typical Ronald Reagan fashion, the young fellow confounded them all by proving so competent and popular with beach-goers that the summer job was his throughout high school and his years in college.

While much has been written about Ronald Reagan as a lifeguard at Lowell Park and his more than seventy rescues of errant swimmers, not as much attention has been given to the way it shaped his character. At a time when most youngsters were satisfied to enjoy the lazy summer days of school vacation playing ball or fishing, Ronald was shouldering serious adult responsibilities. That he took his position seriously was reflected in the tough routine that he followed.

The beach closed at sundown , and when he had all of the swimmers safely out of the water, Ronald would then drive the pickup truck home. The park operator trusted him with the use and overnight possession of the business's truck. The slim young man never shirked the work load or the responsibilities of his position and was to become something of a legend in his own time in Dixon. The local newspaper carried frequent front page stories attesting to his life saving skills. Typical was the following from the August 3, 1928 edition of the *Dixon Telegraph*.

"JAMES RAIDER PULLED FROM JAWS OF DEATH"

"James Raider was rescued from drowning at the Lowell Park bathing beach last night about 9:30 by Life Guard Ronald 'Dutch' Reagan.

The beach had been closed for the day, when Raider, who was a member of a party of four persons, entered the waters in violation of the beach rules.

Raider is said to have ventured out beyond his depth, not being a proficient swimmer. He had gone down once before his condition became known, and the Guard hurried out to rescue him. It was not until after quite a struggle in the water that Raider was brought to the shore. One of the members of the party, who was said to have attempted to rescue him, was forced to abandon the attempt when he too was in danger of being taken down. Raider responded to artificial respiration when he was carried to the bank."

* * * * *

The paper reported that this was Reagan's twenty-fourth rescue since becoming lifeguard at the popular beach. The Lowell Park Beach was not a placid swimming hole. The swift-flowing Rock River was often treacherous to all but the most experienced swimmers.

After his retirement from two successful and eventful terms as President of the United States, Ronald Reagan reminisced in private about those long ago years at the beach. "You know, I've never had to handle as much responsibility in my life as I did those years at Lowell Park!"

Noting my raised eyebrows as thoughts of international summits and many U.S. domestic crises flashed through my mind, he explained, "In those years in California and Washington, I always had dozens of knowledgeable advisors nearby to help me make the right decisions." He paused as he gazed contemplatively out his hotel window at Florida's broad ocean beaches. "But when I was a lifeguard, there was no one to turn to. I had to make instant decisions involving life or death and act upon them on my own!"

With his eyes glistening and the slight catch in his voice that always comes when he speaks of his youth, he added, "Those were the most important years of my life!"

Reflecting on his record of lives saved and the news stories and personal accounts of his life saving skills, I had to agree there was much in what he said!

Dixon's popular lifeguard certainly did not get to keep "bankers' hours" on the job. Rising before dawn to scoot around town in the old pickup truck loading supplies for the concession stand and bath house didn't allow for any lazing around the house sleeping late on those warm summer days. Once at the park, having first helped open the snack stand and bath house, it was into his bathing suit and out to the beach's bathing pier for the day.

When the day wound down at sunset, Ronald had to make sure all of the swimmers were out of the swift-flowing Rock River before reversing the morning procedure by helping to tidy up the concession area and gathering the used towels from the bath house. Back to town in the truck, he seldom arrived home until well after dark, too late for much chance to join the crowd at the ice cream shop or movie house.

Ronald showed little indication that he missed the normal social activities of his classmates during those teen years. We spoke to many who remembered "Dutch" Reagan during that period in his life. Their recollections invariably were of a friendly, good-humored individual who was impossible to dislike. Despite these positive impressions, none of them could profess to any closeness to the young man. One of our interviewees recalled Ronald's frequently picking him and others up for rides in the truck to Lowell Park in the mornings. Recalling that "Dutch" went out of his way to offer the rides, he admitted that he never really got to know Ronald Reagan. One of the young men who ran the bath house for a time and passed out towels and soap all day had similar memories. He remembered Ronald's always pitching in to help at the stand during rush hours and even playing catch together during slack periods at the beach, while also admitting he never really got to know "Dutch".

At the well-attended park, Ronald, the lifeguard, was wildly popular with youngsters who frequently spent the day at the beach. He would gather them around him on the pier as he spun endless stories for their entertainment. It was recalled that he didn't merely tell stories. He acted all the parts, showing some of his mother's mastery of dialects.

The boys in his youthful audience particularly remembered his penchant for exciting sports stories. Presaging his future career when fresh out of college, Ronald gave rousing performances as an excited radio announcer narrating college football games. Drawing from current sports headlines, he painted vivid word pictures of action in the imaginary football arena. His long-term interest in the University of Notre Dame started here as that school's football team frequently dominated the sports headlines of the day. It seems quite fitting that later, when he became a motion picture star, he would play the part of Notre Dame's "Gipper", one of his early football heroes, and thus earn another affectionate nickname.

On the female side, we could not find many who recalled the content of Ronald's performances at the beach, but they all recalled the performer quite clearly. Ronald, by this time, had grown into a taller-than-average young man with a physique seemingly custom designed for a bathing suit. Those undeniable physical attributes, coupled with the famous wavy hair and boyish grin, made him every young girl's dream. The fact that his rapt audience was made up of youngsters six to eight years his junior didn't keep the girls from worshiping him like later generations were to do with "Elvis"! One of the ladies we interviewed, who had been a frequent member of his audience, unabashedly admitted that, as a youngster, she faked trouble in the water several times so she could be "rescued" by the handsome lifeguard. Ronald never showed any signs of irritation over the behavior of the junior beach-goers. They all recalled him as showing infinite patience and good humor over their antics.

That Ronald Reagan was not immune to the attractions of young ladies his own age at the beach was revealed in an essay he wrote in high school. In that literary effort, published in the school's yearbook (reprinted in "A Place To Go Back To"), he recounts the thoughts of a lifeguard meeting an attractive young lady at the beach. Mrs. Graybill, lifelong friend of Ronald and wife of the concession operator who was the lifeguard's boss, recalls that the handsome young man occasionally wrangled time off early enough to keep a date in town with one of his girl friends. Those occasions were not frequent, however, as he steadfastly kept his nose to the grindstone.

Ronald's drive to earn money for his college fund, coupled with his enterprising nature, lead him into sideline ventures. Many stories have been written about how he and his brother raised rabbits and pigeons to sell for food. While a lifeguard, he acquired an old canoe which he fixed up to use on the river. While he was working at the park, he rented out the canoe to anyone who wanted to paddle on the water. Later, in college, that same sense of enterprise helped him to locate positions in which he could earn extra money for his education fund during his spare time. His position at Lowell Park was the most significant, in that it provided him with an income well beyond what he could have earned at any other part time employment. The economics of the position was an important factor in his keeping the job as lifeguard throughout his summer vacations from Eureka College.

In 1990, when Ronald Reagan made a day-long visit back home to Dixon, we had an opportunity to observe his deep emotional attachment and fond memories of Lowell Park on the Rock River. At that time, although supposedly retired, the former President maintained a grueling travel schedule, appearing at political fund raisers and promoting his planned presidential library in California.

The trip to Dixon was a detour from his normal fund raising schedule and only came about because of his insistence on visiting the old hometown. While talking with the President a year earlier, we had suggested he might like to slip back home quietly just to visit the old haunts. We both agreed, however, that it would be an impossible breach of public relations for him not to make it a visit open to all his followers back home. He found the suggestion intriguing, though, and half-way seriously suggested he could slip back into town wearing dark glasses and a mustache for a really private visit!

The President's staff, even after two years out of office, continued to live in a world of perpetual political campaigning. They grudgingly gave ground in agreeing to this deviation from their carefully-crafted itinerary. Even so, their original plan was for Reagan's visit to Dixon to be the usual media performance with every move calculated in light of its prime time impact on television. Usually ambivalent toward the planning and scheduling developed by his politically correct staff, Reagan balked at their plans for his homecoming.

During his years as President, while generally giving the appearance of affable compliance with his advisors, Ronald Reagan, behind the scenes, showed a rigid stubbornness on issues about which he had deep convictions. In the midst of the staff's planning, he put his foot down and let it be known, in no uncertain terms, what he would be doing on his trip back home! The visit was on his terms, but not without some background mumbling from staff members accustomed to catering to the ever-present TV cameras!

The schedule for the day called for picking him up at the local airport and driving directly to Lowell Park. It had been made clear that, no matter what, he wanted plenty of time at his old stamping grounds.

Although the old swimming pier is long gone, and swimming is now largely confined to a municipal swimming pool in town, the rest of the park is largely as it was. The river at that location is unchanged since the old lifeguarding days, the park shoreline is still dominated by stately oak trees, and the opposite shore is still made up of quiet little farms.

With the Secret Service and local police holding the media back (the park had been closed to visitors during this off-season visit), we strolled with Ronald Reagan along the shady shoreline. From the start, it was obvious that we had faded from his consciousness, as he was transported back to those early days. Stopping transfixed by the water, he murmured to himself, "Looks just the same as always." Vaguely waving his hand towards the water, he went on, "The old pier was right here." Then, coming back to the present, he grinned while staring across the river at a small farmhouse on the other side. "I used to swim across the river and back every morning just to warm up. I don't think I could do that now." As some of his itchy young staffers approached to urge him along, he shook his reverie and, flashing the old familiar grin, turned to us — "Got to keep moving, otherwise they get upset!" Showing the kind consideration that has always been one of his trademarks, he was concerned more about their anxiety to do their jobs than about the irritation they often created.

Although he spent the rest of the day visiting his restored home and other haunts in Dixon, he never again revealed the deep emotion his musing by the river had exposed.

Everyone is familiar with President Reagan's frequent nostalgic references to his lifeguarding days at Lowell Park and his scholastic football games. Seldom do we hear much about the depth of his formal and informal intellectual development. The few times that indications of his strong religious training and deep faith have come through, the political handlers and media critics quickly squelched him. Despite this, as we'll explore in a later chapter, that faith was of primary importance and shaped many of his major Presidential initiatives.

For now, let us look at young Ronald Reagan's intellectual development, not only through his formal schooling, but also under the guidance of parents with deeply inquisitive minds.

CHAPTER 13

THE EDUCATION OF A LEADER

There is little question that Ronald Reagan's ability to quickly absorb and later recall massive quantities of information was a key factor in his lifetime of successes. As a good looking, but average, actor in motion pictures, his ability to almost instantly memorize a role played a large part in his climb up the movie world ladder. Casting directors, recognizing that ability, gave him a big edge when choosing actors for major parts. Costs in the cinema industry are so closely tied to the time needed to produce the product that the actors who could get ready to go quickly had preference over the slower learners. Later, in politics, that ability allowed him to rapidly grasp issues and catalog them in his mind for instant reference when needed. Early in his life, that inherent ability pulled him through some difficult times in school and then greatly enhanced his later years of education.

Before his eye problems were diagnosed, Ronald survived school on his quick grasp of information and ability for detailed recall. Unable to follow the teacher's blackboard lessons from his seat in the classroom, those first years rested on his ability to absorb and repeat all the verbal communication. While a decided hindrance, both in and out of school, it did have its beneficial side. Since his education developed mostly from the verbal communication around him, his own verbal skills were greatly enhanced. Teachers and fellow students noted early on that Ronald's ability to express himself was much beyond his age. By the time his visual weakness had been diagnosed and corrected, the youngest Reagan had already acquired the reputation as a "wordy" kid!

From the very beginning, as evidenced by his learning to read before he reached school age, Ronald Reagan was deeply intrigued by the power and knowledge to be found in the written word. In that regard, it is interesting to note that his father became aware of the precocious youngster's reading ability while he was studying the newspaper's front page stories. From the start, he did not evidence the usual childish interest in light reading, but directed his attention to learning what was going on in the real world. That same characteristic was noted later, as many observers reported on his preference for biographies and history in his recreational reading.

Both Nelle and Jack Reagan were avid readers, giving some indication as to where Ronald got his predilection toward the written word. In the old restored Reagan home in Dixon, Illinois, it is easy to see that the family "parlor" was, in fact, a reading room. During the restoration, President Reagan pointed out that his father's comfortable chair in the corner always had a good reading bulb in the floor lamp alongside. In the center of that room was a small round table with a few upright chairs. Almost every evening, Nelle would make up a large pot of popcorn which was transferred from the stove to the middle of that table. On one of his visits to the old homestead, President Reagan recalled, "Every night we would sit around the popcorn bowl and read." Flashing his well-known grin, he added, "We turned our chairs sideways to the table. That way we could keep one arm on the table, free to dip into the popcorn, while we held our books in our laps with the other arm."

During those years, the Reagans did not have a radio or the very popular phonograph in the house. Both Neil and Ronald recalled that their evenings were filled with reading, lively talk or practicing one of Nelle's new productions. There was no room on the agenda for listening to radio or records. Ronald's seemingly unquenchable thirst for expanding knowledge through reading led to a close relationship with the Hall family. Ward Hall, like Nelle an active leader in the Christian Church, had for a couple of years filled in as lay minister during the absence of a regular pastor. The senior Reagans and Halls had become close friends as soon as Ronald's family arrived in Dixon. Ward Hall, active in business and community activities, subscribed to many educational and business periodicals not generally available to the average reader. Ronald's curiosity led him to seek permission to read Hall's intriguing library of magazines. Taken by the youngster's interests beyond his age, Mrs. Ward Hall gave him permission to drop in any time he felt the urge to read. He not only became a regular at the Hall home, but also quickly adopted a comfortable rocking chair in their living room as his reading site. Many years later, as Ronald Reagan began to make his mark as a motion picture star in Hollywood, Mrs. Hall admonished her daughter-in-law, Mrs. Edith Hall, "Save that old rocking chair. It is going to be famous. That boy (Ronald) is going to be President some day." Edith Hall, much impressed, saved the chair!

The reading habit has stayed with Ronald Reagan through the years, even though the pressure of numerous details involved in the presidency always put time at a premium. In a letter to an author several years ago, he stated, "Your book is at my bedside, and I look forward to reading it, since I'm a bedtime reader. I have to wait for breaks in the homework, which has been rather heavy the last few weeks. But I have a hunch I'll make a break very soon." The heavy homework was preparation for a crucial summit meeting with the head of the Soviet Union, Mikhail Gorbachev!

Formal schooling was something of a snap for Ronald Reagan. His quick grasp of subjects and retentive memory insured a smooth passage through high school and college. He saw no particular need to achieve high academic scores. He was satisfied in his own mind when he knew a subject and had no desire to impress his elders with high grades. One of his former teachers, Freya Lazier, who taught French, reported that he did very poorly in her class. She noted that he showed little interest in school activities outside of drama and sports. Lazier further recalled that he had a part-time job after school and was always anxious to get to it.

His record in high school French class was quite typical of Ronald throughout his life. He saw no particular usefulness in the French language; it held no relevance to those things he saw as important in life and world affairs. Subjects like history and English (all communications, written or spoken) were important, and at these he excelled. As always, his sights were set on the future, and his determination to be successful was unwavering. To Ronald, spare time was wasted time, if not put to good use. He was never without a paying part-time job to fill his otherwise idle hours. Dorothy Pottervelt, a fellow member of the Dixon High Dramatic Club and the Christian Church, recalled talking with Ronald one day at Lowell Park about their futures after graduating from school. She recalls Ronald's stating firmly, "Believe you me, I am never going to be satisfied with a $60 a week job!"

Rather heady ambitions when $60 was a very good weekly income! As usual, Ronald came through. Less than twenty years later, he signed a contract with his movie studio calling for over $1 million annually.

Although Ronald was not generally interested in school activities outside the classroom, there were some notable exceptions. Bernard J. Frazer, principal of the high school and Ronald's English teacher, recalled the formation of the school's first drama club. Here, of all possible extracurricular activities, was one tailor-made for the handsome, articulate young man. Ronald's mentor, who we suspect organized the drama club primarily to give his talented student an outlet, analyzed his protégé as well as anyone who ever had contact with the future President. He saw the young student as extremely introverted unless he was acting in a drama. He reported Ronald, while performing, as supremely self-contained and in command at all times. The young actor's approach to every part was with a scholarly probe into the psychological motivation of the character he was to portray. Frazer remembered his student as asking endless questions about the characters and plot of every play. Ronald would not accept any ambiguity or evasiveness in response. If Ronald did not understand and accept the believability of the part he was offered, he would not play the role. In light of the emotional depth of Ronald's participation in those dramatic productions, it's no wonder that Bernard Frazer became a second father figure to the young man. Ronald Reagan maintained a warm personal relationship with his old teacher throughout Frazer's life.

Ronald's enthusiasm for drama and his natural leadership led him to be chosen unanimously as president of the Dixon Dramatic Club. A related note in passing: Margaret Cleaver shared his love of the dramatic and was a frequent co-star with him in the popular romantic comedies performed by the young troup.

Despite his ongoing love of sports, Ronald did not set the world on fire in athletics at Dixon High. He ran on the track team and was reported to be quite good at the quarter mile run. For a time, he was a substitute on the basketball team, but he left no lasting mark. At his first love, football, he was a respectable second stringer but he never matched the flamboyant stardom of his brother, Neil, at that sport. Despite his inability to stand out

146

in organized sports, his devotion to physical well-being and strong discipline turned him into a superb physical specimen. His swimming and lifeguard work at Lowell Park went a long way toward maintaining that physical condition as well. Despite a father who was a chain smoker and his stint in motion pictures when Hollywood appeared to be an active agent of the tobacco industry, he never took up the habit.

It is no accident that Ronald Reagan came into office as one of the most physically fit presidents, albeit one of the oldest. Those early exercise and clean living habits have stuck with him throughout his adult life. One of the more important modifications to the White House upon his arrival was the Ronald Reagan exercise room! On his nostalgic return to Dixon in 1990, while visiting his old South Central School, he indicated his continuing fitness by out-dribbling this writer and making a couple of youthful "lay ups" on the old basketball court.

As a high school student, Ronald was pressed into leadership positions he generally accepted rather reluctantly with an engaging "who me?" attitude. As student body president in his senior year, though, he approached his public speaking duties with relish. Even then, it was evident it did not require a great deal of urging to propel him up in front of an audience. His natural sense of humor and touch for the dramatic made him a spellbinder, whatever the subject. That reputation and his overwhelming popularity made him a natural to take the position as master of ceremonies at the city's combined high school graduation activities. His class yearbook showed where his talents had been developing. While dutifully listing his participation in football and track, it was in his other activities that an indication of his future can be found.

Local newspaper articles, as well as the yearbook, attested to his skills displayed in the drama club. Seldom did a picture appear of one of the club's performances without Ronald Reagan as the focal point in a starring role. As is usual with most amateur dramatics, most of the productions were light in nature. Ronald's instinctive aptitude at comedy and his ability with foreign dialects made him a community favorite. Then, just as later in the motion picture industry, little note was taken of his deep dramatic ability. Good looks, charm and a natural sense of timing in comedy were his major assets. That ability at comedy might have broadened his career in Hollywood and stopped his career in public service aborning, had not the experts in the industry decided he was just too darn good looking to be funny

Ronald's artistic abilities were not limited to the stage, however. The school yearbook suggests he had unheralded talents in visual arts as well. He designed and drew all of the artwork for his class publication. His graphic art, leaning towards the modern, today would fall under the nostalgic "Art Deco" category. For the yearbook, he developed a theme around a "movie" motif, showing an already-budding ambition to be fulfilled later in life.

His broad artistic abilities, besides the dramatic and drawing talents, extended to the written word. As a high school student, he gained attention with his essays and short stories (his forays into poetry are best forgotten) by doing well in literary contests.

This talent, apparently inherited and certainly fostered by his mother, was to stand him in good stead throughout his life. In later years when Ronald sought and held public office, that writing ability was put to good use in composing many of his speeches. One of the reasons Ronald Reagan always appeared so natural and became so popular with the public was that his ideas and phrases were his own. Despite cynical commentators who insisted he was just blindly parroting someone else's words, Ronald Reagan prepared most of his own stuff and did not hesitate to make substantive changes in the words prepared by his staff when conflicts developed.

During Reagan's years in Dixon, the City had an unusual school system. Students went through separated "North Side" and "South Side" schools all the way through high school. At the high school level, however, the two schools joined in sports as one combined team and in some extracurricular functions. Final graduation was also a joint affair; the two senior classes went through single graduation ceremonies and final parties. Ronald went through the north side system, while Margaret Cleaver, his supposed high school sweetheart, was in the south side system! She was as popular in her high school as Ronald was in his, serving as president of her senior class and as a member of the student council. Besides starring with Ronald in productions of the joint drama club, she was one of the editors of the consolidated high school annual.

One of the activities in high school seldom mentioned in Ronald Reagan's history, but of paramount importance to him, was the Hi-Y club, an arm of the YMCA. During a period when the Y was not ashamed of its Christian roots, the Hi-Y was itself quasi-religious in nature. The stated aim of the organization, to promote the "highest standards of Christian character, clean speech, clean sports, clean living and clean scholarship", left little doubt as to its background and mission.

The Hi-Y was an important part of Ronald's high school life, and he enthusiastically served as the organization's president.

Ronald Reagan's Christian background and training were preeminent in his early life and critical to his future success as President of the United States.

CHAPTER 14

BUT THE GREATEST OF THESE

IS CHARITY

Nelle Reagan, the young woman and soon-to-be mother of Ronald Reagan, underwent a profound change in her spiritual life just before the arrival of her second son. Although always a person of deep compassion and concern for her fellow humans, her early life showed no special affinity toward religion or, more specifically, toward fundamental Christianity. Nelle and her husband Jack, throughout their lives, exhibited deep compassion for the less fortunate. Neither could conceal

151

impatience or disgust for governments or social orders that ignored or helped cause the anguish often visited upon some segments of society. Neither of them had found in existing churches any real attempt to address these concerns. Most congregations of church worshipers they encountered tended to be closed social structures with little interest outside their own memberships.

In Tampico, Illinois, before the birth of Ronald, Nelle Reagan found what her dormant faith had been longing for. The Disciples of Christ Christian Church filled the void. Although, to the uninitiated, the Disciples appeared a narrow and quite strict Christian organization, their form of evangelism struck a responsive chord in Nelle.

We can only surmise how she was initially drawn to the Christian Church in Tampico, since it was such a complete change from anything in her Methodist background. Whether it was through friends or just from seeing or hearing their message, Nelle joined the little Tampico congregation and was baptized in the Disciples of Christ faith prior to Ronald's birth. While not able to see the inspiration that brought it about, we can certainly see the subsequent effect it had on all the Reagans, most particularly Ronald.

The Apostle Paul, generally acknowledged to be the father of most Christian doctrine, wrote many instructional letters to early church groups. In his letter to the ancient Corinthian Church, he admonishes, "And now abideth Faith, Hope, Charity, these three, but the greatest of these is Charity."

Although not officially proclaimed in their denomination's

formal doctrine, the Disciples of Christ left little doubt that they were charged to follow the Apostle Paul's exhortation. Their aggressive approach toward doing good works in the community mirrored that charge and fell right in line with Nelle's personal feelings.

From that initial union with the Disciples, Nelle's Christian faith and charity towards all were the lynch pins of her life and activities. From what we know of those years, her emergence as a strong and compassionate voice for Christianity was not a purely emotional affair. Her sharp mind and constant study made it quite clear that her rapidly-growing faith was based upon intellectual acceptance through knowledge. This was especially important to the maturing and development of Ronald's equally strong Christian character. With the same inquisitive mental traits as his mother and a natural drive to know the "why" of everything, Ronald found the bible and Christian history an unending trove of knowledge and guidance. This trait has carried on throughout his life, leading to frequent, deep philosophical and technical discussions with scholars like Dr. Billy Graham in his later years.

The fortuitous combination of his evangelistic mother and learned leaders of the Christian Church, who quickly took to the deep thinking youngster, became critical factors in the molding of Ronald Reagan.

Reverend Ben Cleaver, the new minister of the Dixon Christian Church, took a special liking to Ronald, eleven years old and already an active member of the congregation when Cleaver arrived in 1922. Cleaver, a stern disciplinarian who liked to run a "tight ship", found the youngest Reagan an ideal candidate to assist in his church administration. Although not given to placing great reliance upon the younger members of his congregation, like most who crossed paths with Ronnie in those early years, he seemed to instantly recognize and accept in him a maturity beyond his calendar years.

Reverend Cleaver, in keeping with his natural instinct for maintaining close control over his flock, took responsibility for teaching the boys' Sunday school class in his church. Recognizing that these youngsters represented the future of the church, but realistic enough to understand that they also constituted a major discipline problem within the congregation, Cleaver's Sunday school class was second only to his preaching duties. His early designation of young Ronald Reagan as the number one substitute teacher of the boys' class tells us as much about the good sense and stability of Ronald Reagan as did his tenure at the lifeguard job.

Even though he was supposedly just filling in as a substitute teacher, Ronald became pretty much of a permanent fixture at the head of the class, as Cleaver found he could safely devote more of his time to other church duties on Sunday morning. It seemed to make little difference to the Sunday school students that many of them were older than their supremely self-assured teacher. His was not merely a time-filling Sunday morning performance. We found that many people still retained detailed memories of the content of his lessons and his unorthodox teaching methods. Again, as in so much connected with Ronald Reagan, it was startling to find people remembering specific lessons from the young teacher sixty to seventy years after the fact. Much akin to his story-telling while on lifeguard duty, his sermonettes in that early Sunday school class found lasting niches in the memories of his young charges. A little farther along, we'll take a deeper look at his actual teaching techniques and how those skills carried through his life, even into the White House years.

Reverend Cleaver's reliance upon the young member of his congregation shows up in many reports of church functions during those years. Ronald Reagan's name constantly pops up as a leader of church activities and prayer meetings throughout his teen years. Even in his regular school activities and his leadership of the Hi-Y's, the evangelical tendency was evident. There can be little doubt that his constant exposure to bible study with his mother and the development of his confident stage presence through her plays were keys to his acceptance so early as a church leader. There seemed to be little awareness or concern about the youth of the young Reagan while in his teaching and leadership roles in the old church. In interviews with old-time contemporaries and church members, as questions were raised concerning the ability of the young teenager to shoulder such adult responsibilities, they seem genuinely surprised to think back and recall that he was that young! Again, as we had been finding in all our research, it seems that Ronald Reagan was born grown up!

Ronald's maturity and deep sense of responsibility, well noted by Reverend Cleaver in the running of his church, also played an important role in the close relationship that developed between the handsome young man and the pastor's family.

In recounting the early life of Ronald Reagan, many commentators make frequent mention of his early "romance" with Margaret Cleaver, youngest daughter of Reverend Ben Cleaver. There has been much speculation, aided and abetted by local stories and mythology, as to why the two never married.

Many of the older residents who recalled some details of the Reagan family remembered Ronald and Margaret (or "Dutch" and "Mugs" as they were fondly called) as a steady couple. Although most seemed to assume the two youngsters would eventually marry, none could recall that either of the pair showed any highly emotional attachment. When they both moved on to enroll at Eureka College after high school, it was just automatically accepted that their ultimate mating was inevitable. That assumption was not necessarily the feeling of the two principals.

When Ronald Reagan was elected President of the United States in 1980, the news media, after its normal fashion, searched diligently for every detail they could find from his early life. Because romance is always popular with the reading or viewing public, that phase of any public figure's life is always a high priority. Since the story of Reagan's first failed marriage to Jane Wyman and his spectacularly successful one to Nancy Davis had been played and analyzed from every possible angle, something new was needed.

Margaret Cleaver, who had married a few years out of college, was besieged by reporters seeking information about her romance with Ronald. Showing far more class than the persistent media hounds, she stood firm in refusing to discuss her early personal life. She logically pointed out that her high school and college dating habits had no bearing on either her or Ronald's subsequent life. The President, while notoriously open with the media about most aspects of his life, showed his long lasting respect for "Mugs" and her family by refusing to pander to the seekers of sensationalism.

Looking back on the surface evidence, conventional wisdom would support the appearance of a deep romance between the two, but the actual facts fall more in line with the insistence by "Mugs" that it was just a close, youthful friendship.

Ben Cleaver, who ran a tight ship at the church, did not let his family off lightly; he was just as firm a disciplinarian at home as well. His youngest daughter, Margaret, was, without a doubt, the apple of her father's eye. Like most parents, Dad was quite aware of the predatory nature of young men where pretty, young girls like his daughter were concerned.

In Ronald Reagan, the otherwise-stern pastor saw a straight-laced young man who, while handsome beyond any normal human allotment, did not exhibit the aggressive mating tendencies of his contemporaries. Ronald, in effect, became an eminently safe companion for his protected daughter. The young Reagan was readily accepted by the worried father into the Cleaver family social circle. For the two young people, their friendship and her father's doting approval made it convenient for them to participate in social activities that normally required male and female pairings.

With Ronald and Margaret attending separate high schools, their time together was limited to church activities, their joint participation in the drama club and, during their senior year, working together on the school yearbook.

During those teen years in Dixon, Ronald seemed to draw unusual attention and support from his elders who saw great future potential in the handsome, quick witted young man. Nelle Reagan's guidance in his religious training and the confident public presence created through her dramatic counseling were paramount in drawing this backing for his every move along the way.

Reagan's high school principal, Bernard Frazer, who literally built a dramatic course around his protégé; Reverend Ben Cleaver, deeply moved by his biblical knowledge and teaching ability; and Ward Hall, family friend and Disciples of Christ lay leader, who recognized his deep intellect, all became like doting fathers to the young man.

It appears that both Ward Hall and Ben Cleaver saw in Ronald Reagan the potential of greatness as a minister of God. It was these two, both Trustees of the Disciples' own college at Eureka, who guaranteed his entry into the small Christian college. With an indifferent academic record and no special talents in such activities as sports or music, Ronald was a poor candidate for special preference at any college. His two mentors, Hall and Cleaver, however, saw to it that he received a special scholarship to Eureka College and guaranteed that next vital step on the long road to ultimate greatness.

The "Mugs-Dutch" relationship was destined to continue for four more years, as Margaret Cleaver also enrolled at Eureka College after their high school graduation. Ronald's start at college was inauspicious, and, after the first year, he was ready to chuck any further academic training and strike out as his brother had done after high school. Again, the strong Cleaver influence was to exert itself. The Dixon minister, retiring from his pastorate, moved his family to Eureka before Ronald's second year at the institution of higher learning. It was Ben Cleaver, again, who persuaded Ronald that college was critical to his future and convinced him to stay. Cleaver was to remain a strong counsel to the young student during his remaining years at Eureka.

For Margaret Cleaver, now living with her parents while continuing classes at Eureka, her relationship with Ronald continued on the same plane as during the Dixon High School years. With Ronald returning to Dixon each summer and resuming his time-consuming job as Lowell Park lifeguard, his friendship with Margaret suffered great breaks in continuity. Certainly there was little chance to develop it into the deep romance some observers speculated about during those years.

If there were to be no romantic union of the Reagan and Cleaver families during those years in Eureka, the spiritual bond and guidance remained strong. All of the officials in the Disciples of Christ church organization, including strong family friend Ward Hall, saw in Ronald Reagan a stirring evangelical zeal they interpreted as guiding him toward a church pulpit. There is plenty of evidence indicating he would have been a stemwinder before any church congregation, or an outstanding Christian evangelist, but such a future was not to be. As he left college and struck out in the world of radio broadcasting, indications are that his mentor, Ben Cleaver, was particularly disappointed in the apparent direction his career was taking.

Although the evangelical juices were flowing, and the young man was beginning to focus on his ultimate destiny, it was going to take many more years before his true mission in life crystallized.

Norman Wymbs

CHAPTER 15

THE PARABLES

"He Taught Them Many Things by Parables"

Even in the non-Christian world, Christ is acknowledged to have been the prototype teacher. In today's hyped, electronic world, where we strive for simplistic labels, He would probably be tabbed the "Great Communicator" (to our astute readers that probably sounds familiar). Even among those of the Jewish faith who do not accept Christ's divinity, He is still greatly revered as a "Rabbi". The Rabbi does not have the same function as a priest or minister in other faiths, but is quite simply the ultimate teacher and interpreter of weighty intellectual subjects. Throughout the bible, it is apparent that Christ was fulfilling his role as a teacher, converting difficult concepts of religious doctrine into simplified narratives. The techniques He used even puzzled his Disciples at times, causing much grumbling and eyebrow-raising during his public ministry.

Christ's Disciples, who in today's political world would be highly-opinionated campaign managers, like their modern counterparts, were supremely confident that they had a better grasp of public communications and issues than did their leader. To their continued irritation, Christ frequently used parables to make a difficult point in the usually short time he had to preach to his followers.

"Parable: A short allegorical story designed to convey some truth, religious principle or moral lesson."

In the biblical book of Matthew, Jesus gives a straightforward answer to his testy Disciples as they ask, "Why do you speak to the people in parables?" He responded in his usual cryptic manner. "The knowledge of the secrets of the Kingdom of Heaven has been given to you, but not to them." Probably shrugging his shoulders as though they should already know without asking, he continued, "This is why I speak to them in parables."

In that short exchange, repeated in other parts of the bible, Christ expressed a point to his staff that is so frequently missed by those who are intimately involved with complex subjects. It is human nature to forget, when you have devoted most of your life to a specialized field, that many people outside your sphere of interest simply do not understand what you are talking about. While the Disciples knew the subject in depth and had probably heard the same sermons many times before, they tended to forget that many in Christ's audience were hearing it for the first time with no preparatory background knowledge.

In politics, as well as in government, the techniques that irritated the Disciples of Christ cause the same problem with writers, commentators, bureaucrats and public officeholders. Those individuals who spend most of their waking hours in the pursuit of things political and governmental get so caught up in their own expertise that even their language begins to sound foreign to the ordinary citizen. The popular talking heads and learned-sounding analysts are particularly adept at trying to talk above the heads of their viewers. Frequently, you will hear references to matters of importance only "inside the Beltway". (To the uninitiated, the "Beltway" refers to an express highway — which is really not very express — that completely encircles the city of Washington, D.C.)

Although politics provides the base of our national government, which the naive among us believe belongs to us all, the participants in our political system prefer to think of it as an exclusive club. The secret rites and mysterious rituals they engage in during their tenure inside the Beltway are guarded with the jealous understanding that the ordinary public "out there" is probably not capable of understanding their profundity anyway! Only occasionally does a political figure come along, attempt to penetrate the literary obfuscation and inform the general public as to what is happening behind the concrete barriers of the Beltway.

Such rare political mavericks who try to "bust" the club with its secret handclasp and carefully coded communicators are referred to with disdain as "outsiders", clearly implying that only "insiders" can keep things running inside that whirligig fortress. Sometimes these upstart outsiders capture the attention of the folks out there and must be dealt with by those who have assumed the mantle of exclusive club leadership.

Ronald Reagan was the ultimate maverick, the despised outsider, one who was to be portrayed, wherever possible, as a "Don Quixote" thrusting his lance futilely at windmills. Just as Christ had to attack the money changers in the Temple, Ronald Reagan had to attack the entrenched forces inside the Beltway.

In interviews researching Ronald Reagan's background, we got to talk to a number of individuals who had been students in the Sunday School class he taught so frequently at the Dixon Christian Church. With the actual interviews being at least sixty to sixty-five years after the fact, it was remarkable how sharply memories of those old classes stood out in the minds of his former students. Although I, myself, was a devoted attendee at Sunday School (receiving a beautiful lapel pin for five years of perfect attendance), I must confess to being totally unable to remember any specific class lesson. Our interviews of Reagan's old students revealed unusual recollections of specific biblical messages imparted by their young teacher. Each specific lesson recalled was tied to clear memories of the youthful teacher's method of making his biblical point. Ronald converted the bible lessons of the day into stories more attuned to the normal daily lives of his charges. Lessons on courage and devotion to their Christian faith, while coming from the somewhat stilted phrasing in the bible, were clearly illustrated by their teacher with stories from his own active imagination.

Many of Ronald's former students recalled his riveting narratives of action on schoolboy fields of honor such as football and baseball arenas. They recalled tales of courage and individual initiative by young men lost in the jungle or battling raging, flood-swollen rivers. His stories always moved back and forth with references to specific biblical passages from the lesson of the week. His exciting dissertations, while well-remembered, were always recalled in the context of the biblical lesson he built them on.

Ronald Reagan, always a quick study and a keen observer of those around him, had learned well the message imparted through the pages of the New Testament of the bible. In an enduring characteristic of his entire life, he was not reluctant to pick up and put to good use the principles or teachings of others that reached the goals he had in mind. His many hours of reading and discussing the bible with his mother, who always used illustrative stories to clarify biblical concepts, helped greatly to develop his own narrative abilities. Ronald Reagan saw in Christ's parables the most effective way to drive home very important points to a listening audience.

From the earliest days of Ronald Reagan's public life, commentators and media news experts almost universally deplored his "anecdotes" or little stories so liberally sprinkled throughout his speeches. Many of them attempted to degrade or destroy his message by their heavy emphasis on his "phony" stories.

Author Lou Cannon, showing a personal conflict between his admiration for Ronald Reagan as a person and his ill-disguised contempt for Reagan's philosophy of government, referred to the President's parables by stating that he "demonstrated a willingness to substitute dramatic fiction for prosaic fact when it served a moralizing purpose". This attitude, expressed by many other critics, was calculated to leave the impression that there was something inherently evil about using such illustrative anecdotes.

Many times over his years of campaigning as an outsider, shunned by the Beltway Club, Ronald Reagan made reference to the "Welfare Queen". This mythical character, a composite of supreme slyness and political guile, was able to live a life of consummate luxury at the expense of the public. Her accumulation of tens of thousands of dollars through government relief checks was frequently cited by Reagan in his campaign against abuses in Federal welfare programs. Whether the "Welfare Queen" was an actual person, or whether her local government welfare agencies were so unbelievably slipshod is beside the point.

The message in Reagan's parable of the Welfare Queen was clear and well-understood by his audiences. The Federal Government's social programs were in disarray and badly in need of fixing. His story, often repeated despite the teeth grinding from his critics, made his point, and the voters clearly understood the underlying message.

Continuous and critical harping on Reagan's frequent use of fictional anecdotes to illustrate important points was either a naive misunderstanding of the reasons behind them or, more probably, a calculated attempt to stifle an effective campaign and oratory tool. Were Christ himself subject to the kind of critical analysis heaped on Ronald Reagan, you can imagine the prime time TV news coverage!

The opening camera zooms in on popular TV talking head *Dan Blowdry.* With his broad and all-knowing smile, he opens with, "Good evening, ladies and gentlemen. Continuing our in-depth coverage of the campaign, the opening story tonight takes us on the campaign trail of Jesus of Nazareth. Our political correspondent, *Bill Shirtsleeves,* has some background."

The scene shifts to Bill holding a microphone while standing on the edge of a large lake. In the background, a small fishing boat bobs just offshore. "Dan, today the candidate from Nazareth muddled his photo opportunities, addressing the farm problem while standing in that small boat you see behind me. None of his campaign staff could explain to me why he chose an audience of fishermen to launch into his farm policy!"

The camera flicks back to Dan in the studio, who, with his famous smirk, asks, "Bill, anything new in his farm message?"

Back to the lake scene. The camera runs earlier footage of the candidate sitting in the little fishing boat with a small, but attentive, audience gathered along the shore. The bit opens with Bill's explanation of the setting, then picks up the candidate's words spoken casually from the boat. "A farmer went out to sow his seed. As he was scattering his seed, some fell along the path and the birds came and ate it up. Some fell on rocky places, where it did not have much soil . . . "

Cutting into candidate Christ's speech, the scene returns to Bill, now live, standing by the deserted lake shore.

"Dan, he went on to point out that the seed the farmer threw on good soil produced . . . OK! back to you."

In the studio, a now broadly-smiling and all-knowing Dan turns from his monitor where he has been watching Bill.

"Thanks, Bill, for that on-the-scene report. It appears that the Nazareth Party is beginning to refine their farm program."

The camera zooms back, revealing a moon-faced, smiling, companion talking head with his hands full of papers. "With us tonight is our regular analyst, *John Sincere*. John, what do you think of today's developments in the campaign?" Zooming in on John, firmly straightening his sheaf of notes while nodding at the star, Blowdry, John states, "Dan, while it appears on the surface that Jesus of Nazareth has finally come forth with a farm policy, I don't think it's going to fly. As we all know, He is the son of a carpenter, and, while He may know something about building, it's obvious He knows very little about farming!

His story today about a farmer, scattering seeds along a paved path and on rocks indicates an abysmal lack of understanding of the farm problem. It's a gross insult to depict the farmer, who has made this country great, being so ignorant as to sow seed in areas where it cannot possibly grow! The Nazareths are going to have to get their act together and begin to address the real issues rather than downgrading our country's great farmers!

That is our commentary for tonight. Back to you, Dan."

"Thanks, John. Well-thought-out as always. Tomorrow we'll continue our in-depth campaign coverage." Cut to commercial.

Not so far-fetched as it may sound, television, which has become the major, and in many cases the only, source of information for millions of individuals, has created its own standards of accuracy in reporting. While thinking nothing of presenting staged events as "news" or commissioning self-serving surveys or polls as plots for news stories, the media generally seeks to hold public figures to a higher standard than their own. Thus, while never apologizing for their own straying away from pure facts, they gleefully attacked Ronald Reagan for his "fictitious" stories. But despite that, just as Christ established his truths through his "phony" parables, Ronald Reagan got his basic message to the voters through his "phony" anecdotes! In the face of such criticism and even the often-expressed concern of his own disciples, Reagan's parables have become an indelible trademark of his public career.

Norman Wymbs

CHAPTER 16

DIVINE GUIDANCE

Nelle Reagan lead a life that was a constant, unwavering beacon of her deep Christian faith. While what we have reported so far, along with her ceaseless activities of helping jail prisoners and working with the physically and mentally ill, would seem to paint a picture of a consummate "do gooder", she was not remembered that way. Old friends and contemporaries recalled her with a certain amount of awe and wonderment that she could have been so thoroughly a good person. Her good works and very tangible efforts towards the rehabilitation of the physical lives of her charges did not in any way subvert her sincere striving for the spiritual revival of those individuals scraping the bottom of society's barrel. She never let it be forgotten that, although a good meal and a warm place to sleep were basic foundations for their well-being, nothing was achievable without the most important ingredient, a firm faith in God!

With her bible always at hand and with the trademark Reagan unflagging optimism, she won over many converts to her message of reliance on Divine Guidance coupled with strong family love and support. With Nelle, there was no discussion concerning "traditional values". To her, there was no alternative. Looking back on her ministry, for it was a real missionary saga in every sense of the word, it's noteworthy that we found no indication that anyone considered her "preachy". Had she, after the fashion of so many evangelists, exhorted her audiences solely by waving the bible and endlessly quoting scriptures, she would, in all probability, have been dismissed as just another religious fanatic. Nelle, however, possessed of deep intellect and compassion, sensed the overall needs of the troubled inmates in the local institutions and conducted her ministry to address all of them. An excellent cook, she made good use of her culinary skills to initiate quick attention and interest. In what became the trademark of both of her sons, she did not neglect the importance of humor in her dissertations. With full stomach and in a good humor, there was no way her audiences would not be ready to receive and absorb the message.

A review of Ronald Reagan's many public appearances reveals that, except on the most solemn of occasions (with his upbeat attitude there were relatively few of those), he followed his mother's pattern. He almost always opened with one of his light-hearted, humorous anecdotes to relax the audience and invariably closed with another story calculated to draw a laugh, while still conveying an important message or moral. Usually, these stories and humorous asides were inserted by Reagan into his speeches without the knowledge or approval of his formal speech writers.

Both Nelle and Jack Reagan were natural story tellers who found gentle humor in virtually every life situation no matter how grim it might first appear. It is no wonder that Ronald's most appealing personal trait exhibits this same ability. Although he exhibited all of his parents' natural abilities in this area, so far he has never publicly displayed another of their notable talents. Both Nelle and Jack loved to sing, although his voice had more of a professional quality than hers. Nelle lead her audiences in hymns and popular songs of the day, offsetting any lack of vocal quality with her own musical accompaniment on a much-used ukulele. Although Ronald Reagan has frequently been seen singing, usually in groups, I find no record that he ever resorted to the ukulele at any public meeting!

The use and study of the bible were constants in the Reagan household. The bible was not a "coffee table" book in their family. It was always nearby and in daily use. Ronald Reagan has carried his mother's old bible with him throughout his public life and has given it particular attention as he penciled notes for proposed speeches on every subject. By the time he retired from the Presidency, it was a testimony to the original bookbinder's skill that the old volume was still reasonably intact. Today, Nelle's old standby rests in the Presidential

Library in California and is still held reasonably intact by multiple applications of mending tape over the years. Its well-worn condition was caused, in a large part, by the President's constant thumbing through for suitable passages and phrases to use in his public messages. Nelle's many notes of help and reference are nearly illegible now as a result of those constant references.

In the front flyleaf, Nelle noted the following favorite passages of reference used often by her popular son.

"If in sorrow, read John 14.

If people fail you , read Ps 27.

If you worry, read Matt 6:19,27.

If downcast, read Ps 34.

If discouraged, read Isaiah 40.

If your faith becomes weak, read Heb 11."

Thoughtful guidance left by a loving mother to a devoted family.

During his public life, Reagan made frequent reference to his mother and the influence of her Christian faith on his own life. During an impromptu question and answer session at a meeting midway into his first term as President, he put it this way, "Isaiah reminded us that the Lord opens his gates and keeps in peace the nation that trusts in Him. I hope you won't mind my saying — Nelle Reagan, my mother, God rest her soul, had an unshakable faith in God's goodness, and while I may not have realized it in my youth, I know now that she planted that faith deeply in me. She made the most difficult Christian message seem very easy. She knew you could never repay one bad deed with another. Her way was forgiveness and goodness, and both began with love."

Jack and Nelle's compassion and concern for others were not just a localized or neighborhood thing. They were well-aware of the state of affairs in the entire country and its relationship with the rest of the world. Jack's concerns were manifesting themselves in a strong activist position in the world of politics. This little-known part of his life, which had an important influence on his son's future, we will get into a little later. Nelle's ecumenical reach is best exemplified by a penciled notation on the margin of a page in her bible's Second Book of the Chronicles, "A most wonderful verse for the healing of the nations". On that well-thumbed page, the verse she noted has been quoted many times by President Reagan in foreign policy remarks.

> "If my people, which are called by my name, shall humble themselves and pray and seek my face and turn from their wicked ways, then I will hear from Heaven and will forgive their sin and heal their land."

Ronald Reagan's reliance upon Christian faith and his broad knowledge of the bible and its philosophical concepts were not just a show biz thing to be turned on for campaign purposes only. Not only did he draw upon his strong religious background to establish important policy points, but also he frequently went out of his way to draw attention to those values in personal living. The following statement at a public appearance sums up his philosophy of living quite well.

"Within the covers of that single book (the bible) are all the answers to all the problems that face us today, if we will only look there. 'The grass withereth, the flower fadeth, but the word of our God shall stand forever!' The bible can touch our hearts, order our minds, refresh our souls."

Reagan's deep Christian faith, so much a part of his personality and background, simply could not be suppressed. His spontaneous references to biblical texts and frequent exhortations to apply the power of prayer did not sit particularly well with his political handlers. Although the news media, generally, tended to ignore his frequent biblical references, seldom even mentioning their use, his speech writers and staff tried to head him off at the pass wherever they could. His irrepressible enthusiasm and inborn reliance on a strong fundamental faith constantly lead him to pencil in bible references on the carefully-crafted speeches they printed for him. Although most of his speeches were born through long, almost illegible handwritten notes scribbled off quickly by the President, the finished product always tended to reflect the personality of the faceless speech writers. With his own notes and favorite anecdotes, he always managed to bring them back to his own inimitable style and strong views.

Reagan never swerved from his conviction that Christianity was the ultimate answer to all the world's problems. Even on the secular subject of civil rights, he indicated that strong belief. "All of us, as Protestants, Catholics and Jews, have a special responsibility to remember our fellow believers who are being persecuted in other lands. We are all children of Abraham. We are children of the same God."

There were times during his public life when President Reagan's unswerving faith and boundless optimism caused raised eyebrows and not a little bit of knowing snickers on the part of those who were convinced he was an idle dreamer. Speaking of what some saw as a resurgence of Christianity in the then-still-oppressive Soviet Union in the early 1980's, he stated, "Think of it, the most awesome military machine in history, but it is no match for that one single man, hero, strong-yet-tender Prince of Peace. His name alone, Jesus, can lift our hearts, soothe our sorrows, heal our wounds and drive away our fears. He gave us love and forgiveness. He taught us truth and left us hope. In the book of John is the promise we all go by. 'For God so loved the world that He gave His only-begotten Son, that whosoever believeth in Him should not perish, but have everlasting life.' "

At the time he sounded like, at worst, a questionable leader for the country, or, at least, a naive optimist out of touch with the world situation. The Soviet Union, then at the apparent peak of its power, was ruthlessly striking down any vestige of independent thought or religious faith in its oppressed population. Although his words sounded like the empty "feel good" preaching of an uninformed religious zealot, as the leader of the United States, he was already wielding the big stick against the "Evil Empire" which we'll get into later on. At this point it is sufficient to note the accuracy of his statement about the latent Christianity behind the impenetrable walls and barbed wire of the Soviet Union. In 1990 when the Evil Empire of the Soviet began to crumble, the whole world was amazed to see how quickly the Christian churches were up and running after the yoke was removed. Despite the godless repression of over seventy years, as Ronald Reagan had pointed out, it was impossible to squelch the inherent faith of the Soviet people.

During the entire first term of President Reagan, the opposition political and news media leaders could find nothing of substance with which to attack his popularity with the public. This high level of acceptance lead to the news media's adopting the term "Teflon President". Used derisively by his political opponents, it nevertheless fairly accurately showed the continued citizen acceptance and affection for the very popular President. No amount of criticism, disdain or downright dirt they threw at Ronald Reagan seemed to stick. All their vituperative attacks rolled off, like water off a duck's back, or in the popular idiom, like cooking waste off a Teflon-coated frying pan!

In 1985 the American news media thought they had finally found the weapon to defeat, or at least seriously wound, Ronald Reagan. Ironically, as they so frequently showed, they did not really get the message, as they chose to attack the President in the area of his strongest resolve. The occasion was a projected trip to Europe, and the slings and arrows of the opposition zeroed in on his solid Christian faith.

The President, on a planned stop in West Germany for a conference with that strong ally's Chancellor, was scheduled for a pro forma visit to one of that country's military cemeteries. Much like our country frequently escorts distinguished foreign dignitaries to Arlington National Cemetery for a ritual wreath-laying, Reagan was scheduled for a similar visit to the German Military Cemetery at Bitburg, Germany. Bitburg, containing the graves of over two thousand fallen German soldiers of World War II, holds much the same solemn significance to Germany as Arlington does in our country.

Reagan's ever-alert and mostly frustrated critics, ever-anxious and digging for ammunition against the man, suddenly found what they thought would finally crack the President's deep reserve of national popularity. Some brilliant shovel wielder dug up the facts that there were some German soldiers of the infamous SS Corps buried in the hallowed ground at Bitburg. They conveniently ignored the facts that there were less than fifty SS members out of the two thousand interred there, and that a large proportion of the two thousand were hardly more than teenaged boys hastily recruited for Germany's last stand during the war. Brushing aside the fact that an overwhelming majority of those lying there had died honorably for their country, the critical media wolves began to howl and snap at Reagan's heels.

Ignoring the central purpose of the President's trip to Europe, the sensationalists played the Bitburg theme almost exclusively. One prominent Jewish leader became the instant darling of the news media as he indignantly announced he would not appear at the White House to receive an award scheduled to be presented by President Reagan. In the convoluted reasoning of those out to get Reagan, the argument was put forth that, since the German SS Corps had been in the forefront during the German persecution of the Jews in World War II, and there were those few SS bodies beneath the surface of Bitburg, Ronald Reagan was endorsing the German holocaust by his proposed visit to the site. After the manner of edgy political handlers, most of Reagan's White House staff joined the chorus urging him to cancel his planned visit.

On this one issue, Ronald Reagan displayed two of his most enduring, although seldom seen by the public, characteristics. Angry at the deeply personal attacks over what he considered a non-issue, he stubbornly set his jaw and announced the visit to the Bitburg Cemetery was still on! Seldom did anyone outside his immediate staff get the opportunity to witness Ronald Reagan's stubborn determination when he took a stand on matters of firm principle. In this case, with the political opposition and the news media joined in raucous attack, some of which was viciously personal, the public got a chance to witness his firm determination and, for the most part, applauded it!

The other, and deeper, mark of character was his strong sense that the criticism and any subsequent retreat would not be Christian. Genuinely puzzled by the furor over the few buried SS soldiers in the vast Bitburg Cemetery, Reagan stated, "The final word has been spoken. I think it is morally right to do what I am doing, and I'm not going to change my mind about that." Continuing, he said, "All of those in that cemetery have long since met the Supreme Judge of right and wrong, and whatever punishment that was needed has been rendered by one who is above us all."

Later, while speaking beside the many rows of graves at the German cemetery, he stated, "We do not believe in collective guilt. Only God can look into the human heart. All these men have met their Supreme Judge. They have been judged by Him, as we shall all be judged."

In those simple truths, Ronald Reagan displayed the essence of his strong Christian character. One can imagine the smile of pride that would have suffused the face of Nelle Reagan had she been there to share the simple, but eloquent, faith of her son.

Norman Wymbs

CHAPTER 17

A POLITICAL FAMILY

One of the most cherished traditions in our American culture is the folklore of the "self-made" man. Whether in finance, business or the political world, we tend to honor, even worship, those we think reached their lofty pinnacles of success with little or no outside help. Just as in most folk tales, there is more fiction than fact when you probe to the source. While most of us hang on every word concerning the life and times of the famous, we are apt to overlook the real factors that made them reach the top. In much the same way many dream of the day "their ship will come in" or fantasize about hitting the jackpot, we prefer to believe that is the way it really happens. The truth, of course, is that we are all the results of multiple influences from our families, schools, churches, friends and life experiences. The self-made success is, in reality, the fortuitous combination of all those influences. Final achievements and place in history come from the way those lifelong influences are combined and used. Ronald Reagan is no exception to that pattern. We have already looked at how his family life and education contributed to his later leadership of his country, but there is another very important factor that has received relatively little attention in analysis of his impact on the world.

Temperament and leadership qualities are, of course, critical elements in the making of an outstanding President, but these are wasted talents in the absence of another vital cog. Under our governmental system, the greatest leader in the world would never have the opportunity to display his talents if he lacked political smarts! Under our political process, it is not unusual for an individual, lacking any real leadership qualities, but with excellent political astuteness, to reach high office. It almost never happens the other way around. Without political understanding, many natural leaders never reach the top. The United States, fortunately, has been richly blessed with politically smart natural leaders throughout its history.

Granting Ronald Reagan had the vision and ability to lead the country, how did this guy whose opponents still deride him as only a "second rate-actor" get the political moxy to reach the top? I'm glad you asked!

As happens frequently, we tend to gloss over important details, while looking for attention-getting highlights when

184

putting together a story. Although many writers have had a go at Ronald Reagan, both positively and negatively, there is little of his political education in any of the narratives. While it is not logically realistic to assume he suddenly blossomed out of the motion picture industry with a full-fledged political agenda and philosophy, that is the story we have been given.

In the early buildup preparing him for his entry into elective politics, a concerted effort was made to sell the idea he learned politics from his activities in the screen actors' union in Hollywood. To attribute his later success in capturing the Republican Party and neutralizing its long-entrenched leadership to his activities in an obscure, narrowly-limited labor union is preposterous. It would be no more ridiculous to credit his political education to the campaign for high school student body president!

Some small hints at the political influence in Reagan's early life come from his frequent references to the fact he registered as a Democrat when he first became eligible to vote and, in fact, cast his first national vote for Franklin D. Roosevelt for President in 1932. There is little doubt his registration decision was a direct result of his father's strong support of and membership in the Democrat Party. Ronald Reagan's frequent statements concerning Roosevelt's influence on his early political thinking, while driving his opponents in the Democrat Party right up the wall, is nevertheless a strong indication of how his political thinking evolved.

In that early book, "Where Is The Rest Of Me?", produced primarily to promote his entry into serious elective politics, his advisors allowed only an offhand reference to his father's political persuasion. In that volume, Jack Reagan's beliefs were slipped innocuously into a general description of his father.

"Jack (we called him by his nickname) was a handsome man, tall, swarthy and muscular, filled with contradictions of character — a sentimental Democrat, who believed fervently in the rights of the workingman."

Note that, in the book, Ronald speaks of his father's contradictions of character. Although that statement gets no further elaboration, it appears it was inserted to make sure not too much weight was placed upon Jack's being a Democrat! In the peculiar way that politicians warp history, Roosevelt has become the icon of all liberal thought within the Democrat Party, even though much of what has transpired since Roosevelt's administration bears no resemblance to his programs and theories. The same offhand approach used in that book has been used over the years to slough off Ronald Reagan's own early Democrat leaning. We are presumably supposed to accept that fact as a sentimental action corrected in his later life as he grew more politically aware!

A careful review of Jack Reagan's background suggests he was anything but a "sentimental" Democrat. He was not only politically knowledgeable, but also active enough to draw serious attention from the Roosevelt campaign and a substantial reward for his support after Roosevelt went into office, as we will see later. Events in Jack's life at that time indicate he was every bit as much an activist in politics as Nelle was in her social reform activism. Putting together all the facts on Jack reveals he was a worthy tutor for his youngest son's plunge into the dog-eat-dog world of politics! Although we could find no specific indication that Nelle took any direct part in politics, because of their closeness and support for each other, it is safe to assume she was in full accord with her husband's feelings in this regard.

Bits and pieces of information from Ronald and from old friends reveal Jack Reagan to have had a deep compassion for those who had not been dealt a winning hand by fate. We have already noted how he took an active hand and participated with Nelle in her ministry to the sick and helpless. Although apparently not quite as attuned to her fervent evangelical Christianity and the raucous campaign against alcohol, he was shoulder-to-shoulder with her other efforts at righting some of the perceived social injustices. In retrospect, particularly with the devastating depression starting to grip the country, it is not hard to see how Jack gravitated to the Democrat Party.

To understand the powerful influences at work in those days, which were to culminate in the enormously popular and effective Ronald Reagan Presidency, a little domestic history needs to be recalled.

After the shock and disruption of World War I, when for the first time Americans went to die in another land, the United States collectively hitched up its pants and got back to worrying about its own future. Vowing never to again become involved in foreign problems, they concentrated on old-fashioned American enterprise and its individual rewards. The effort was successful, as most of the 1920's produced the cherished Yankee "good life" for most of its citizens.

Politically during this period, the country was dominated by Republican politics and officeholders. With things appearing to go so well, the Democrats were unable to mount any sort of effective political opposition. Dixon, Illinois was, in most ways, typical of the rest of the country in those heady "boom" days!

Browsing through the history of that period, as found in the pages of the *Dixon Telegraph* newspaper, it is hard to find any indication that things might not have been going as well for the country as it appeared. Recalling that the *Telegraph*, at its inception, almost coincided with the initial birth throbs of the Republican Party, as exemplified by Illinois' favorite son, Abraham Lincoln, it is not hard to understand the newspaper's viewpoint. The *Telegraph* and its founder, Ben Shaw, were in the nature of parents to the Midwestern Republican Party and highly instrumental in the promotion of Lincoln into the Presidency. In the 1920's, as it still is today, the *Dixon Telegraph* was a conservative, Republican-oriented newspaper still run by Shaws descended from the politically savvy Ben! With no other newspaper in the area coming anywhere near the circulation of the *Telegraph*, the paper's old issues give a rather clear picture of the prevailing political majority, while revealing little of any opposition to the accepted wisdom of the day.

Much of those days of political education and activity in the Reagan family we have to deduce from the results of subsequent events. We know that Jack and Nelle had well-developed concerns for the unfortunate minority, rapidly growing toward a near majority, who were not enjoying the fruits of the country's earlier apparent prosperity. There were no government social programs at the national level, and the only local social efforts were administered by county mental hospitals and municipal jails. In most cases it was hard to distinguish the difference between the so-called hospitals (usually called homes in an attempt to hide their misery) and the jails packed with more down and out vagrants than criminals. The most effective social welfare and charity came from the voluntary institutions, such as churches, and from private homes. In those difficult years, charity did, in truth, literally begin at home!

Jack and Nelle Reagan were in the forefront of such personalized help to the downtrodden and gave unstintingly of their limited resources and time. While Nelle concentrated more on the area of moral reform through faith in God as the ultimate solution, Jack took a more secular view, as he spoke out, increasingly forcefully, on the need for help from the political system. The influence of the two, with differing approaches to the same problem, apparently was an ideal combination in the guidance and education of their youngest son.

Jack, a successful and popular independent businessman in Dixon, was struck a near mortal blow by the severe depression of the late '20's and early '30's. With as many as 50% of all small businesses wiped out and unemployment running over 25% during those years of despair, there were few who were not affected. Jack, a feisty Irish fighter, did not surrender to the difficulties, but kept going, holding a series of hand-to-mouth jobs during the worst years. Nelle, just as dogged in her determination as her husband, pitched in by working as a seamstress at home and in a friend's small dress shop. Even during those trying years, the Reagans never forgot the plight of others, as their home and meager resources were always shared with those in worse circumstances.

Jack, like many formerly successful small business and professional people, was developing a heightened awareness for the need of government to take a larger part in easing, or even preventing, the economic and personal shock of such devastating collapses in the business and social structures of the country.

With over one-quarter of the nation's work force without jobs, there were no important government programs or even projected plans to help the unemployed. Many able-bodied individuals, unable to find work, were reduced to bare existence through local charity and volunteer soup kitchens. Small businesses, out of capital and unable to continue, simply closed their doors and expired, as did Jack's long-successful shoe store. Banks were unwilling or unable to risk their depleted resources in what appeared to be a losing cause and quit making business loans to the small operators. With no effective government banking regulations or assistance, thousands of seemingly solid financial institutions folded, increasing the snowballing effect as millions lost their life savings.

Even given the chaos and despair of the times, there appeared to be no real feeling at the head of government that political action would play any part in the struggle to recover from the nearly total collapse of the country. Never having had government very deeply involved in their personal lives, most citizens were not looking in that direction for help. That feeling was beginning to change, being boosted by the severe drought in the early '30's, which wiped out thousands of farms and brought about food shortages and higher prices when the economy simply couldn't handle another blow!

Now there were deep political rumblings that were to lead to the greatest shift in the way people viewed their government since the arrival of Abraham Lincoln. Jack Reagan and millions like him were not unaware of the fact that while the little guys were dropping like flies in the collapsed economy, the big and strong seemed to be getting bigger and stronger. While not begrudging the good fortune of that relatively small group, Jack and his counterparts across the country felt the system needed a basic change. Free enterprise was still the battle cry, but something needed to be done to protect the small enterprise from free fall during an economic recession. Jack's fighting temperament cast him into the role of political maverick, as he joined the increasing chorus of voices calling for a major political change.

National leaders in Washington, never good at perceiving grass roots changes in the country, appeared to be frozen in place. Not knowing what to do, they did what Washington has always done best. They argued and did nothing.

Into this vacuum of innovation and spiritless leadership quietly slipped Franklin Delano Roosevelt. Aside from his personal growth in spiritual faith, nothing was to have the impact on Ronald Reagan that President Roosevelt did during his administration. It is fair to say that the influence on Ronald of FDR would have been minimized, or even non-existent, had it not been for the increasing political activism of Jack Reagan. Jack's active support and work in Roosevelt's first campaign and the result they had on his life made a deep impact on future President Ronald Reagan!

Norman Wymbs

CHAPTER 18

JACK'S NEW DEAL

After Ronald Reagan's election to the Presidency in 1980, the news media and other writers found there was much about him they did not know. It is not surprising to find that public communicators tend to follow predictable paths. Until the American public finally expressed their overwhelming endorsement of the Reagan challenge by awarding him the Presidency, reporters had blindly followed the conventional wisdom that he was a flawed actor with little chance of success in his quest. So anxious were they to harp upon and repeat the politically correct theme of the times, that few of them, if any, really knew anything about the family background of the new President.

Coming into his high office, Reagan's life in the Hollywood motion picture industry had been replayed by the news media more often than old "I Love Lucy" reruns on TV! Probably because it entailed more old-fashioned effort and real investigative ability than was common to the news industry, virtually nothing was known of the new President's life before motion pictures. Working with only bits and pieces, mostly in the nature of short, limited anecdotes from his past, those years before movieland were a real mystery. The physical facts, such as where he was born and where he grew up and went to school, were well known. His mother's church activity and his father's supposed drinking problems had been touched in a superficial manner. Nowhere in all the writing and commentary had anyone come up with anything to show how his early years had contributed to his triumphant quest for the White House.

In all fairness, it should be pointed out that the news media and analytical writers were not entirely at fault for the lack of information on the Reagan family and its early years in Illinois. Ronald Reagan has always been a master at communicating what he wants us to know and even more adept at keeping from us those things he thinks we don't need to know! Always a thoroughly private and self-contained individual, he feels very strongly that his private, personal life should remain just that. By deftly and good-naturedly parrying or ignoring personal questions he didn't want to answer, he developed a reputation with the media of being uninformed and forgetful. Closer examination of his observations on his early life, however, reveal much about the closeness and single-minded purposefulness of the entire Reagan clan and how these traits guided him to his successful role in politics.

In an interview shortly after his election in 1980, Ronald Reagan in a few well-directed words, as he does so frequently, projected a volume of information on his past. The interviewer, anxious to unearth something new and, preferably, sensational, was quizzing him on his early life in Dixon. The President, as usual in such interviews, was in high good humor and was tossing out his usual innocuous anecdotes that were, by this time, well-known to everyone who had ever tried a similar discussion. Hoping to draw some kind of statement about the harshness of his youth, the interviewer turned to questions about the poverty in which he thought the Reagan family had lived. This was not a new approach, as many writers had bitten on the apocryphal stories of Reagan's rise from abject poverty. After once again assuring the interviewer that the Reagans, while not rich, were far from poor, the President paused in reflection. With that familiar mist in his eyes and a noticeable catch in his voice, he said of those years growing up in Dixon, "It was a good life. I couldn't have asked for anything more, then or now!"

About to start an eight-year reign as President of the United States, a venerated and astoundingly popular leader just moved into the luxury and pampering of the White House could still sincerely state that nothing could be better than those years in Illinois! In that simple, heartfelt statement, Ronald Reagan neatly summed up the positive and grateful view of life that was at the core of the entire Reagan family.

Jack Reagan, a proud man who was confident of his abilities and purpose in life, had rolled with some hard punches which would have knocked out a lesser man. His prized business, which had given him independence and stature in the

195

community as he raised two sons and sent them off to college, had been wiped out by the Great Depression. While many in similar straits were succumbing to the sheer weight of the disaster, Jack kept his chin up and fought back. Never losing his sense of humor or optimism, he kept the Reagan family together while scraping a living out of a number of less-than-rewarding jobs and enterprises. It was because of this difficult period that one unkind and ignorant writer tabbed Jack as a drunken, itinerant shoe salesman! He was certainly not a drunk and he held jobs while up to 50% of his contemporaries were begging charity. His sales ability and irrepressible upbeat nature kept the family solvent while he sold shoes and did clerical work.

Although he was sure that the American spirit was such that things would inevitably get better, Jack had little confidence that the country's leaders were going to be of any help. In this atmosphere, fairly common across the country, it suddenly appeared that the national Democrat Party had produced an answer. Franklin Delano Roosevelt, a relatively unknown Governor from New York (we'll examine that parallel later), was a presidential candidate seemingly incarnated out of Jack Reagan's hopes and frustrations. FDR sounded the bugle note in his first campaign that rallied the country. Having a particularly deep impact on the Reagans, his simple, but forceful, rallying cry, "We have nothing to fear but fear itself," struck just the right upbeat tone for the Reagans.

Nelle's often-heard admonishment that, no matter how bad things looked, the Lord always worked them out for good, and Jack's fierce conviction that hard work and positive thinking would win in the end made them natural supporters of Roosevelt.

Even without minimizing the seriousness of the national situation and lacking any special conviction that Roosevelt's promises could really help, Jack Reagan and thousands of other non-politicians threw themselves into the Democrat Party's presidential campaign. The main draw of the aristocratic Roosevelt was his positive, upbeat attitude towards the future. During this year of rising hopes in 1932, Ronald Reagan graduated from Eureka College and was back home seeking work.

Ronald, with the enthusiasm of youth and the unquenchable optimism of all the Reagans, had set his sights on a career in commercial radio. Despite the general decline in the nation's economy, radio was prospering and becoming an ever greater factor as an educational and an entertainment medium across the country. Spurning the opportunity at local retail clerical positions which Jack's connections had produced, the brash graduate set out to conquer the big radio stations in Chicago. After the not unexpected short shrift he received in the big city, Ronald was back in Dixon, reluctantly ready to face the less-than-exciting local job market.

At this critical point in Ronald Reagan's life, his father, as he had done so often in the past, offered some down-to-earth counsel. Not only recognizing the overwhelming desire Ronald had to break into the radio business, but also confident that his determined son could make it in any competitive field, Jack talked the young man into lowering his sights somewhat. He convinced Ronald that his best opportunity in that rapidly-growing field would be with a smaller, growing station in the Midwest. Lending his son the family Oldsmobile, Jack pointed him west and sent him off with a heavy dose of encouragement.

Ronald Reagan didn't have to travel too far west, as he managed to land a job as sports announcer at a small station in Davenport, Iowa. He thus launched a career which spanned two decades within the entertainment giants of radio and television and was sandwiched around his great success in motion pictures. As an aside, at this point it is interesting to note that Jack Reagan, so often degraded as an abject failure, during the height of the world's most severe depression, still owned and drove an Oldsmobile auto that he made available to his son for that job-hunting trip!

During that summer and fall of 1932, besides helping one son get launched on a new career and supporting another still in college, Jack found time to get active in the campaign of Franklin Roosevelt. That activity was a difficult move, as the area was quite solidly Republican in sentiment and support. Researching the media of the time, we could find little in the news showing Jack's position within the Democrat Party or his personal activities in the election campaign. The locally dominant newspaper was openly pro-Republican and never featured articles concerning activities of the Democrat Party. The issues of that paper daily featured front page stories on President Herbert Hoover's reelection efforts, with lots of pictures, while the challenger (FDR) was relegated to minor back page reports without pictures! Despite the lack of local press coverage, Jack and many others doggedly kept at their efforts to elect Roosevelt.

As would be expected, Jack's fervent support and advocacy of Franklin Roosevelt's "New Deal" were having a deep effect on Ronald. In his new position at the radio station in Davenport, even though his specialty was sports, and he was not involved in general news, Ronald could not help being exposed to much of the campaign opinion. That area of Iowa was as solidly partisan toward the Republican President as any part of the country, since it was only thirty-five miles from the birthplace and continuing home of favorite-son, Herbert Hoover! Despite the local pressures, Ronald Reagan had developed the same hope for and support of the projected "New Deal" as his father and, that fall, cast his first presidential vote for Franklin Roosevelt!

That Jack Reagan was not just another run-of-the-mill supporter of Roosevelt became apparent shortly after FDR was sworn into office in March, 1933. The new President, moving swiftly to set in motion the proposed programs that had created his overwhelming public mandate, showered Congress with new proposals to help the moribund U.S. economy. One of those efforts was the "Federal Emergency Relief Administration", which was personally headed by Roosevelt's closest and most trusted aide, Harry L. Hopkins. Modest by modern standards, the new agency, FERA, was funded with a $500 million Federal appropriation. Its mission was to provide direct grants to state relief agencies. This represented a major departure from the prior practice, in which the national government made loans only to the states. With the new approach, this program required a whole new administrative organization.

Jack Reagan was appointed District Manager for FERA that summer and opened an office in Dixon. To understand the importance of this appointment and its indication of the political clout Jack had developed with the Roosevelt forces, we need again to look at the country's condition in 1933.

Roosevelt's election, while creating hope, did not in itself create any boost in the nation's economy. Unemployment was still over 25%, business was dormant and most banks were surviving only on a day-to-day basis. The new administration in Washington had few jobs to offer under the usual political spoils system, despite thousands of loyal supporters' seeking work. The modest start of FERA was one of the few federal programs which actually created new jobs with the Administration. There is little doubt, under the circumstances, that the pressure and maneuvering to get one of those limited positions were intense and competitive. That Jack Reagan so quickly received one of the coveted appointments as a District Director is the best indication of his importance in the election campaign. No "sentimental Democrat" here! He was a political activist of the first order!

Jack's political clout with the Roosevelt Administration was to manifest itself again when his eldest son, Neil, graduated from Eureka College a year behind Ronald. Encountering the same difficult job market as his younger brother, Neil was finding the same closed doors. Always in the forefront when his sons needed help, Jack used his contacts and influence to get Neil appointed to a new position as District Representative for the Federal Re-employment Bureau with an office in Dixon! The Roosevelt Administration knew about and appreciated the support of the Reagans, particularly "sentimental" Jack!

Jack's successful entry into and obvious enjoyment of the game of politics had a long-lasting effect on his youngest son. Ronald's interest in and close following of the programs of President Franklin Roosevelt were to become important factors guiding the later Reagan Administrations.

200

After the heady excitement of the political campaign of 1932 and his direct entry into government service in 1933, it would appear that Jack Reagan, at middle age, had finally found his real mission in life. Unfortunately, his health was to stifle that potential. After a couple of heart attacks, he died eight years later at the age of fifty-eight.

Although he did not live long enough to pursue his belated career in politics, Jack Reagan motivated his son, Ronald, and left his country with a lasting legacy of accomplishment in the Reagan name!

Norman Wymbs

CHAPTER 19

THE ASSEMBLY

In this look at the roots of Ronald Reagan, heavy emphasis has been placed on outside influences, as well as that of the family, on the development of his character and intellect. During those formative years at home, the family was paramount in creating what was to become the public conception of Ronald Reagan, the man. Of almost equal importance were the outside factors of culture and education bearing upon those same early years. As with all of us, Ronald's hometown, with its own peculiar traits and character, played a critical role.

We have earlier alluded to the mystique of Dixon, that hard-to-define but distinct aura that seems to set it apart from other similarly-sized American communities. Although sometimes hard to pinpoint, the appeal to a natural human desire for knowledge and personal growth seems to have been a part of this Midwestern area since the early pioneer days. Nowhere does this reveal itself more strongly than in the phenomenal development of the Chautauqua Movement in the latter part of the nineteenth century and the first quarter of our age.

In the middle 1800's, a Methodist clergyman in New York, seeking a more effective way to train Sunday school teachers, started what was to be a cultural bonfire throughout the United States. Convening a meeting in the Chautauqua Lake country of New York state in 1874, that minister and a few of his colleagues held their first retreat to train church teachers and lay leaders. Their avowed aim was to broaden and expand the church Sunday school program to encompass more of the intellectual world beyond the bible. Choosing an area well away from the heavily populated and, in their minds, religiously stagnant metropolitan centers, they put together a lecture session the likes of which had never before been seen in any church organization. Recognizing that church dogma and teaching largely ignored the realities of the non-secular world, they sought to blend pure biblical instruction with intellectual lecturers from history, science and government.

It is doubtful, that even the most enthusiastic founders of the Chautauqua Movement, as it was to become known, had any inkling of what they were about to unleash on the country. TheUnited States, torn apart by a bitter war, was in the throws of rebuilding and was undergoing a serious introspection about its destiny. Citizens in all parts of the nation, especially in the semi-isolated, small communities, were reaching out beyond their formally narrow parochial concerns. The Chautauqua approach turned out to be tailor-made for that compelling need. The first indication of what was stirring came in the second meeting when, impressed by what was planned, President Grant agreed to be their featured speaker. It is of more than passing interest for the purposes of our study to note that this sitting United States President, who put the power and prestige of his office behind the new endeavor, was a native of Galena, a pleasant short drive from Dixon in northern Illinois!

Expanding rapidly from the east, Chautauqua meetings were sprouting throughout America, especially in the Midwest. Although essentially a small town phenomenon, the scope and depth of the program were indicated by one of its early assemblies in the city of Chicago. That meeting became so popular it was expanded to a year-round affair and eventually incorporated itself into what is now the world-renowned University of Chicago! Certainly a significant example of the cultural depth of the movement in that already highly sophisticated city!

In 1887, the Lutheran Synod of Northern Illinois decided to hold a "Sunday School Institute" in the Rock River area. In the summer of 1888, under the auspices of the Chautauqua Movement, they held a three-day meeting along the banks of the river near Dixon. It proved so successful they formed a committee to plan another institute to be known as the Rock River Assembly for the following year. The program for that first formal assembly was broadened to place a heavy emphasis on speakers and experts on worldly subjects. By 1890, the annual meeting was becoming so popular that the few small buildings and tents were insufficient to handle the crowds. A stock corporation was formed, with all the stock quickly subscribed to, and a 34-acre tract of land along the Rock River in Dixon was purchased to establish the new Assembly grounds.

In a history of the Rock River Assembly, published in 1923 by the Lutheran Synod, the function and purposes of the meetings were made clear. Speaking of the Chautauqua Movement, it stated, "It is not a wholly religious movement. Yet the Church of the Lord Jesus Christ has been its originator and chief promoter. Trends toward Christian principles and life have been its distinguishing characteristics, as it has undoubtedly been the secret of its perpetuity. 'Chautauqua', defined, is a system of popular education which seeks to give what has been called the 'College Outlook'. Its endeavor has been to give the advantage of education to all. It goes on the principle that education, begun in youth, should continue throughout life."

The Dixon assembly grew so rapidly that the tents and modest structures originally provided proved inadequate. A "tabernacle", larger than any local church, was built to hold the meeting audiences, but even as it was dedicated, it proved too small. People from miles away were pouring into Dixon to attend the learned lectures and evangelical sermons! Sunday crowds rapidly grew to the point where they exceeded the total population of the town!

Two major railroads fed passengers into Dixon, and an elaborate local electric railway was constructed to pick them up and deliver them to the Assembly grounds. Faced with this unprecedented national popularity, the Assembly leaders made a bold move, deciding to erect an auditorium capable of seating over five thousand visitors, with facilities for additional hundreds on a giant stage. From Dixon's seemingly unlimited reserve of talent emerged Mr. Morrison H. Vaile, an unprepossessing local architect, who agreed to design the new building.

Vaile's structure, circular in design with a diameter of 160 feet, was the largest building in the country completely clear of interior supports. After the fashion of some of today's modern "superdome" stadiums, this building contained nothing to disturb the view of the giant stage from any angle. Most remarkable without today's modern engineering advances at his disposal, his building was constructed entirely of wood!

The Dixon Assembly now offered facilities unexcelled by any of the other Chautauqua centers, almost all of which used circular circus tents to handle their meetings. To put the Dixon accomplishment in perspective, it should be noted that by 1923, there were over ten thousand individual Chautauqua Assemblies meeting in towns throughout the United States! Total attendance nationwide was more than thirty-five million people (equal to more than a third of the nation's population)! Of all those ten thousand annual gatherings, the Dixon Assembly was second in attendance only to the original Chautauqua still meeting annually in New York!

At the peak of popularity and attendance in Dixon in the early 1920's, the Assembly was a dominant cultural and religious factor in the community when the Reagan family arrived. Those nationally famous meetings were, in fact, one of the factors that drew Nelle and her family to the President's permanent hometown. The sessions had long since grown beyond the ability of the local Lutheran Synod to handle alone and had become a cooperative venture shared by all the churches and civic organizations in town. The Dixon Christian Church was a leader in planning and running the meetings, and it didn't take Nelle Reagan long to get deeply involved. The extent of her enthusiastic participation was indicated by her standing membership on the prestigious and active Assembly ticket committee, along with her equally aggressive Pastor, Ben Cleaver.

Nelle, without the old temperance movement to absorb her excess energy, gave full attention to the promotion and support of the local Assembly gatherings. The whole-hearted local participation and the high quality of the programs were indicated by the continued large attendance maintained at the summer sessions. Weekend participation frequently exceeded fifteen thousand per program. Over the Labor Day weekend holiday in 1921, the local paper confidently predicted fifty thousand people would participate in the extensive programs.

The standard format of the meetings provided for Christian-church-related subjects and speakers during the early part of the day, with mornings devoted to seminars and classes designed to help church leaders. By noon and early afternoon, the big guns from churches and major Christian endeavors from around the world took over. By late afternoon, the programs became more ecumenical, as the related arts of music, drama and humor took center stage. By evening, the really heavy hitters took over, with such divergent featured speakers as the flamboyant evangelist, Billy Sunday, and learned political orators like the Honorable William Jennings Bryan holding the audiences enthralled.

The Chautauqua Movement was conceived as a means to bring metropolitan culture and the "college outlook" to small rural communities without the supposed advantages of the big cities. From the start, the Dixon meetings reached beyond that rather limited scope. The quality of the speakers and the intellectual depth of the overall programs in Dixon were such that their audiences were drawn from miles away.

I remember my father-in-law's fondly recalling his frequent pilgrimage as a young man from his hometown of Rock Island to enjoy the spirited performance put on by the Reverend Billy Sunday and other motivational speakers. The substantial and luxurious hotel, built on the Assembly grounds, came about as a result of the heavy influx of visitors from the Chicago area! It appeared that the great Midwest cultural center of Chicago was unable to provide some of the stimulus available in Dixon!

When the "Ronald Reagan Boyhood Home" was dedicated by the President in 1984, memories of the Chautauqua meetings were brought back to both Ronald and his brother, Neil. As the two entered the old home for the first visit since their boyhood, President Reagan immediately noted an old Assembly program displayed on the parlor table. Picking it up and turning to Neil, he said, "You remember these, don't you? I surely do!"

Neil responded, whereupon the two brothers, ignoring the impatient dignitaries and staff trying to push them along on a tight schedule, poured over the program, murmuring and chuckling over shared memories of the Assembly meetings.

While exposure to the intellectual and motivational world of these annual meetings played a big part in the maturing of Ronald Reagan, of equal importance was his contact with the many outstanding visitors at the sessions. Dixon's cultural draw was so persuasive that hundreds of families from Chicago and more distant points made annual vacation trips to the Assembly's substantial facilities to participate in the meetings. Many children of these visitors made their way to Dixon's public beach at Lowell Park. The handsome and personable lifeguard quickly became the favorite of the younger set, many of whom learned to swim under his patient tutelage. From these contacts, the handsome teenager got to meet the families in for the summer meetings. The big city sophisticates, obviously intrigued by the quick-witted and knowledgeable youngster, accepted him into their circle, as his grasp and interest in the outer world continued to broaden.

One of the always-enduring characteristics of Ronald Reagan has been his ability to strike a balance between idealism and pragmatism. In politics, as well as in his personal life, this knack of weighing diametrically opposite approaches to problems has much to do with his continued popularity. Those early days in Dixon were critical in the development of this dominant character trait which was guided and honed by those people and events to which he was exposed. From such diverse learning experiences as the Assembly meetings and his Christian training guided by Nelle, the pattern is apparent.

Ronald's mother's strong Christian faith and her conviction that people would always do the right thing if properly approached and given a fair chance had a counterpart in one of the most consistently popular speakers at many of the nation's Chautauqua meetings. It may well be that her evangelical zeal for the Prohibition movement was partially a result of the leadership of that nationally-known lecturer, William Jennings Bryan, who was one of the Reagan family's favorite speakers.

210

Bryan, a Democrat politician who was that party's losing candidate for President three times, had a large and loyal national following. Although unable to achieve high office other than a short period as President Woodrow Wilson's Secretary of State, he was still popular as a speaker on politics and national affairs in general. His oratorical skills were unquestioned, and he drew large audiences, even when he took unpopular stands.

His last hurrah came when he prosecuted the famous Scopes trial concerning the teaching of evolution in a public school. Although he won the battle which involved violation of a law prohibiting teaching of anti-biblical theories, he lost the war to the growing political correctness theories which opposed the bible. In his later life, he wrote a book concerning the war against the bible. Echoes of his ideological campaign can still be heard in the current controversy over prayer in public classrooms. President Reagan has carried this banner high in his continued drive to return prayer to public classrooms. Although Reagan has been just as viciously attacked by liberal media and politically correct gurus as was Bryan, his personal popularity carried him through. Reagan, although truly keeping much of the Bryan faith, was successful at achieving the high political office that eluded that earlier orator.

Bryan was a firm believer in the native goodness of the American people. Despite his political setbacks, he persisted in unfailing enthusiasm for his country's future. A prolific speaker throughout the country, he held a special affinity for the Dixon gatherings and appeared there regularly before large supportive crowds. In his later years, speaking to the Dixon Assembly he said, "Yours is one of the distinguished Chautauquas of the country. Very few have had the continuous existence that yours has had. Nowhere else could you get so much for so little money. Ordinarily, it is difficult to find auspices under which to speak, and these Chautauquas furnish the best platform for one who has a worthwhile message to give an audience. Through Chautauqua audiences, I have kept in touch with the best of friends, thousands upon thousands of them, and this is my only justification for a quarter century on the lecture platform."

The life of this idealistic orator, whose philosophy and beliefs were so mirrored in Nelle Reagan and her younger son, was beautifully eulogized by President Franklin Roosevelt at the dedication of a memorial to Bryan in Washington in 1934. Quoting from a speech by Bryan given before the Democrat National Convention of 1904, Roosevelt said, "You may dispute over whether I have fought a good fight; you may dispute over whether I have finished my course; but you cannot deny that I have kept the Faith."

There is no better memorial for any man, and this one certainly fits Ronald Reagan as well, since, throughout his public life, he too has kept the faith!

Ronald Reagan's exposure to the political and social idealism of Dixon Assembly speakers like William Jennings Bryan made a lasting impression and helped shaped a mature political philosophy. Of no less importance was the Christian idealism and purity of faith expressed by evangelists such as Sunday and many others who appeared on stage at the meetings. Ronald Reagan, however, would have had no more lasting impact on the world than the almost-forgotten Bryan was it not for his innate ability to blend pure idealism with workable pragmatism.

In his later years, while leading his country into preeminence in the complex field of world politics, Ronald Reagan's skill at expounding and selling his vision of an ideal world was supported by his almost instinctive ability to chart a practical course toward his goals. Throughout his public and seldom-seen private life, his deep religious faith has shown that same blend of pure evangelism that was enunciated by proponents like Billy Sunday as well as the straightforward theology of similar masters of the pulpit with a more intellectual approach. During the critical years of his presidency, he developed a close relationship and often sought the counsel of Reverend Doctor Billy Graham. Always close at hand was his mother's battered old bible and her many notes and lessons conveying her own blend of faith and practicality.

That ability to merge the purity of idealism with the reality of what was do-able became the hallmark of Reagan's political career. It is not hard to detect the echoes of William Jennings Bryan's many jousts with the windmills of unbending government in many of Ronald Reagan's public speeches. Nor is it possible to miss his unswerving faith in the United States and its people. Like Bryan, Reagan has never had any doubts that the American people, through their God-ordained inherent goodness, would always ultimately do what was right and proper. In that strong faith, you can easily detect Nelle Reagan's confidently assuring her son that God's will, no matter how harsh it may appear at the moment, always works out for the best.

What insured Reagan's success, as opposed to the frustrations of Bryan, was that pragmatic view of how much of his policies could actually be accomplished. In that regard, Reagan learned and expanded upon the abilities so well deployed by President Franklin Roosevelt. Even though his frequent references to Roosevelt could always be counted upon to raise the hackles of his political opponents, the similarities between the two are unmistakable. Roosevelt, while embracing Bryan's unique idealistic blend of social liberalism and conservative fiscal and foreign policy views, recognized that practical governing required recognition of the basic immobility of the governing body. That ability to see and use the opposite ends of the same stick made Roosevelt one of the country's most successful leaders!

That same quality made Ronald Reagan a President who will rank shoulder-to-shoulder with Roosevelt in the historic annals of the United States!

CHAPTER 20

IMAGERY

In the political world, especially the weird atmosphere of Washington, D.C., it is gospel that the perception of influence and its resulting power is of as much value as the real thing. A great deal can be accomplished by projecting the image of someone with ready access to the centers of decision making in government. Logically examined, it is obvious that it would be physically impossible for the thousands of practitioners of "The Connection" to actually have access or rapport with the relatively few power figures in the legislative or administrative branches of government in our nation's capital. Since logic seldom has anything to do with what happens in Washington, and the nature of the business precludes few from having the nerve to challenge the perception, the art of such imagery continues apace. Although Capital insiders, most particularly the news media, know this, the perception has its advantages for their purposes, so the scam continues.

The White House maintains a full staff of photographers so that, besides official government photographs, every visitor, no matter how casual, can have his very own photo with the Main Man. This practice became such a logistic burden by the time John Kennedy entered the White House that an automated signing machine was installed to apply the President's signature. Since then, all photos provided to eager visitors can be carried home to show off the intimate image and signature to prove the high contact.

While most such photos, and even the supposedly signed personal notes and correspondence, are cherished by their recipients as a pleasant memento, many are used to help develop power images. You need only check the office walls of even the lowest local political leaders to note how these photos are used for image building at every level. One major Washington manipulator of recent years refined such image building to high art. He actually employed a full-time photographer to trail him on his frequent forays into the power centers of Washington and some state capitals. The photographer's job was simple: take pictures of the boss whenever he got within focus range of anyone even remotely important. Those pictures worked wonders for the slick con artist as he swept through government regulatory agencies, seeking and generally getting lucrative concessions for his business enterprises. The perception he created, with its image of easy contact with key national leaders, worked well until he reached too far and caused public embarrassment to a gaggle of powerful Senators. The system turned on him like a wounded tiger, and he is now exerting his influence as a full time busboy in a Federal institution out west! Word is that he can expect little chance of a near term parole, even while others step into his shoes in the major league image game!

Even though the perception of power and connections through the image game is important to those seeking personal influence, the image of leadership at the highest levels is even more important. Great potential power resides in the office of U.S. President, some Senate and House positions and even, occasionally, top Cabinet or department heads, but none of it is usable or effective without a positive image or perception of leadership. While our electoral and governing system is the best yet devised by man, there is no way any system can guarantee the quality of the leadership provided.

Recognizing that weak point in the system, it becomes the primary function of political image makers to create the impression that their charges are, indeed, the best, brightest and most able individuals for the job. That function of political handlers has always been paramount, but it is only in the modern age of electronic communication that it has become refined into more of a science than an art. The television screen has been merciless in its ability to reveal that the silk purse being sold us is, in reality, a portion of the porker's head. To reinforce their sales job and to head off such unflattering revelation, the political image makers like to reach back into history and build the contemporary image in the past's glowing light.

In any campaign for a major office, it is important, if not mandatory, that the candidates have a charismatic or a heroic role model to follow. Hardly an office seeker worth his salt can get more than five minutes into a campaign spiel without casting himself in the mold of a Washington, Jefferson, Lincoln or Roosevelt. Their coattails are easy to ride, belonging as they do to historic characters dearly beloved by the American people. If you are creating an image, it certainly doesn't hurt to use the best pattern available. After all, when was the last time you heard a candidate compare himself to President James A. Garfield? Image makers know that the shadows and memories of past heroes often give a favorable boost to their modern-day wannabes, no matter their lack of substance. Little extra touches in the same direction always help, such as gushing social page interviews or TV profiles depicting that the candidate's favorite books are on the life and times of Lincoln (although actually he goes first for the comic pages in the daily paper). In the same vein, pictures of the hopeful seriously at work in his office surrounded by action paintings of George Washington or Teddy Roosevelt are very helpful!

A great deal of attention in recent years has been drawn to the battle between social revisionists and traditional historians over the rewriting of history, during which the practice of image making sometimes becomes ludicrous. Noteworthy in this modern trend has been the recasting of Christopher Columbus and his part in the history of the Americas. Long looked upon as an explorer of great stature and personal courage, for five hundred years he has been thought of as no less than the father of our civilized continent. He is now portrayed as a greedy, corrupt and ruthless destroyer of a pristine land and its simple, good-hearted peace-loving people. In such re-imaging, it becomes necessary to recreate everything around Columbus, so that the primitive American Indian (now more properly "Native American") becomes a simple, land-loving preserver of the natural environment. One revision, even now appearing in the Sunday paper magazine sections, has Columbus really trying to find a home for persecuted Jews being driven from Spain! Without getting into the ongoing battle over whether there is any substance to the new imaging after five hundred years, our concern is the ease with which such changes are made and the lack of serious questioning of the methods. That type of recasting of past historic figures is not uncommon in the political world.

Long before social activists recognized the benefits to be derived from retroactive image building, the political professionals had perfected the process. Although it sounds insulting, or at worst condescending, the imagery pros know that most members of the American public have short attention spans and memories activated only long enough to store short visual and sound bites of information. The prime time TV news producers have exploited this characteristic for years. While none of us would agree with the concept that all the world's important happenings could be covered in less than three or four hours of exposition, we all consider ourselves fully informed after only twenty minutes of hard news on the typical video program. Candidate handlers are well aware of this and strive mightily to get their charges as much as thirty seconds of presentation from a network star talking head. To accomplish this, they have developed great skill at devising ten to twenty second sound bites they can place in the mouths of their candidates to be dutifully picked up by the prime timers.

While few political candidates are really good at producing catchy or memorable phrases, history provides a great treasure trove of socko words uttered by long-gone public figures. The beautiful part of dipping into history for these important-sounding phrases is that you do not have to be scrupulously accurate about the circumstances from which they are drawn. By having their moldable candidate lean heavily on the memory of a past hero, the image makers show no compunction in placing those historic sound bites as brand new pronouncements. Plagiarism has never been considered a sin in the rough game of politics!

Some ringing statements are so famous they belong forever to the individual who originally produced them. While there may be few alive who experienced the legitimate thrill of hearing presidential candidate Franklin Roosevelt rally the electorate with his stirring cry, "We have nothing to fear but fear itself," most of us have heard it mouthed frequently by political wannabes, usually out of its original context of the great financial depression. Probably the top favorite of a current image candidate is the stirring, "Ask not what your country can do for you. Ask what you can do for your country." Again, the original context is lost, and it is made to apply to whatever the current candidate deems to be most important to his campaign. Political campaign managers can insert such phrases from the past into the mouths of their charges, since most people think they know what they mean, and the good image of the past hero rubs off on their man.

Historic imagery, whether factual or slightly bent, has become an important staple in contemporary American politics. Past Presidents are particularly important when building the image of a current hopeful. Catchy concepts from a bygone era can become handy substitutes for a poorly-thought-out current plan. Roosevelt's so-called New Deal becomes handy shorthand for the contemporary campaigner who wants to assure the voters that he will effect compassionate change for the good of all. Conveniently ignored in such imagery is that the actual New Deal was a loose assortment of government social efforts, many quite bad, that were hammered out over more than ten years of fitful effort!

Similarly, modern office seekers frequently try to portray themselves in the imagined tough mold of President Harry Truman — usually with some reference to his famous desk sign, "The Buck Stops Here". While drawing freely on the "feisty" image of that past leader, the modern image makers conveniently forget that the "feisty" was born of Truman's firing of popular General Douglas MacArthur, his resultant near impeachment by Congress and his intemperate attacks on the arts critic who had the temerity to suggest that Truman's daughter was not a world class musician! The many emulators of courageous President John Kennedy (notice the popularity of the Kennedy hairdo among modern candidates) tend to forget his disgraceful failure to provide the promised support for the heroic Cuban freedom fighters slaughtered at the Bay of Pigs in Cuba!

Even when a strong academic case can be made for the historic inaccuracy of the political hero images used in campaigning, the fact is that they are so effective that they will probably be a part of our political heritage for many years to come. Because of that very effectiveness, a fierce possessiveness toward those images has developed within the two major political parties. It is considered nothing less than an act of desecration should a Republican attempt to drape himself in the mantle of a long-dead Democrat, or vice versa. The sheer anger and sometimes vicious reaction to apparent violations of this sacred dogma were illustrated by an event during the 1988 Presidential campaign.

Vice Presidential candidates Dan Quayle for the GOP and Lloyd Bentsen for the Democrats squared off in a nationally televised debate. When questions were raised concerning Quayle's youth and lack of government experience, he responded by pointing out that he had as much or more actual experience in office than did John Kennedy on the eve of his election to the Presidency. Quayle had crossed the line and dared evoke the name of a Democrat legend in his Republican campaign! All hell broke loose as Bentsen quickly attacked Quayle's personal character and ability for even daring to breathe Kennedy's name. This attack was to continue unceasingly throughout that 1988 campaign and even through his subsequent four years as Vice President of the United States! In the same vein, President George Bush was quickly attacked for having the effrontery to mention Harry Truman during his reelection efforts!

Ronald Reagan was a constant thorn in the sides of the Democrat image molders and their supportive media, as he insisted on making frequent reference to President Franklin Roosevelt in his campaign speeches. Although Roosevelt was the all-time untouchable in the Democrat hero stable, they were unable to lay a glove on the affable Reagan as he continued to evoke the sacred image! Ronald Reagan was, in this area of competition as well as most others, an enigma to his opposition. How could this paragon of conservatism possibly succeed using the father of liberalism as his favorite role model? That the Democrat image makers and their fawning media supporters could not understand this says much for the superficial manner in which political legends are created.

Ronald Reagan approached high office with a knowledge and understanding of image making far superior to the political professionals in either party. As a nationally popular star of the old Hollywood movie studio system, he himself had reaped great benefit from their continual image building. The studio star system was built upon creating highly saleable public images for their top performers. Critical to the individual success of those stars was the ability of their fans to identify with the personal image of their screen idols. There is little difference between the adoration shown a movie idol and the slavish devotion of the voters to a popular public figure. No matter how the full-time professional politicians may sneer at actors, as they did for so long with Ronald Reagan, deep down they understand that actors and politicians have more in common than not. For the high office holder, it matters not so much what you do, but how you are perceived in the act of doing. Just as the glamorous movie queen can win plaudits playing the lovable girl next door while running through a half-dozen lurid affairs in real life, so can the wavy-haired Senator preach compassion for the "little man" while living the debauched private life of a rich playboy!

All this is not, of course, to say that all political office holders are insincere and do not perform well for their constituents. The sad, unfortunate fact is that no good can be accomplished without first getting elected to office. It is in that process that every candidate must play the image game to some extent. Which circuitous route brings us back to Ronald Reagan!

None of the Washington stars, officeholder or background manipulators has ever shown the skill at image building displayed by Ronald Reagan. A text book example of that skill can be made from an image he drew from a relatively minor part in a motion picture. The little substance behind his endearingly affectionate nickname, the "Gipper", will have latter-day historians scratching their heads in wonderment. Even among his many devoted followers today, there are probably many who have no idea where it came from.

If you want a real case history on image building, you could not ask for anything better than this one! Here was a fictitious story line about an individual who certainly had created no historic impact on the nation's history, yet his name becomes part of a major historic legend. To compound the magnitude of the sales job done on this "Gipper" line, everyone knew it to be fiction from the start. Even though most of the quotations from the past used in today's slick political image building are somewhat mangled, they generally have a strong core of fact behind them. I don't think there is any other public figure in history who could have done so natural and effective a job of creating historic substance out of pure fiction as did the "Gipper", Ronald Reagan!

Ronald Reagan's ability to present a strong, but simple, image of himself is something that future historians may well ponder over. That seemingly unconscious knack is best illustrated by his public association with the kids' candy, jellybeans. It is hard to say where it all started, but shortly after Reagan became leader of his country, he also became king of the jellybean lovers to his countrymen. Always with a keen and perceptive eye to public relations, the President soon acquired another trademark, as in virtually every official Oval Office photo, a canister of the colorful candies appeared. Indicative of the strong rapport he always had with the public, nary a discouraging word was heard concerning the possible ill health effects the jellybean craze may have had on young, growing teeth, let alone older waistlines.

To understand these positive personal images that always seemed to grow out of actions and surroundings of Reagan no matter what he did, consider the sad case of his protege George Bush.

Bush, after eight years in the shadow of Ronald Reagan as Vice President, finally achieved the Presidency by riding Reagan's shadowy coattails through the election of 1988. Bush, a snobbish aristocrat of the old Republican school, tried to emulate Reagan by re-imaging himself into a more acceptable common man. Bush's image makers pumped the story of their mentor's liking for pork rinds and barnyard horseshoe pitching to remold him into a more universally acceptable light. Their efforts went over like a lead balloon, leaving Bush to forever bear the burden of blue blood aristocracy. This episode, much like the effort to lighten up President Jimmy Carter with his bulky sweaters in front of the fireplace, were doomed more because of the nature of the subjects than because of the form of the image making.

Ronald Reagan's many images were acceptable to the general public because they mirrored the true character behind the projection. Ultimately, this is what determines the success or failure over the long haul of today's professional image making. It is still true that you "cannot make a silk purse out of a sow's ear"!

One final word on the sacred status of old political images. The Democrats and other critics of Ronald Reagan had no cause for alarm over his apparent preempting of the memory of President Franklin Roosevelt. As we move along, the truly strong philosophical bond between these two seemingly different Presidents will become evident. Ronald Reagan, with his father leading the way, found a real role model in the leader who pulled the country through its worst recession and biggest world war.

CHAPTER 21

THE ROOSEVELT FACTOR

History, when viewed from a great distance, breaks down easily into clearly-defined milestones which mark epochs in human progress or, at the very least, major changes in the perception of what constitutes progress. From afar, the saga of the United States shows unmistakable sharp turning points through its first century and a half. As is characteristic of history, strong individual leaders appeared at those turnings to lead or initiate the changes. Milestones of history reflect these leaders' individual personalities and character.

From the country's inception, when an unruly group of colonies expressed its distaste for England's iron-fisted rule by revolting, the United States seemed in command of its destiny. The Declaration of Independence and, later, the Constitution appeared to make clear what everyone in the new country wanted and expected. Freedom from central monarchical control was the rallying cry. Ironically, after breaking that strong dominance, the new United States turned to George Washington, a leader who strongly advocated a powerful central government not a great deal unlike the despised England. Washington's strong personality and his emotional link to his countrymen, while propelling him into its leadership, did not totally convert the fiercely independent colonies.

In the beginning, the differences between the strong central government activists, the federalist supporters of Washington and the states' rightists manifested itself only in closed-door debates within the new Congress. Despite the increasingly strong and more open conflict, the system muddled along, and the growing country prospered. When those fundamental differences became unreconcilable and the country's leaders turned into raging partisans, order broke down, and the Civil War erupted. Once again a strong leader emerged in the person of Abraham Lincoln, and the collapsing union was saved by yet another stalwart of history.

Strangely, Lincoln was not a federalist by nature or political background. Even though he presided over a bloody war that saved his country, he felt, as did most American leaders, that the unique independence of the individual American states was too precious to destroy. That conviction prevented the Congress from enacting punitive measures that would have effectively eliminated the individual states. That very independence of initiative and enterprise that Lincoln so revered in the old colonies was what enabled the union to survive. The divergently growing and prospering industrial states, with their innovative approaches to production and finance, provided the margin of victory for Lincoln and his preserved union.

Although it would seem that a greatly-enhanced federalism should have naturally emerged from the Civil War, the United States still consisted of a rather loose alliance of independent governments. Central currency triumphed over independent scrip, but the bulk of the banking and finance system remained under local control. With a few lesser wars and alternate recessions and booms, that economic system continued to survive, and the citizenry prospered. The ongoing conflict between the federalists and the states' rightists did not go away, however, but gradually evolved into what we now label "liberal" and "conservative".

The standoff, with liberals wanting more central control and conservatives holding out for more local independence, might have continued as a permanent stalemate with neither gaining an edge was it not for a major economic upheaval in the late 1920's and early '30's.

In 1918, the United States' victory in its first really foreign war started irreversible changes. Soldiers returning to the United States after the war brought with them new ideas and a much less inhibited approach to life. The country embarked upon an economic and social binge unprecedented in history. After the strains exerted upon families and careers by the war, everything seemed to break loose in an "anything goes" decade-long block party!

Rapidly expanding and increasingly efficient communications brought the country physically closer together. The national interplay blurred once-sharp regional differences in the country. Simultaneously, the old, still largely puritan moral codes, dating from the original colonies, began to disintegrate. A philosophy of "live for the moment and get yours while you can" took over. Conservative business ethics were cast aside as a majority became converts to the "get rich quick" religion.

The country did, in fact, appear to be booming, as fortunes were made almost overnight. Although much of the seeming prosperity was paper created by dubious and frequently fraudulent investment schemes, few of the country's leaders seemed to be concerned. It was no longer fashionable to produce anything tangible. Why sweat it when everyone could become wealthy just by manipulating buy and sell orders of beautifully engraved pieces of paper called stocks and bonds?

Inevitably, the big bad wolf blew down the pigs' house of paper, and the country plunged into an economic depression. It was not just local. Spreading throughout the world, it became the worst economic collapse in history! As often happens, the good fell with the bad, and the depression took with it virtually all of the legitimate productive enterprises in the country.

As the United States moved into the decade of the 1930's with unemployment exceeding 25%, the financial institutions dormant and its once vibrant industrial might silenced, the country wallowed in confusion. When the citizens cried out for help, their leaders shrugged their shoulders without a clue as to where to turn.

Now, the pendulum in the centralized versus diverse theories of governing began to swing toward Washington.

From the beginning, the people of the United States had weathered hard times by rallying around family and church to prop up their faltering members. By 1932, the suffering was so widespread that the traditional support systems could not manage. With the whole country "going to hell in a handbasket", frantic citizens turned toward their government for help. Local governments, dependent upon locally generated taxes on personal and commercial prosperity, were themselves destitute and unable to help. The Federal Government, still essentially bogged down with a statist mindset, had no structural programs capable of dealing with the severe trauma at the local level. That's not to say there was not much handwringing and pontificating over the country's plight by many politicians, but that didn't result in any positive action.

With all these overwhelming personal problems weighing on their backs, the American public could generate little enthusiasm for the approaching national elections of 1932. That ennui disappeared almost overnight, as one man electrified a dispirited population and generated a core of hope!

There need be no more exposition on Franklin Delano Roosevelt for historians, present and future, to recognize his impact on history. Almost from the start, because of the dark times and lack of leadership in the country, he stood out as a milepost of the stature of Washington or Lincoln. Besides his commanding personality and intellect, he is remembered equally for the governmental changes generated (not all of his own volition) during his presidential administration.

The largely unrealized centralized government power that Washington envisioned and Lincoln began to assert really began to crystallize only under the mantle of President Franklin D. Roosevelt. Whether all the central control initiatives set off by his administration will endure only future historians can assess. Whether the pendulum has swung too far to one side is still subject to hot debate.

That Ronald Reagan, the last great hope of the conservatives, and Franklin Roosevelt, patron saint of the liberals, should have so much in common is not as odd as it might appear at first glance. The United States still is, as it has always been, an unlikely marriage of fierce individualism and happy group thinkers!

Had Ronald Reagan been a few years younger or older in that election year of 1932, he probably never would have moved on from the show business of Hollywood to the show business of Washington in later life. As it was, that was the year he came charging out of college, degree in hand, full of all the enthusiasm and optimism such higher learning can give a man. Although his parents were suffering mightily from the depression, having lost their cherished family business, they retained the optimism that none of the Reagans were ever without. Jack and Nelle, confident the Lord would provide and their country would prevail, never got down. That enthusiasm carried on through their always optimistic son, as Ronald attacked the marketplace, unfazed by the fact that more than a quarter of his fellow citizens were without jobs or hope.

By that election year, the United States had reached such a level of despondency and disorder that its preeminence in the world stood in greater jeopardy than even during the darkest days of the Civil War. The old "can do" Yankee spirit was all but dead, and nothing appeared able to turn things around. For the first time in its history, a solid majority of its citizens looked to their government to solve what they would previously have considered a personal problem.

On the surface, FDR would not have appeared to be the leader to take the country into the coming new age of Federal activism with its stronger control of its citizens' personal lives. He was, after all, a wealthy aristocrat whose family had prospered under the free-wheeling pioneer atmosphere of the growing country. Actually, Roosevelt was by no means a socialist. He was a forceful leader, however, who saw that his country, more than anything else, needed the perception of a strong guiding hand at the helm. Young Ronald Reagan, just embarking on a fresh career and well aware of his country's leadership dilemma, recognized that needed strong leadership in Franklin Roosevelt.

In today's world of often bitter partisan politics, it is still hard for many to accept any notion that RR and FDR had anything in common. Everyone is sure that they know the difference between conservative and liberal philosophies and that those two Presidents just couldn't possibly be bedfellows. Why? Just consider their differences, as exemplified by the following Presidential speech excerpt. "The stark fact before us is that great numbers remain unemployed. A large proportion of these unemployed and their dependents have been forced on the relief rolls. The burden on the Federal Government has grown with great rapidity. The lessons of history, confirmed by the evidence immediately before me, show conclusively that continued dependence upon relief induces a spiritual and moral disintegration fundamentally destructive to the national fiber.

To dole out relief in this way is to administer a narcotic, a subtle destroyer of the human spirit. The Federal Government must, and shall, quit this business of relief. We must preserve not only the bodies of the unemployed from destitution, but also their self-respect, their self-reliance, and courage and determination!" This was certainly a typical, down-the-line Ronald Reagan attack on the welfare system, in the same vein as his frequent "Welfare Queen" anecdotes!

The previous quotation is from President Franklin Roosevelt's public message to Congress delivered on January 4, 1935 and better known today as a "State of the Union" address. FDR, upset over the two billion already spent by Congress to expand an unemployment compensation program that he had intended only as a temporary measure, was expressing his growing concern over the tendency of Congress to expand the Federal Government's intrusion into its citizens' personal lives with a growing social welfare system. This basically conservative nature of Roosevelt has long been overshadowed by the broad social programs Congress continued to expand during his administration.

Ronald Reagan's attraction to FDR and his later pattern of governing was based on that underlying conservative philosophy. Roosevelt and Reagan both felt very strongly that the role of government was solely to do for its citizens those things that individuals and independent enterprise could not do for themselves. In all other areas, both felt the government should get out of the way and let the system function.

That basic principle of Roosevelt was best illustrated by one of his first acts upon becoming President in 1933. The American finance system was near collapse as its widespread banking institutions teetered on the brink of failure. FDR immediately halted all banking activity by declaring a bank holiday and ordering all of them closed. The already ultra-liberal Congress jumped with joy and quickly moved toward nationalizing the banking system. From now on, the Congress and Washington's bureaucrats would run the banks and take full control of all the country's assets!

Roosevelt quickly exerted his leadership, as he would have to often in his administration, firmly reminding the country of his unswerving faith in the free enterprise system. Scorning the raucous cries from Congress, he ordered the banks reopened within a week, still under their original ownership. Rather than taking them over, he ordered some needed regularity changes, then patted the bankers on the back and told them to get back to the business of making the country go!

Roosevelt's action on the banking system did more to reassure the country's business leaders than anything else done to that point. Confidence began to rebuild as the country began to realize that the Federal colossus had no intention of bulldozing them under! The country was heartened at this show of leadership and his firm control of the system. FDR's action, which really changed nothing in the system, accomplished its purpose by restoring confidence in a finance process which was to grow and strengthen from that point onward.

Roosevelt knew and understood the importance of appearances and apparent action in establishing leadership. He was so good at the part that he gained immediate acceptance with the American public as a man who could lead them through any obstacle. Ronald Reagan saw this early in Roosevelt's career. Although he may not have consciously picked up FDR's techniques, he displayed all the same characteristics when he won the Presidency in 1980.

Much of Roosevelt's reputation for social and welfare activism came about more as a result of the aggression of Congress in those areas than through his own initiative. The irony of the U.S. system of government arises from the fact that the very governing body, Congress, that was designed to be a direct link to and representative of the average citizen, has grown to be the least connected. The elected representatives of the people have grown into a self-reproducing body with a life and personality of its own, not necessarily bearing any resemblance to the reality of America. The best witness to this phenomenon has been its creation of an elitist world, centered in Washington, with its own private bank (not subject to banking laws) and a House post office serving primarily as a money laundering center. To further divorce itself from the citizenry, Congress exempts itself from virtually all of the employment laws and social security regulations ordinary citizens must follow. The elite society of Congress is completed with its private gymnasiums, stores, restaurants and transportation. All in all, it is little wonder that Congress ignores the direct representative of all the people in the Presidency and goes its own self-centered way!

Roosevelt's straightforward unemployment plan to temporarily compensate those out of work was expanded by Congress into the monster he spoke against in 1934. FDR made clear, from its inception, that he viewed the new social security system as a personal retirement annuity in which only those who participated reaped rewards commensurate with what they had put into the fund. It did not take Congress long to expand that one into a program totally unrecognizable from Roosevelt's initiative!

This tendency of Congress to expand every program to provide as many vote-generating benefits as possible has been the bane of virtually every modern President. Like the unruly patient who takes the doctor's prescription of two aspirins and a glass of orange juice a day and turns it into a dozen pills and a gallon of fruit punch, Congress cannot seem to leave well enough alone. Their action, when criticized, is always turned into "blame it on the Administration", while the President frequently has difficulty gaining credit for his initiatives left untouched and successful. There is little doubt in this writer's mind that Roosevelt would have been every bit as critical of many of the uncontrolled actions of Congress as was Ronald Reagan.

Ronald Reagan recognized in Roosevelt the strong leadership that produced simple, firm and effective ideas and learned well the lessons from FDR on how to get the most important matters past a muddled Congress. Early in his first administration, working against an antagonistic Congressional leadership, Reagan applied those lessons well. During his term, the breakaway support he garnered for his program acquired the label "Reagan Democrats", one of the great oxymorons of our time! Present-day commentators tend to forget Roosevelt had just as much opposition from Congress, even though it was mostly from his own party, but he got around it through direct appeal to the public.

Roosevelt, aware of the powerful influence commercial radio was wielding on the opinions of the public, instituted a regular, direct address to the country in programs he called his "Fireside Chats". Speaking informally and "one on one" with his audience, he developed a rapport that no member of Congress or Senator could overcome during important legislative battles. That same technique was tried by President Jimmy Carter with televised messages. Carter's fell flat, as he attempted to create an unlikely new image by wearing a bulky, turtleneck sweater on camera.

Reagan, more a master of the electronic media, following Roosevelt's original and effective pattern, also used the short radio spots to win the public and, coincidentally, drive his Congressional opponents right up the wall! His long study and understanding of FDR paid off in this area as it did in many others. Later along we will see how that Roosevelt connection clicked in foreign affairs, as Congress was cut off at the pass!

On a campaign note, we cannot move on without a sidelong glance at yet another RR/ FDR link. Jimmy Carter's Presidency had been plagued by bad economic times and unfortunate policy decisions, weaknesses that Ronald Reagan was quick to exploit during the 1980 campaign. It's hard to forget the impact of Reagan's often-repeated campaign shot, "Ask yourself are you better off now than you were four years ago?" As he relentlessly drove Carter into a hole by implication, he let it be known that things were bound to get better with him in the Oval Office.

On June 28, 1934, Franklin Roosevelt, during one of his now regular Fireside Chats, defended his first year in office with the following. "The simplest way for each of you to judge recovery lies in the plain facts of your own individual situation. Are you better off than you were last year?"

Here was the other side of the same coin! All great figures in history have been able to look at the past and adapt the most effective actions of prior leaders to their own ends. Roosevelt was a master at using history to achieve his goals, and Ronald Reagan, with the same ability, made good use of one of his historic leaders, Franklin Delano Roosevelt!

Norman Wymbs

CHAPTER 22

FOR GOD AND COUNTRY

For those who have never had the great privilege of meeting Ronald Reagan on a personal basis, he appears to be a simple man to understand. For millions of voters, on a number of occasions, there did not seem to be any unfathomable complexity there. He always speaks clearly in language everyone understands, and his clear-cut principles and ideologies are always evident to most listeners. Even years after completing his second term as President of the United States, it is not unusual to hear citizens comment on difficult national policy issues by declaring, "I wish old Ron was back to handle that one!"

Probably the greatest paradox of Ronald Reagan's period in U.S. history is the sharp divergence between the general public's affection for and confidence in their "Ron" and the negative opinions of the public analysts usually found in the print and electronic media. Now really, how could there be two such different Ronald Reagans? The obvious answer, of course, is that there are not two Reagans, but two amazingly different perceptions of the same person. Actually, Ronald Reagan has maintained a steady course throughout his life, and what you see, if not distracted by irrelevant outside analysis, is what you get!

Those differences, which we have all seen over the years and which we usually attribute to partisan political positions, are not necessarily ideological in nature. Frequently, individuals who would generally be expected to be on the same philosophical path as Reagan end up showing confusion when they get close to him and try to probe his inner character. At that point, the soft silk curtain usually falls, and Reagan deftly directs the curious visitor away from whatever track of inquiry he was on. This was quite evident a few years ago in the published comments of an individual who would normally be expected to have more insight on Reagan than anyone else outside his immediate family.

Nationally noted historian Edmund Morris was invited by President Reagan at the start of his Presidency to write a personal biography of his life. To accomplish the task, Morris was given unprecedented access to the normally introspective Reagan. Over the years, he had innumerable opportunities for private interviews and frequently sat in on important Presidential meetings to observe the guiding of the ship of state. Few writers, even those of the stature of Morris, have ever been given such a golden opportunity to observe and "get inside" such a major international figure. He had carte blanche to interview the President's staff and his family members (including the children, who have generally been fairly outspoken). He got to read much of the Presidential mail and had at least monthly occasions when he could personally quiz the President.

When President Reagan retired to his less-than-docile post-White House life in California, little public information had been released on the progress of the much-anticipated Morris biographical work. In 1991, more than two years after Reagan left Washington, the subject surfaced through an Associated Press report of a meeting Morris attended at the University of Virginia. His remarks, apparently inadvertently released by that institution, were picked up and published by the press service. In the reported comments, it appears that the noted biographer, despite his long personal access to Ronald Reagan, suffered the same frustrations as many others who thought they were getting close to the President!

Morris, after his years of one-on-one access to Reagan, was quoted as stating at that Virginia meeting, "He is the most mysterious man I have ever confronted. It is impossible to understand him."

He went on to indicate to his audience that even Nancy Reagan has difficulty understanding him. "I went through a period of a year or so of depression because I felt that with all my research, how come I can't understand the first thing about him? He grew more puzzling the more I tried to study him. I only came out of this despair when I found out that everybody else who had ever known him, including his wife, was equally bewildered."

That sense of total frustration, encountered by many besides Morris, was tempered by his assessment of Reagan's confidence and personality. On the access to information he was allowed, Morris said, "He had the guts to let somebody come in from the outside, stare at him, read his mail, go off and talk to his children. Whatever you say about Ron Reagan, he has guts!" Morris, at that meeting, was quoted as finding Reagan's personality "irresistible" adding, "World leaders were seduced by (his) extraordinary personal sweetness."

From the very start, based on research and our own personal contact, we felt that a true understanding of Ronald Reagan could not be achieved without a thorough knowledge of his background. Particularly critical were the years he spent with his remarkably strong parents and the impact of their diverse personalities. The nature of the times during his maturing years, his schools and active Dixon Christian Church were all important to understanding what drove this world leader. The personal mood and aspirations of his contemporaries growing up in the heartland of the country are critical to any real understanding of this incredibly complex, simple man!

In this book thus far, we have dwelt heavily on Ronald Reagan's religious background through his mother and their strong church as well as the family's close friends in the Christian community. We have attempted to reveal the strong sense of social consciousness and community support exhibited by Jack and Nelle Reagan and to tell how these traits have been reflected in their youngest son. We have even brought politics into the picture through Jack's activism and an explanation of how it had a bearing on Ronald's ultimate destiny.

Of equal importance, if somewhat more difficult to pinpoint, is the source of the extraordinary patriotism of Ronald Reagan. This characteristic was definitely inherent from his youth. He did not, like so many politicians, drape the convenient cloak of patriotism over his shoulders solely for campaign purposes. This love of country and confidence that his United States was righteous and good were tenets of faith almost as strong as his Christian faith in God. The two, in fact, as we will see later along, were really very much intertwined. To assess his patriotic drive and the way he approached his country's relationships with the rest of the world, we must understand Reagan's geographical roots.

That portion of the Midwest, as represented by northern Illinois, with Dixon at its center, was right in the path of the explosive westward growth of the country in the last century. The area didn't just sit there and watch the parade go by. It was easily a major component of that movement. There can be little question that the individuals responsible for that historic expansion were among the most innovative and strongest of the fledgling colonies' citizens. Many of those rugged patriots stayed in the area and built the businesses and institutions needed to accelerate and support the massive growth. To those early Americans, there was no task so formidable they could not accomplish it, nor any obstacle they could not overcome. They had no doubt they were in God's best part of the universe, and they were there by divine destiny!

The Civil War, so disruptive to most of the country and leaving hard-to-heal scars, did not have such a negative effect on northern Illinois. Shaking off the trauma of that war, Dixon and the whole area enthusiastically returned to peaceful, but aggressive, efforts to remake the United States into the best of all worlds. Their pride and confidence were understandable. After all, it had been their very own Abraham Lincoln who had saved the Union, and another neighbor, General U. S. Grant, who had engineered the victory!

Later, the Midwest and southern rural areas of the country provided a disproportionate share of the citizen soldiers who participated in the victory in Europe during World War I. That war put the United States in the forefront of world leadership, and the citizens of the midlands were not unmindful of their considerable contribution to that accomplishment.

The fervent patriotism of the region was an important part of the ethic of the Reagan family. Ronald grew up among family and friends who had little doubt that their country was, by far, the finest country in the world! The military profession, or temporary emergency service for one's country, was not looked down upon. To the contrary, such patriotism was a mark of honor. That natural and fervent love of country had a natural example in Abraham Lincoln's multiple voluntary enlistments in his country's military.

This, then, must be looked at as a major guiding influence in the background of Ronald Reagan. For biographers and historians to truly understand the motivation behind the philosophy and drive of President Ronald Reagan, they need to know and understand the strong influences on the young man before public life.

Reagan, quickly finding his natural groove in the show business aspects of radio announcing, did not take long to get moving up the ladder of success. Not long after starting at the small radio station in Davenport, Iowa, he had the opportunity to move up to the more sophisticated metropolitan station in Des Moines. Here, in what was the biggest city of residence in his young life, he quickly became absorbed into a very busy broadcast schedule and its related time-consuming social requirements. It was in Des Moines that another important milestone which was to bear heavily on his future approach to governing the country occurred in his life. He joined the U.S. Army reserve corps.

Again, unless the time and circumstances of this move in the young radio announcer's life are understood, a significant link to understanding certain acts of his Presidency is missed. In Reagan's early book, "Where's The Rest Of Me?", he tells of his efforts in Des Moines to get into the military reserve. Remember, that book was produced primarily as part of the build-up to launch Reagan into big-time politics in California. At the time of its publication, the country had staggered into an unpopular stalemate in the war supporting South Korea against a northern communist invasion. Military life was not the first choice of many young men, and the popular news media were no longer touting uniformed military leaders. The country's older citizens were crying "enough already" as the sad news poured in from the hardly-known country of Korea. The political promoters who sought to move Reagan front and center onto the campaign trail were faced with a dilemma. His youthful voluntary act of joining the military would not go down well in the then-growing antimilitary climate. The facts, however, could not be changed, so the image molders had to make do!

The solution appeared to be for Reagan to treat his action back in the mid-thirties with his familiar and often used self-deprecating humor. Thus, in his book, he professes to having joined the military only as a means to get to ride horses in the Army Calvary!

Baloney! In that part of the country, and with the social contacts a popular young radio sports announcer generated, he would have had all the horse riding opportunities he needed without looking for an army nag! To become an officer in the U.S. Army Reserve, he had to undergo a rigorous course of self study and to attend weekly formal classes to qualify. Even after long periods of study, he still had to pass a series of examinations. The final hurdle was to pass the physical exam before getting the commission. Ronald Reagan could not pass the Army physical because of his seriously deficient eyesight. The ever-aggressive Reagan, through some ingenious maneuvering, managed to get the authorities to accept a civilian doctor's exam which he somehow got through. He received his commission as a Lieutenant in the Army Reserve! From a dispassionate view, this is not the kind of convolution that quick-witted and able Ronald Reagan would have gone through just to ride a horse!

Reagan joined the Army Reserve because of that deep-seated desire to serve his country, although in 1965 it was an act that his political handlers shuddered over. That act on the part of Ronald thirty years earlier was typical of a trait common to all the Reagans. They always put their money where their mouth was! He had a good job, so he did not need the pittance paid to reservists. The country was not anywhere near a war, so there was no urgent need to join up. Ronald had made his first decisive step into public service for his country.

As a further disclaimer to the silly horse riding story was the fact that Reagan maintained his reserve officer status right up to World War II. At that point, as a successful and popular movie star, the last thing he needed was an interruption for military service. Still (not often mentioned by Reagan biographers), when he was called to active duty just before WW II, he again tried to get around the physical exam so as to be fully-qualified for active combat service. The Army, however, now a little more circumspect about its physical exams, became immediately aware of his eyesight deficiency and would qualify him only for limited noncombatant service.

Although cinema star Reagan loyally did his part for the Army in a special services unit during the war, when he later entered political life, his critics would frequently insinuate that he had deliberately avoided combat duty. Typical of Ronald Reagan, he never attempted to publicly correct those erroneous assumptions, but always preferred to move on to the current tasks at hand.

When Ronald Reagan campaigned for the Presidency, he concentrated upon and held firmly to a few major policies he deemed important to the country. None did he pursue more relentlessly after election than his promise to make the United States Military Services preeminent in the world. More than anyone before or since, he made service to one's country in military uniform honorable again. His own personal patriotism became the standard by which his administration was measured. The increased respect accorded the men and women of the country's military services was a major hallmark of his Presidency.

Norman Wymbs

CHAPTER 23

BRINGING IT TOGETHER

The foundation for the structure was in place. The fundamental religious and educational tutoring, the strong family life, the professional success, capped off with broad political experience — all combined with a well-honed personal philosophy — pointed toward a solidly finished result. Even though, like a finely-crafted jigsaw puzzle, no single item hinted at the final picture, the artwork was becoming clear. The picture emerging well before that climactic election year of 1980 depicted Ronald Reagan as President of the United States.

Given the accumulated individual pieces, the result was not as surprising as the fact that the seemingly-introverted and self-contained young man would become such an immensely popular and effective world leader!

Scanning our country's past, it is evident that many of our Presidents had one common characteristic. They were men carefully groomed for leadership by family and strong traditional and cultural influences. Not to disparage Nelle's apparent grooming of her young son for the Presidency, as declared by older brother Neil, but his preparation had been primarily of faith, ethics and inspiration. Prior Presidents, preprogrammed for the job, had been mostly prepared for the physical trappings of the position. Their backgrounds were such that leadership and philosophy were considered inheritances.

Although technically true that any youngster in the United States can grow up to be President, the odds are strongly against anyone without a preplanned and "proper" life path. The system is so firmly structured, in fact, that those few who rise from the ranks of the "average" citizen have much less chance at success than those born to our republic's ruling class.

Early in the life of the country, there was a more clearly-defined, culturally elite ruling class, producing such leaders as Washington, Jefferson and the Adamses. As the country matured, that upper class became broader and less clearly defined, while at the same time, its power over the system became stronger. Later Presidents, like Franklin Roosevelt, John Kennedy and George Bush, came from politically and socially powerful families who molded their offspring to fit the country's top executive office. It must be noted, also, that in these later years, wealth has become an even more dominant factor, although from the time of George Washington, apparent wealth at least equaled culture. The best indication of the importance of personal wealth was shown in the election of 1992 when multi-billionaire, Ross Perot, certainly one of the most unlikely candidates in memory, bought a big chunk of the electorate.

The hierarchy of family power can be found in almost every free country, no matter what form of government is followed, and there is much to be said for its ability to maintain stability in governing.

Despite this, the United States, probably due to its long-cherished pioneering ethic, has turned more frequently than any other nation to leaders drawn from a non-ruling class. We are a country that reveres heroes. While some nations worship royalty, we relate to leaders who reach beyond human limits and become larger than life. Presidents like Ulysses S. Grant, dashing Civil War hero; Theodore Roosevelt, in boots and sword, charging up San Juan Hill; and calm, assured Dwight Eisenhower, engineering the victory of World War II, have become beloved legends in our historic annals.

Because ours is a highly politicized system of governing, it is not surprising that many of our Presidents should have arisen from purely political backgrounds. Mostly, the professional politician claimants of our highest office have been among our least successful leaders. That is most likely the result of the natural American's striving toward idealistic goals, and the politician's natural tendency toward compromise for the sake of votes.

As expected, some of our most successful Presidents, as measured by their long lasting popularity, combine more than one of the criteria generalized above. Franklin Roosevelt and John Kennedy added to their basic elitist background considerable portions of political smarts in order to achieve their successes. Both leaders were also possessed of the somewhat heroic streak that had made Grant and the earlier Roosevelt so attractive to their followers. Of all the characteristics contributing to the success of those reaching the Presidency, by far the most important to their immortality in history was their inspirational leadership. That inspiration sprang naturally from their sense of heroics or, in the context of national leadership, their patriotism.

The compassion of the American public is such that during an actual political campaign, while we may hold fixed issue positions, we tend to give our hearts to the underdog. In a society devoted to human sporting activity, the football Superbowl and the baseball World Series provide strong national guidelines for judgement. We thrill and relate to the .200 hitter who laces the game-winning homer, or the sub, off the bench, who bursts over the line for the winning touchdown. The tailender in politics draws the same sentimental support — sometimes gaining eternal fame, in the manner of Harry Truman's spectacular win over favored insider, Tom Dewey, or sometimes achieving less-than-satisfactory, long-term results, as in Jimmy Carter's rise to the Presidency. Such political underdogs are usually so classified because they arise from outside the tight political control of the major party insiders who have anointed someone else. Since the dominant news and opinion media work closely with those political elite, the media are the ones who quickly affix the "underdog" label, usually in a less-than-complimentary manner.

Those not tabbed by the inner decision makers, but who win election anyway, have one great advantage: the sporting American public generally is highly tolerant of their performance and sincerely pulls for their success. Unfortunately, that advantage usually cannot overcome the disadvantage represented by the undermining of their position by disgruntled media and the left-out insiders. It takes an exceptional leader to overcome the disadvantages, and few outsiders succeed.

In recent history, the endless shots taken at President Carter's family (who can forget what the media did with the Billygate stories) and his personal penchant for the minutiae of White House operations were in sharp contrast to the hands-off treatment of President Kennedy's wild family life and the continuous flow of White House girl friends. The difference, of course, was that Kennedy was the prototype political insider, while Carter had pushed his way in from the back lot.

Approaching the 1980 Presidential election, the elitists in the Democrat Party found they had shot themselves in the foot by helping to downgrade Carter. Their less-than-enthusiastic support had contributed considerably to his failed Presidency. Now they were in a snit and faced with the prospect of having to go with their President for another term try, which they saw as well-nigh impossible. Following the predictable pattern of the rigid mentality within political party structure, they tried to dump Carter in favor of insider Senator Ted Kennedy. To no one's surprise, the dissipated and disgraced brother of martyred President John Kennedy came a cropper, and the Democrats were stuck with Jimmy Carter.

The disarray of the Democrats over Carter in 1980 gave no solace to the Republicans, however, as they faced a similar outsider problem. The Republican insiders, then led by party dictator Nelson Rockefeller, having successfully stopped Ronald Reagan in 1976, were in trouble in 1980. Their inside gopher, Gerald Ford, a loser to the weak Carter in 1976, left them without a viable horse to ride. Reagan, as outside as a candidate could be, was determined to stay outside and could not be compromised. With Reagan even more unacceptable than four years earlier, Republicans, in desperation, placed their bets on George Bush. Bush, referred to as the "resume candidate" because of all the appointed positions he had held, was so much an insider that he had once been chairman of the Republican Party. His biggest drawback was that no matter his strong support from the insiders, he had never been able to muster enough public support to win any major election.

Ronald Reagan won the Republican nomination despite the opposition of insider party leaders, while Jimmy Carter took the Democrat nomination by default. The election of 1980 was shaping up as an unusual confrontation of two candidates whose own party professionals could give only token support. Politics would never be the same again!

Despite their obviously differing political philosophies, Reagan and Carter had remarkably similar backgrounds which contributed substantially to their initial approval from the majority of U.S. voters. Had they not met under the adversarial circumstances of the 1980 election, they would probably have been soul mates. Both came from small American communities steeped in old-fashioned family values. Integral to that basic American life was their gung-ho, pioneer spirit of enterprise.

Neither could, in any way, be considered an elitist in social or family background. They had both been governors of their respective states of Georgia and California, and their terms as governors represented the strongest parts of their resumes for the high office of President of the United States. Most important to their initial appeal was the fact that both represented strong, fundamental, Christian upbringing and personal faith. Carter's strong emphasis on Christian morals was the primary edge in his initial campaign. Vowing to raise the ethical and moral standard of Washington, he aroused the usually dormant, conservative Christians to political activism in his campaign.

In his reelection campaign of 1980, although he was the incumbent President and should have had a strong advantage, Carter was a long shot. Having entered the Presidency four years earlier as a consummate outsider, Carter was quickly perceived to have been absorbed and converted by the entrenched political system in Washington. In addition, his inability to carry through on the campaign promise of moral regeneration turned the Christian vote, so important to his success in 1976, against him. That group, having tasted the excitement and power of their votes in the earlier election and now became even more active and turned to Reagan. Ronald Reagan stood tall as the only legitimate outsider able to promise change, and he played the theme to perfection!

We have written much about the news media and analysts and their influence on politics and political thinking in the country. Although there is a dominant philosophical bias driving their commentary and reporting, a strong geographic prejudice is just as important in forming their ultimate views. All the major television news networks generally acknowledged to be the main source of information for most Americans are based in and distribute most of their information from New York. The dominant talking heads on their shows, as a result, rise from within that narrow geographic base. Even the major subscription print organizations feeding the country emanate from New York City. It should come as no surprise, knowing the source, that the most-circulated syndicated writers also grow out of this same incubator. Although the media leaders indignantly deny that this narrow concentration has any influence on the way they handle news or form their opinions, the facts speak a different story.

It does not take long with the evening prime time news to realize that New York in particular, and the northeast in general, are at the center of the universe. In politics, no matter how inept the leadership or how poorly the state is run, the national news media always look upon the Governor of New York as a major national leader. Occasionally, they will dredge up a few kind words for the New York suburbs of New Jersey or Massachusetts, but seldom does anything more than a few miles west or south of their home base merit favorable attention.

Ronald Reagan had served eight highly successful years as Governor of California, a larger and more economically important state than most of the countries in the rest of the world, but you would have been hard-pressed to hear anything about it from the national media. California, after all, was only that sunny place of great golf courses and fun-filled parties you got to only after a long uncomfortable airplane flight over the wilderness! As for Jimmy Carter and his time as Governor of Georgia, forget it. That place left the news after Sherman finished his march! From the viewpoint of the national opinion molders, better that these two men had been Mayors of New York or at least members of Congress from Maine!

The tunnel vision of the expert news and political pundits was actually an advantage for the Reagan campaign of 1980. So much of the negative sniping at Reagan concentrated on two areas, his age and his motion picture career, that the message he was purveying so powerfully to the public was missed by his opponents. The average voter, always more discerning and knowledgeable than the media believed, quickly dismissed the two major hits on Reagan. His effervescence and good-humored approach to the campaign killed the age argument. Ronnie came through as ageless! The "second rate movie actor" charge fell on equally barren ground, as the public watched his flawless campaign performances every night on prime time TV. Since he had not made a movie for more than twenty years, most of his audiences wondered what the critics were so up-tight about!

Ronald Reagan pitched a powerful message right over the heads of the political experts and the news commentators. His message was for the hearts of his countrymen, and the voters got it. They liked what he said and recognized that it was directly from his heart, but was never understood by the experts, who, for the most part, even to this day, have not gotten it! History will note, however, and understand its simple, but effective, message!

Norman Wymbs

CHAPTER 24

THE GIPPER'S APPEAL

Surprisingly, while Reagan's critics have always been rather uniform in their attacks on his every move and policy initiatives, they have not exhibited any uniformity in putting a finger on what made him so popular. Although they found it difficult to admit to his successes, when they did, they could find no way of explaining the result. Finally, most of them fall back to crediting his electoral and administrative victories solely to his personal popularity and his "likableness"! For the historians of the future, this is going to seem a very weak explanation for the success of his two terms as President. To put that viewpoint in perspective, aren't all political officeholders likable? Well, they are, at least at the start. I can't recall any major politician who was ever elected because the public disliked him (or her)! It appears we need to find some better reason to justify this man's being given the reins of the country for eight years!

One of the knocks on Reagan most often used was that he was only a "second rate" actor who continued to fool the public with his transparent act. That his detractors were administering the ultimate insult to U.S. voters, asserting they were so easily fooled by inferior acting, never seemed to occur to them. Their continued attacks along that line probably had an effect opposite that intended, actually creating stronger support for the Gipper.

Even harder to understand was the sometimes sardonic label of "Great Communicator" which has stuck with Reagan as closely as his Gipper nickname. For the media to label a second rate actor as a great communicator seems something of an oxymoron. For the media commentators who draw high pay and prestige for their ability as communicators, pointing out a sub-standard actor could insult their own professional standing.

Dismissing Reagan's popularity as merely a talent for communicating philosophies and policies, his detractors missed the point, thus spearheading his success.

During this 1980 campaign, Ronald Reagan concentrated on three primary platform planks, none of which were new or original with him. Certainly, none could be considered revolutionary enough to account for his resounding success. Many articulate Republicans and political conservatives had been preaching from the same pulpit for years. His call to rebuild the country's defense capability and draw a firmer line against Communist intrusion into the free world was echoed and supported by many of his political opponents. His call to reduce the Federal Government's ever deeper intrusion into personal and business lives was standard political philosophy for all but the most dedicated social engineers. His clarion call for lessening the Federal tax burden could be traced all the way back to the birth of politics. Thomas Jefferson, in what was probably the country's first political position paper, blasted President George Washington for raising taxes!

The pundits were right about Ronald Reagan's astounding popularity with his fellow citizens, but they never could get it right as to why!

Ronald Reagan led by inspiration. He was a super patriot. His every word and action signaled unremitting love of country and devotion to its causes. I do not think that Reagan has ever paused and thought of himself in super patriot terms. It is a natural trait, as deep-seated and as unquenchable as his unfailing good humor and optimism. His unflappable and positive view of the future was a natural outgrowth of that same inspirational - patriotism. Like the great heroes of the past, he knew his country was inherently good and right in its principles and, therefore, must prevail. That inspiration was communicated clearly to the people throughout the land, and they reacted positively. For the first time in many years, he had America collectively lifting its head and swelling out its chest in pride of country.

Ronald Reagan was marching at the head of a gigantic national "Fourth of July" parade! Mom and Dad Reagan would have smiled and nodded their heads in approval, recalling their young son's setting the pattern as he strutted in his brilliant Drum Major's outfit at the head of the Dixon Boys' Band!

A few years back, as we stood curbside under tall, shady, old oak trees watching an Independence Day parade, that spirit was bright and compelling. It was an old-fashioned and typical small town celebration of our nation's founding. Earlier in the day, the whole town had turned out in the downtown park for pancakes, coffee and lots of friendly visiting. The afternoon was given over to the parade, as virtually every child in town participated in the march through the heart of the town. The floats were not glossy "Macy's Day" products, but outdid any professional floats in the obvious love and enthusiasm their young designers had put into them. Old-time war veterans and shiny-faced young Boy Scouts marched proudly together, celebrating the nation's birthday. As the last float, marching group and cheerful band had passed our vantage point, I turned to an older man standing next to me and remarked, "That was terrific, wasn't it?" He looked at me seriously and stated, "I was disappointed. There were only 24 American flags today." Surprised, I told him, "I thought that was great. I haven't seen that much patriotism for a long time." Shrugging as he turned to start down the street, he said, "No real enthusiasm anymore. We always used to have more than thirty-five flags in the parade."

To me, coming from a supposedly sophisticated part of the country, that display of enthusiasm for the nation's Independence Day and what appeared to be a sea of waving flags seemed the ultimate patriotic display. My neighbor on that curbside had put his finger on what many people in the country found of concern. To him, and to many like him, it seemed we were losing our old-fashioned love of country.

That old-fashioned patriotism is still on public display in many of our heartland small towns where today's politically correct sophistication has yet to gain a firm hold. That parade, one of the greatest American shows I have ever witnessed, took place on the quiet, oak-shaded streets of Ronald Reagan's hometown, Dixon, Illinois!

But, what does old-fashioned American patriotism have to do with a popular election and a successful Presidency? I'm glad you asked!

We all know that old stuff went out of fashion long ago. It simply is not politically correct any longer to get dewy-eyed over the flag and the origins of our nation. We're now enlightened, and part of a great new single world. Patriotism is for doddering old men who still wear their old army caps. That is what we hear from every angle and what most of us pretend to believe, because the deep thinkers tell us it is the new culture. The cultural mind benders have insisted for years that patriotic fervor, as exhibited at that parade, is nothing more than latent nationalism. We know that nationalism is selfish and contrary to the new "multi-culturalism", the new buzz word that will level the whole world so that we can all share equally in its unhappiness.

Through all of this modern thought, patriotism is constantly equated to nationalism and is, therefore, automatically to be shunned. Actually, the terms are opposites and should not be interchanged. When the United States Civil War erupted, the South was driven by nationalism. They felt each state should run its own affairs as it chose, with no concern for the other states of the Union. In today's world, we see the same thinking, as Czechs disdain Slovaks, Serbs kill Bosnians, Shiites slaughter

Kurds, and every possible cultural reason is sought to separate me from you. Abraham Lincoln, a pure patriot, realized this country could not survive with narrow nationalistic divisions. He knew that, if the Confederacy was allowed to split the nation on a North/South line, it would not be long before Virginians struck Carolinians or New Yorkers launched a vendetta against Pennsylvanians. As an American patriot, Lincoln also knew that such nationalistic divisions would only open the door to some other aggressive power to move against the whole country. The United States rallied to Lincoln's patriotism, and the Union survived.

Like so many mass cultural movements followed by emotional rote rather than reason, the anti-patriotism attitude in the United States does not have substantial roots. Ronald Reagan instinctively recognized that most of the high points in the history of the United States have been presided over by leaders of great patriotism and followers who understood it. Such inspirational leadership has always struck a hidden nerve of self-esteem within the country. Ronald Reagan was tapped directly into that nerve, and his countrymen loved him for it!

Over the years, there have been a number of challenges to the country which have given rise and impetus to super patriot leaders. Franklin Roosevelt was one who saw the serious threats to his country and rallied his countrymen to the battle. Such patriotic drive is not always involved in war or warlike actions. Roosevelt used the power of love of country to rally the people against the debilitating effects of the Great Depression in the 1930's. Later, he was again to rally that great force in the 1940's in an heroic war to put down one of the world's most ruthless dictators. As we noted earlier, Ronald Reagan was deeply impressed and guided by the example of Roosevelt.

While we have had successful patriots as leaders at many critical points in our country's history, we have also had a number of low points at which such leadership was needed, but not forthcoming. After World War II, the overall quality of national leadership declined, with only one or two exceptions. The country again reached a peak of patriotism with the idealistic leadership radiated by President John Kennedy. As has been the case with most heroic figures from our past, he had the charisma and natural instinct to inspire the country. He pulled the country out of its blue funk of despondency over looming Communism with his challenge, "Ask not what your country can do for you. Ask what you can do for your country!" In addition, he made a firm vow to take the lead in world technology by having the United States put a man on the moon in ten years! With that challenge, the country hoisted the flag, initiated a massive scientific and industrial charge, and marched off to win the world status war!

Unfortunately, the almost unlimited patriotic and inspirational promise of John Kennedy was snuffed out by an assassin's bullet. His successor, President Lyndon Johnson, was not up to the task, and the country started a long slide downhill in national esteem. A cynical backroom politician, Johnson killed whatever bit of national idealism existed after Kennedy's death. The country was thrust into a bloody war in Vietnam with no clearly-delineated high purpose and with a national leader obviously not at the head of the parade. This sad period started what was to be the longest period of anti-patriotism in the history of the United States.

Things did not get better during and after Johnson, as the general cynicism of the national government permeated the whole country. Great rhetoric was mounted to promote massive programs constituted to help the helpless. Paradoxically, the more the country spent on social programs calculated to make everyone feel righteous and good, the less esteem the people felt for their own country. Flag burning and permanent shanty town protests in our nation's capital became representative of the national mood.

Outside the borders of the United States, the rest of the world, especially the non-performing "third world" nations, took delight in trashing the country. The giant Soviet Union, bastion of bumbling communism, took pleasure in humiliating the United States at every opportunity, while the country's leaders spent endless hours in public hand-wringing.

The response of the United States Congress and the President to the sad state of the country's status in the world was to point the finger of blame at its citizens. The people of the country were suffering a deeply-imposed inferiority complex.

President Jimmy Carter, who was at his executive best while making sure his fractious staff maintained a fair schedule on the White House tennis courts, professed to see great malaise sweeping across the country. At the height of this non-leadership, the country's former friend, Iran (at this point everyone seemed to be a former friend), stuck its finger in the eye of the United States. In the ultimate humiliation, Iran held hostage the entire staff of the U.S. Embassy in its capital. President Carter, after much initial bluster and then unseemly pleading, finally retreated to the White House in a pout.

Finally, succumbing to national indignation at the country's being made an international laughing stock, and with his reputation sinking out of sight, President Carter ordered a military rescue strike on the Embassy in Iran. By this time, with a military system decimated by Congressional diversion of funds into favorite pork and social projects, his orders should have been suspect from the start. With poorly-operating equipment and a leadership lacking coordination or morale, the outcome of Carter's rescue attempt was predictable. The United States force did not get anywhere near its objective, as equipment and leadership broke down in the desert, and the supposedly elite U.S. strike force turned tail for home.

At this point, morale in the United States was lower than a snake's belly! In the face of all this, the two major political parties, along with most opinion experts, still didn't get it!

Ronald Reagan, running his own campaign with his trusted associates from the California days, sure got it, though! From the very start, he preached the greatness of the United States and declared we did not have to accept second best any longer. We deserved and needed the best in Washington, and we needed to let the world know quickly that the United States was the best! It took awhile for his message to penetrate the crushed national spirit. George Bush, the Republican Party insider, backed by the Washington insiders in the GOP primary, stuck with the same tired old politics as usual. Early in the campaign, he seemed to have the edge on Reagan, mostly because he had the professional party people pushing his candidacy. It looked like Reagan would again come up a day late and a dollar short.

Reagan's determined patriotic pitch for restoring American greatness finally began to penetrate to the lethargic Republican voters, and enthusiasm rose to a fever pitch. The nomination was safely in his pocket when the Republican convention assembled that year.

In the general election campaign, Reagan had to again come from behind, as he doggedly stuck to his theme of America's standing tall once again. The message was taking hold nationally, and flag waving was once again popular, as the country had a new hero to rally behind. From then on, the election was a foregone conclusion, and Reagan won going away! For the first time since popular war hero, Dwight Eisenhower, the country had elected a President they really wanted to lead the country. Most of the elections since World War II had turned on the defeat of the candidate that the country did not want. The winner took office almost by default. Presidents like Truman, a narrow winner over unpopular Dewey, Johnson over a scary Goldwater, and Carter over a stand-in for the disgraced Nixon might not have reached the White House had there been more acceptable opponents. Carter was not popular in 1980, but Reagan's overwhelming mandate could not be attributed to the anti-Carter vote. The country now had a truly popularly-elected leader at a time when leadership was sorely needed.

Ironically, the only two Presidents in modern history to win on a frankly patriotic theme turned out to be the youngest (Kennedy) and the oldest (Reagan) when sworn into office. While critics had put the hit on Reagan as too old for the rigors of the Presidency, he got his strongest support from the younger voters. Conversely, Kennedy, who was criticized as too immature to lead the country, got some of his strongest backing from older voters. So much for the conventional political wisdom!

For years, old-fashioned, flag-waving patriotism has been considered gauche by the intellectual elitists attempting to mold the culture of the country. That attitude has never been able to squelch the latent pride most Americans feel for their country. That national affection for their country was always waiting there for the proper direction to move the nation into world leadership once again.

Ronald Reagan entered the Presidency with two strikes against him. The economy was a shambles, and the country, both militarily and diplomatically, had fallen to second rate status. But, like any true American hero, all the Gipper needed was that third swing, which he used to hit a towering home run!

Details to follow.

Norman Wymbs

CHAPTER 25

REAGAN, THE ADMINISTRATOR?

OK, the election was over. Somehow personality, appealing television and better campaign ads had propelled Ronald Reagan on his way to the White House. Now the public would see what a colossal mistake they had made to entrust management of this great country to a mere actor! After all, the conventional wisdom went, everyone knows that Ronald Reagan is bored and turned off by the details of management. It was assumed to be common knowledge that he was a shallow thinker and certainly could not be expected to cope with the complexity of being chief

273

executive officer of the world's largest corporation. Political pundits, already convinced the task would be too big for the amiable dimwit, began looking forward. Now, let's see who appears to be the frontrunner for 1984 when we will surely have to clean up the mess left in the White House by Ronald Reagan?

Reagan's critics, who usually prefaced their sharp razor slashes with, "I like him personally, but...", were about to make another of their embarrassing mistakes about Ronald Reagan. Seemingly unable to learn from past errors in judging the man, they still did not get it!

When Ronald Reagan made his long-thought-out decision to run for Governor of California, one of his early moves was to put together the nucleus of a group to become known as "Citizens for Reagan". There was nothing particularly unusual in that. Every politician starts with such a support group, usually called "Citizens For. . .", "People For. . .", or the more homey "Friends Of. . .". Such organizations have the primary function of raising money for the candidate's campaign and sometimes even provide working bodies to do the mundane chores of campaigning. Such associations generally consist of a mix of money producers buying into the action, idealists who look to the shining future with their candidate, and plodding workers who like to talk on telephones and lick stamps. In that respect, "Citizens for Reagan" was no different from the standard. In one particular and unusual respect, however, it stood out from all the rest and represented a sharp departure from historic campaign committees.

As we have repeated frequently, Ronald Reagan, if nothing else throughout his life, was a consummate optimist. He never approached any task with an "if we can do it". His philosophy was always "when we do it". His campaign committee was not just for the election effort. Winning, in his always upbeat assessment, was a given, and planning for the post-election workload was a primary function of "Citizens for Reagan". Every facet of policy implementation and administration of the office was analyzed and prepared for. His "Citizens" did not just produce policy and position papers. They produced topnotch administrators who confidently prepared to run Governor Reagan's programs after his election. Before the voters went to the polls, Ronald Reagan had a complete staff assembled, thoroughly briefed and ready to take over the administration of the state.

As is usual with any government headed by a minority political party, Governor Reagan took more than his share of sharp criticism and determined opposition. One of the hallmarks of his two terms, however, was the quality of his administrative staff and top lieutenants in the state government. Even his most severe critics grudgingly gave him high marks for the team he assembled to run his governorship. That team was recruited, trained and provided by "Citizens for Reagan".

Like much of what Ronald Reagan had done in the past, his masterful assembly of a working staff in California was largely ignored by the mainstream news media. As he prepared to move into the White House, a little rudimentary historical review should have given pause to the naysayers.

Reagan had kept his old "Citizens for Reagan" group going, even after he finished his second term as Governor of California. The core membership and leadership of the organization consisted of devoted Reagan loyalists who were ready to follow wherever his path might lead. Regular meetings of the old gang were like enthusiastic alumni gatherings of a solid, old, ivy league school. They were truly family, fully attuned to each other, accustomed to working as a team and ready to win another one for the Gipper when the time came.

The rejection of Ronald Reagan by the entrenched national leadership of the Republican Party made the California-based group all the more important to his expanded political plans. The "Citizens for Reagan" almost pulled it off in his aborted challenge to the party hierarchy in 1976, and then registered a solid victory in his challenge to the GOP leadership in 1980.

Although the Republican Party establishment showed little shame in rushing out in front of the 1980 parade and claiming credit for Reagan's electoral landslide, it was the old, devoted California gang that really won the day. Now the team from the West tied on their cleats and prepared to take on the Washington bureaucracy in a political Superbowl!

Unless you've stuck your nose inside the tent, it is hard to realize the cumbersome nature of the organization that runs the government of the United States. Theoretically, the huge, largely intractable, permanent bureaucracy takes its lead from the elected instruments of government. In actual practice, the elected warts on the back of this colossus face a formidable task just being acknowledged. In the end, effectiveness of these few elected leaders in their ability to dent and move the bureaucracy decides the quality of governance we receive. While the President and his top staff members, including the Cabinet, get all the attention, it is the hundreds of middle management personnel that determine the success or failure of any President.

With some three thousand direct Presidency management jobs to fill, any new administration faces a formidable task to prepare for action. With all the news media focusing on and pressuring for names of the top positions, such as Secretaries of State, Defense and Treasury, it is to be expected that those should be the first positions filled by an incoming President. Head hunting for these vacancies is by no means as easy as recruiting performed in the interest of an auto company. For example, in the business world, there is always a good supply of well-trained and experienced executives ready to be tapped for any top job. Finding a new Secretary of State is a much different ball game. No other organization has someone you can easily move into place. With that very major project at the top, it is easy to see how the middle levels become largely ignored until the last minute.

The personnel problem is one of the curses of our governing system in which, every four or eight years, we throw out all the babies with the wash water. That one factor has done more to spoil initially promising Presidencies than any domestic or foreign crisis. Ronald Reagan, no more or less than any prior President, faced the usual staffing hurtle.

History shows that Ronald Reagan, so often criticized as a disconnected President, entered office better prepared for immediate, full time operations than any other chief executive in recent years. As soon as he was elected, his top Cabinet choices became known, and they moved quickly to get their shops planned for full operation. This is where the real value of his "Citizens for Reagan" became evident, just as it had years before in California.

Hundreds of middle management posts in the new administration were assigned to his California gang. Those news reporters who were paying attention began to refer to this group as Reagan's "California Mafia". Of more importance, though, and not really understood by reporters, they were not only dedicated Reagan policy supporters, but also experienced managers who were conversant with every policy and planned initiative in Reagan's master plan. They immediately set about putting together target teams with specific goals and plans of operation fully spelled out. When Ronald Reagan took the oath of office as President, his efficient team of administrators was already moving into the executive offices and clearing their desks for action!

This was not just a filling of jobs by the new administration. It was an extension of their leader's own vision for leading the country. Virtually none of the important mid- management positions went to purely political appointees. They were staffed by individuals as dedicated to the cause as Reagan himself. Those who did receive purely political appointments were placed in positions where they could enjoy the maximum in status while wielding the minimum in authority, so as to not mess up the important goals of the administration.

Unlike most Presidents, Reagan was fully functional from day one. With experienced and aggressive people on board, he could move immediately on major initiatives and legislation proposals. His outstanding success in those first few years could be largely credited to the fact that he was ready before his Congressional opposition was grouped to react against him. His early programs glided through the system with little serious difficulty under the powerful combination of Reagan's personal ability to rally the country and his crackerjack staff, which blew down the roadblocks.

When President George Bush rode into office on the popular coattails of Reagan, his transition was made easy by the still-in-place staff of his predecessor. Bush, in fact, kept the bulk of that staff with him until the third year of his administration. It is not just a coincidence that the Bush Presidency began to fall apart in those later years just as he was purging the old Reagan carry-overs from his team. Without his own team of qualified midmanagers to move in, the Bush White House began to come apart at the seams.

In 1992, newly-elected President William Clinton publicly acknowledged that he hoped to move his team into place as smoothly and efficiently as Ronald Reagan had in 1980. Clinton's transition failed to measure up, as he lacked the talented and dedicated people to take over the important inside functions of governing.

Ronald Reagan, during his campaign, had promised to cut back on the excessive bureaucratic staff entrenched in government operations. There was nothing unusual in that. No politician worth his (or her) salt ever runs without such a promise high on the campaign agenda. Seldom do such promises amount to more than campaign rhetoric as, after the elections, all the newcomers become absorbed into the existing, immovable structure of government. Since the staff coming in with the new President is almost always inexperienced in the ways of inside governing, the entrenched bureaucrats with years of turf building experience have little difficulty thwarting any attempts at streamlining or, heaven forbid, reducing the bloat! With Ronald Reagan, things were going to be much different from what they had confidently expected!

Reagan's pre-trained and ideologically-oriented middle management team took charge, with his major goals foremost on their agendas. He wanted the Federal Government to back away from its ever-growing intrusion in private and business lives. Immediate administrative orders were forthcoming to reduce excess and overlapping regulations. Procedural actions were streamlined to reduce the growth of forms, reports and other paperwork. All these reforms lessened the internal need for large numbers of government personnel. During Reagan's first two years, his team eliminated more than 90,000 career bureaucratic jobs in just those areas subject to Presidential administrative control. Although a drop in the bucket for a government employing over a million bodies in operations not including the military or the Post Office, it showed that there need be no drop in administrative efficiency with the pruning of dead weight. Reagan had kept his campaign promise of government cutbacks, not by traumatic across-the-board cuts, but by logical downsizing of unnecessary functions. It is surprising that the operation was so smoothly handled, that the expected rage from Congressional and lobbyist supporters of internal "pork" didn't materialize.

During those early years of the Reagan Administration, I became acquainted with many of those dedicated performers from the old "Citizens for Reagan" organization. That organization, incidentally, changed its name to "Citizens for the Republic" after Reagan took office, but its primary function remained the same. I learned from them many of their initial assignments when the administration was just starting. All were charged with directing specific departments toward consistent compliance with the overall goals and objectives of Ronald Reagan. Very few of them were career political or government workers, and most of them stayed on board just long enough to get their assigned departments on the right track. These dedicated "Reaganauts", mostly nameless and faceless to people outside the team, took only one or two years in those Washington positions to complete their missions. Quite a few of them were called back at later periods to take on new, but similar, tasks as the Administration moved along.

Reagan used his task force from California like an experienced military commander. While he took the strategic lead, always with a sharp eye on the final goal, his loyal corps commanders led the tactical forces which paved the march toward those goals. Of all the fiercely loyal partisans in that team that I've met over the years, never did I encounter one who sought any personal recognition or glory in the mission.

Having been a campaign supporter of Ronald Reagan for many years, and fully supportive of his vision for the country, it was not until those years in the White House that I came to fully understand his inspirational leadership. Few individuals, as typified by biographer Edmund Morris' puzzlement, ever really understood the tremendous attraction of this seemingly simple, self-effacing man. One of the best public indications of the mystique of Ronald Reagan came, inadvertently, from President George Bush.

After eight years as Reagan's Vice President, and then riding his mentor's popularity into the Presidency himself, George Bush showed frequent puzzlement over his years with the Gipper. Bush, an unknowing master of fractured syntax and startling non-sequiturs, admitted he just didn't get "that vision thing"!

"That vision thing" was what Ronald Reagan was all about and what drew his devoted and almost fanatical followers. Not only was his vision of the future, particularly for the United States, inspirational, but also he was possessed of the unique ability to cause others (apparently excepting Bush) to see it as clearly as he did. His projection of "that vision thing" created most of the strong personal devotion of his followers. At the risk of sounding irreverent, Ronald Reagan aroused the kind of passionate following that Christ did when he asked his followers to "take up the shield of faith" in their crusade against the evils of the world!

The inspirational support of those around him was not the result of any attempt by Reagan to "schmooze" or become best buddies with anyone in his closest circles. The media frequently made light of Reagan's apparent lapses of memory relating to those around him. This phenomenon once created quite a stir among the late night comedians, as Reagan apparently forgot the name of one of his own Cabinet members. It probably seems a strange characteristic to many, but we found that, throughout his life, he had difficulty remembering specific people unless they were being presented in the context of what they had accomplished. He, in effect, liked everyone equally without singling out anyone specifically (excepting Nancy, of course), but he always respected and honored individual performance and results. Once, while speaking to a former close aide who had been with Reagan from the early California days until his retirement from Washington, I asked, "Isn't he going to miss you after all these years? You've actually been with him as many hours during the years as any member of his family." This individual, who was also retiring to private life, looked at me strangely and replied, "Of course not. There will always be someone else there to do what I was doing, and he'll keep doing what he does best." More reflectively, the former assistant went on, "I know he appreciated what I did over the years, and I'm proud and happy that I could have been of some help to him. He has never been a person who shows outward emotional responses to people, but we always knew when we were pleasing him with our support." With a proud smile, he concluded, "There aren't very many of us in this life who have had the opportunity to be so close to such a great and good man!"

That was a common feeling we found among those who had been part of what the press likes to call the "Reagan Revolution". It wasn't that they held him in any particular awe. Most of them privately referred to him as the "boss", as he never held any grandiose pretensions about his position. While not showing outward emotional attachment, he was always aware of family and personal situations and quietly offered help and support in difficult times.

Everyone who participated in that Reagan revolution knew he might well forget their names when they next met, but also they knew he would always remember what they had done to further his "vision thing"!

Norman Wymbs

CHAPTER 26

OBSTACLE COURSE

From the Constitution of the United States:

Article I, Section 8:
The Congress shall have the power ... to provide for the common defense and general welfare of the United States ... to declare war.

Article II, Section 2:
The President shall be commander-in-chief of the Army and Navy of the United States and of the militia of the several states, when called into the actual service of the United States ... he shall have the power, by and with the advice and consent of the Senate, to make treaties.

Almost from the day our founding fathers composed the Constitution, it has been considered a model incorporating document for a representative government and has, in fact, been used as a pattern by many other countries. The architects were justifiably proud of the way it covered almost every conceivable governing contingency in its few pages. None of them, however, could possibly have anticipated the great confusion and constant change in interpretation of their simple words which have occurred during the ensuing 200 years. Thousands of volumes have been written analyzing the assumed thoughts of the writers, and hundreds of careers have been built on the base of "Constitutional scholarship". Most of our Federal Courts could close up shop were it not for the continuous flow of challenges, revised views and new principles offered to that simple document now residing in the National Archives. You would think we could now assume, after 200 years of picking, pecking and twisting, that everyone concerned knows and understands the Constitution of the United States, right? Well, let's not jump to conclusions.

The excerpts from the first two sections, on the face of it, appear to be simple enough for anyone to understand. Congress provides a military service for the defense and welfare of the country, and the President is commander-in-chief of that force. Any good dictionary (even those in use 200 years ago) will agree that to "command" is to have or exercise authority or control over or to be master of. Clear enough. Congress sets it up, and the President runs it!

When you get to some of the other powers, things begin to get murky. The President has the power to make treaties, and that certainly implies the power to conduct all necessary negotiations and concessions to the point of presenting a document to the Senate for its "advice and consent". Now we're getting a little more complicated in running the government.

During the course of international relations, it is not at all uncommon that actual force, or the threat of force, becomes an integral part of negotiating settlements or "treaties". Remember that the President, who has the clear power to negotiate, also commands the military, our country's only agency of force. If the President, in his treaty-making power, has the authority to use all facilities at his call, we must assume that includes his Army and Navy. How far, then, can a President go toward actual use of the military while conducting his administrative duties and powers? Such are the questions of interpretation facing every President who has ever held office, and no clear line has ever been drawn.

When we debate the legitimate questions of Constitutional interpretation, we run head on into the always-dominant problem in Washington — the overwhelming egos of the participants. There will always be a natural antagonism between the Legislative and Administrative Branches of government as long as questions over operating turf remain. It is no great feat to pick out dozens of senators or congressmen who know deep down that they are far more capable of running the White House than the incumbent President. Similarly, few Presidents worth their salt have not chafed at the idea of presenting any of their brilliant handiwork for the "advice and consent" of those turkeys over on Capitol Hill. How far can the President go in challenging Congress by acting on his own in these grey areas?

The political ego factor and the constant jockeying for de facto leadership of the country present the major obstacles to any Presidency. Strong Presidents usually gain at least temporary ascendancy over Congress for their major initiatives, while weak ones succumb to the pressures and abdicate leadership to whatever committee of Congress assumes jurisdiction.

This tug-of-war, while critical to any administrative policy, becomes most critical in the area of the United States' relationship with foreign countries. Since Congress' dominating mood is often contrary to that of the sitting President regardless of political affiliation, the ego and leadership battles are sure to be joined.

President Franklin Roosevelt had a running battle with Congress in this area, although they were both nominally of the same political persuasion. As the danger to world order became critical because of the aggressive actions of the European Axis nations, Roosevelt faced major problems as to how much he should defer to Congress. Legislators, both Republican and Democrat, were strongly anti-war and particularly firm in their desire to keep the United States out of any "European War". Roosevelt was forced to use every persuasive tool at his command to coerce Congress to beef up the nation's military machine, as was its function under Article I, Section 8. After pushing them, kicking and screaming, into action, including institution of the country's first peace time military conscription, the President went one major step beyond!

Roosevelt, through every means at his command, mostly covert, provided support, both moral and material, to the European Allies fighting the German/Italy Axis. Fortunately, Roosevelt's judgement and unilateral action prior to our country's formal entry into World War II produced a fortuitous and positive end result and assured his eternal place as a hero of the United States! Keeping in mind that Ronald Reagan was a great admirer of Roosevelt and a perceptive student of his administration, what followed during his eight years as President, not surprisingly, reflected strong Rooseveltian influence.

Roosevelt's overpowering personality and persuasive powers, coupled with the inability of Congressional leaders to command equal news media attention, won the day for his actions. Ronald Reagan had equal, if not better, persuasive ability, but it was pretty well offset by the expanded news media, particularly television, which gave top Congressional leaders broad public exposure and made them star personalities in their own right. Roosevelt also had the advantage of being able to run his administration with a higher level of secrecy than is available to a modern-day President. In the late 1930's, President Roosevelt was greatly helped in his "cause" by the actions of a ruthless German dictator who was already killing and destroying his neighbors. Reagan had to face an equally ruthless Soviet Union which was every bit as much at war with the rest of the world as had been Nazi Germany, although the U.S.S.R. was achieving dominance through bullying and intimidation without as much overt force.

Ronald Reagan came to office knowing he had a war to fight that was every bit as critical as Roosevelt's, but he would be facing just as antagonistic a Congress which was supported by a much stronger national news media. As has been so true in the past, the United States was to be blessed with strong leadership at a time when it was most needed. Ronald Reagan was up to the task. Raw political power and bombast were not to be his weapons. Rather, he was to accomplish the mission with disarming good humor and a deep insight into the psyche of the American people. That much-ridiculed "second rate" acting ability played no small factor in his coming success.

In twenty years of occasional contact with Ronald Reagan, traveling convention speaker, political candidate, President, and the country's best known retiree, one characteristic has remained constant. His almost unfailing good humor and determined optimism have been his hallmarks. As we learned in all our historic probing, those were characteristics he seemed to have been born with. Had he been able to speak at birth, I have no doubt he would have had some cheerful one-liner for his mother, who had just endured a difficult delivery of an overly large baby. The world saw a heartwarming manifestation of that Reagan character in his light-hearted quips with the doctors and nurses as he lay near death from an assassination attempt while President.

Calling these traits of Reagan "almost unfailing" was not a slip of the printer, for there was one point at which we found Ronald Reagan definitely down and showing little optimism. The free give-and-take of politics was a game that Reagan always seemed to enjoy thouroughly. No matter how rough and personal any campaign became, afterward, win or lose, he moved forward with no regrets or second guessing. There is little doubt that he received a severe baptism under fire in the rough, and often dirty, infighting during his show business career. That business, just like politics, often means substantial personal gain and ego gratification to the winners and oblivion for the losers. That battle training, which goes well beyond the polite drawing room competition, was to serve him well in the coming battle of the Potomac inside the show biz world of Washington!

The infamous double cross engineered against Reagan at the 1976 Republican Convention went well beyond what could be considered normal and natural political competition. When President Ford stiffed Reagan for the Vice Presidential nomination that year, he violated one of the most sacred tenets of our governing system, in the eyes of Ronald Reagan. The President of the United States had gone back on his word. To a dyed-in-the-wool patriot like Reagan, almost anything could be justified in the heat of political battle except violation of the honor of the Presidency!

As reported earlier, at the meeting and after Ford had pulled his switch, Ronald Reagan was as morally crushed and dispirited as we have ever seen him. While he showed no concern over the personal affront or anger for what had been done to him, he did show profound distress over what he saw as a disgrace to the country and its Presidency.

We did not see Ronald Reagan again after that tearful session until 1979 in Florida. The occasion was a Republican Party conference of state committee members from the Southeast. The meeting was held at Disney World, with much advance publicity, as a showcase for potential GOP candidates getting in line for the following year's presidential race. President Jimmy Carter was in such popular and political disfavor that the Republicans showed a surge of enthusiasm the likes of which had not been seen since the resignation of President Richard Nixon.

All the Republican hopefuls had been invited to attend the weekend meeting. Reagan, Senator Bob Dole, former Texas Governor John Connally, Congressman Jack Kemp and a gaggle of others, soon to be forgotten, were invited to make their pitches to the party elite. The format of the meeting would have the contestants appearing together in what is irreverently referred to as a "cattle show". The organizers, consisting of the inside movers and shakers of the Republican Party, were confident all the invitees would fall all over themselves at the opportunity to parade before the king makers. Their assessment was correct in all but one respect. Ronald Reagan refused to attend!

Reagan, who was not about to forget what this same party leadership had done to him at the Kansas City (Ford) convention, made it clear he would not again expose himself to their double dealing. His refusal to attend put the Republican Party leadership in a real box. Despite their own ill-concealed preference for an insider like George Bush, they knew the rank-and-file of the party, as well as the general news media, looked upon Ronald Reagan as the clear frontrunner. In a near panic, fearing a failure of their much ballyhooed meeting sans Reagan, the GOP elitists sought a face-saving way out.

Reagan, knowing he had them in a corner, agreed to appear as the featured speaker at a dinner the night before the general meeting was to convene. He still would not answer the cattle call on the following day. Tickets to the preliminary dinner, featuring Reagan, were to be made available to all comers, not just the party management and delegates chosen for the formal convention. The Republican Party got to save face over Reagan's refusal to accept their loaded invitation to the convention by promoting the early affair as a special fund raiser they had planned all along.

We got to visit with Ronald Reagan at a small reception before the dinner that night. Apparently, he was still not comfortable with the party leadership and not at all ready to trust their impartiality in the coming nomination race. His feeling proved to be right on the money, as it became clear the party insiders were following the old Rockefeller guidelines and promoting fellow insider George Bush for the nomination.

Coming away from that Orlando meeting, many of us Reagan supporters were concerned about and debated the effect of his open distrust of party leadership on his chance for the nomination. As it turned out, Reagan and the old "citizens" group from California had all the bases covered. His grassroots campaign overcame the internal opposition from his own political party.

The post-convention meeting with Ronald Reagan at Kansas City in 1976 had given us our only view of Reagan's being despondent and lacking his trademark positive outlook on the future. The meeting at Orlando's Disney World in 1979 gave us our first glimpse of Ronald Reagan, the tough, no-holds-barred, political infighter. That meeting and the subsequent events at the 1980 Republican Convention in Detroit showed that Reagan, despite his inherent niceness, knew how to play the old political game, "Don't get mad — get even."

It seemed to be Ronald Reagan's fate that, during his whole life, friends and foes alike would seriously misjudge him. He is so obviously friendly and warm-hearted in personal contacts and always unfailingly cordial, that many who did not look beyond the surface appearance saw him as a soft touch. That attitude had no effect, as long as those dealing with him did not attempt to interfere with his deeply-held principles and life goals. Reagan was always an affable and compliant pussycat until someone stepped over the line. Then he became as hard as nails! Even when he was being the tough guy, though, his pleasant mannerisms made the bitter pills slip down almost unnoticed. During the heat of the election campaigns, and later carrying over into office, the news media did more to stir up the fighter in him than any opposition political leader.

To best understand the unremitting media spotlight under which the President must operate, you need to take a look at the executive offices at the White House where things are run. The White House West Wing, containing the President's famous Oval Office and offices of his immediate staff, is unbelievably small and cramped. Movement between offices is so restricted that a talent for shoulder blocks and elbow clips is almost a mandatory qualification for service. Compounding the natural problem of conducting quiet management of the country under these working conditions are the ever-present news media representatives. And ever-present they are, with their own room in the Executive Wing and their constant watch on the visitor entry and waiting room of the complex. The President and his staff can, of course, hold private meetings as they wish. They seldom remain private for long, as the news media representatives can easily spot who is present at any executive office gathering. Knowing who is present generally gives a fair idea of the subject, and it doesn't take long for the news hounds to get to their favorite inside news leakers to develop a story. One of the best indications of the way the media has become almost another branch of government is the television networks' permanent camera set-ups. Outside the West Wing, on the carefully cultivated White House lawn, the TV people all have fixed cable and electrical connections. When they want one of their always-ready and carefully made up talking heads to go into action, all they need to do is plug their cameras and microphones into the privately reserved receptacles on the lawn and roll their tapes!

Since every President and major government figure lives or dies through publicity and "good" press, it is a rare official (and one with short tenure) who habitually offends the minions of the media. If they occasionally lose their tempers and composure over the often obnoxiously aggressive press corps, abject apologies are quickly forthcoming. There is little doubt that much of the offensive behavior of the press is encouraged by the perpetrators' knowledge they will get away with it.

Ronald Reagan, who by nature found it impossible to knowingly offend anyone, had a problem with the news media from the very start. His natural inclination to attempt to answer every question, no matter how far out of line it might be, frequently caused shock or derisive commentary. Even while most public figures are well-prepared and ready for almost any subject during direct questioning, there is always at least one questioner who will make a blind side hit with an unexpected query. The best response under those circumstances is no response at all or, as is usually the case with most politicians, a statement that bears no relationship to the question. Such reactions to the unfair hits were contrary to Reagan's natural openness and desire to be cooperative. He was finally forced to find other means of avoiding the "Have you stopped beating your wife?" type of question.

During Reagan's Presidency, his personal staff members were always quite noticeable at public meetings, as they almost physically had to draw their boss away from continuing questioning beyond a meeting's end. In private gatherings, Nancy Reagan ran interference by pulling her husband away from his friends and fans when the affairs ran overtime. As his administration moved on, Reagan came to realize that his very openness could well be the worst obstacle to his ambitious plans. It was here that his acting ability came to the forefront.

Among the trademarks and personally appealing sights of Ronald Reagan given the public were the TV bits of him as he hurried to the Marine helicopter on the White House lawn. Whether leaving for some important international meeting or just a quiet weekend at the Camp David Presidential retreat, he was always followed by shouted questions from reporters. In the beginning, he always tried to shout back answers while on the run, but finally he learned to cup a hand over his ear and indicate he could not hear.

Ronald Reagan's publicly-acknowledged hearing loss and his use of a hearing aid became his best defense against the unwanted question. The cupped hand over the ear and the puzzled shake of the head became standard signals that the talk was over. While visiting his restored boyhood home in Dixon in 1991, Reagan paused in the living room of the little house to answer a series of questions concerning his youth. The video reporter, after the usual schedule of boyhood anecdotes, began to rove afield in his questioning. Reagan suddenly got his now-familiar startled look and, tapping his hearing aid, announced, "I guess my battery just ran out. I can't hear your questions." The interview was abruptly over, and the TV crew gathered its equipment and left. Meanwhile, the President got up and walked to the small dining room where we were to have a private lunch. During the meal, his hearing aid battery staged a remarkable rejuvenation as he and my wife Harriet got into a spirited discussion of the good old days in Dixon. The old hearing aid gambit had served its purpose once again!

The need to conduct some matters not only in private, but also without giving a signal that anything special is under way is a continuing problem in the Presidency. Ronald Reagan became better than most prior chief executives at the game and was able to conduct much without undo leaks and early publicity derailing his most important initiatives.

On one occasion, I became a part of one of the common ploys used at the White House to mislead or shut out the overly inquisitive press corps. I had finished the manuscript on the earlier book about Reagan's youth ("A Place To Go Back To") in Dixon, Illinois, and the President indicated he would like to see it. The suggestion was made that I drop by during my next trip to Washington. An appointment was set up, but confusing to me at the time, the meeting was scheduled with the President's legal counsel (I was told Reagan would see me afterwards).

Upon arrival at the White House, I was duly logged in as a visitor to the Counsel, who met me in the West Wing reception area. After a short, purely social visit in his second floor office, he escorted me down the back stairs to meet the President's secretary. She led me into the vacant Cabinet room which connected to the Oval office through her own private office and advised she would be back for me when the President was ready.

After an interesting, solitary ten minutes trying out all the Cabinet chairs bearing brass nameplates of the members, she returned to usher me through her office into the President's Oval Office. By this time, quite bewildered by the strange procedure, I must have looked startled as I noted photographers behind the President. Reagan, noting my reaction, grinned like a Cheshire cat, advising, "It's OK, Norm. They are friendly. They're on our team."

After a relaxed visit discussing the book and his old hometown with the President, I was ushered back out the way I had come in. The President's Counsel met me again and publicly led me out through the reception area!

It was sometime later that I learned this was a standard procedure when the President wanted no public notice or media inquiries concerning a meeting in his office. My meeting, of course, was of no importance, except that Ronald Reagan, who always kept a pretty closed book on his personal life, considered my visit as personal business. The clandestine meeting was not for the purpose of hiding anything. The White House later sent me the photos taken that day and indicated that I could feel free to use them as I saw fit in publicizing the book. The secrecy was a standard procedure when President Reagan thought a private visit was warranted. With his wry sense of humor, he derived real pleasure out of putting one over on the ever-vigilant news media!

There was a down side, however, to Reagan's tricks to insure privacy. His official White House schedule showed frequent breaks explained as allowing him to catch up on desk work. A number of unkind news commentators took to calling these short blanks in his official schedule "nap time". Late night TV comics picked up on it, and Reagan's need to take frequent naps was used to justify their continuing claims that he was not really with the action, and, just as they had said from the start, he was too old for the job.

Although I'm sure there were many other just as innovative ways the President found to get his job done without the gossip-prone media's intruding, I did have the opportunity to see another ploy in action. Early in President Reagan's first term, we attended a small social reception at the White House. These gatherings are frequent occurrences and are usually scheduled to reward loyal campaign workers or administration supporters who merit a short visit with the President. Since they hold no special governing significance and occur during the early evening, the White House press corps studiously ignores them. On this occasion, as our group was milling around waiting for the President, we noticed his top staff and Cabinet officers quietly slipping into the crowd. Our egos took a larger-than-normal surge, figuring we must be pretty important if the whole Cabinet was showing up to meet us. Unfortunately, we soon noticed they were all unobtrusively slipping out to the private elevator to the upper floor private living quarters. Later we learned that the President had called a private meeting of the Cabinet in his quarters to discuss a brewing crisis, and that this was one of the few ways they could all gather without the news media's getting on their backs.

The elaborate methods used to keep certain critical meetings private was not solely to freeze out the news media members.

Washington, the most gossip-prone community in the world, is a place where the unauthorized leaking of inside information has developed into a high art form. Every experienced reporter builds his or her reputation on the ability to cultivate inside stool pigeons who pass secret information or advance tips on pending actions in order to gain favor. Many otherwise-mediocre administrators, including some as high as the Cabinet level, have risen to high position largely from news media build-up lavished on them solely for their value as tipsters. When the administration can pull a surprise meeting, not only are inquisitive reporters bypassed, but also the participation in such meetings is held to such a select group that any would-be leakers are quickly ferreted out.

Ronald Reagan was a true master at handling the news media. Although he, like all of his predecessors, could not close off all the leaks, he was more successful than most at keeping some of his major policies quiet until he was ready for a public announcement.

President Reagan's special skill at protecting his major moves allowed him to gain the most effective reaction when he went public. This was to be a most crucial factor as he began his major policy moves that were to seal the doom of the Soviet Union.

CHAPTER 27

COMMANDER-IN-CHIEF

The history of the United States echoes with examples of a peculiar love/hate relationship toward its own military forces. During and shortly after most military expeditions, the soldiers and sailors of the armed forces have been held in the highest regard, many actually reaching almost godlike status in the hearts of their countrymen. Even on a casual trip through the country's heartland, you cannot help noticing the statues and monuments in prominent public places honoring the heroic figures from past wars and explorations. The many streets and public places named after those long-gone leaders bear eloquent

301

testimony to the esteem America once held for those protectors and heroes of the nation. In recent history, however, there has been a sharp change in the apparent public attitude, almost amounting to an anti-hero bias. You need only to observe during your travels the lack of monuments or memorials to the leaders of the Korean and Vietnam wars to recognize this extreme shift in public feeling.

Did the country really change? Did the country totally lose its patriotic fervor that has been such a unique hallmark of its history? Ronald Reagan didn't think so, nor did most of Americans, as it turned out! Therein lies an important key to the Reagan Presidency!

The emphasis on individual initiative and the free enterprise system has been so dominant throughout history that it is only natural that Americans would be anxious to get back to their own affairs after outside diversions, such as war, are successfully dealt with. During long periods of growth and peaceful domestic pursuits, it is probably to be expected that the armed forces would fall into neglect or worse. Like a rusty fire hydrant in a neighborhood that has no fires, the community prefers to ignore or hide its presence.

The heady euphoria and pride after World War I, when the hastily-mobilized military might of the United States turned the tide in Europe, were well justified. For the first time, the country had shown its position of global dominance in a foreign conflict. That feeling was to evaporate as the postwar world soon fell into a deep economic depression. With the country unable to sustain its domestic economy while watching businesses and jobs collapse, the military forces faded in national priority. Many citizens became openly antagonistic toward career military personnel, looking upon them as freeloaders drawing an easy living from a government unable to help its destitute, civilian population. During those dog days of the 1930's, no sensible military man would dare wear his uniform outside the safe confines of his base. It seemed that soldiering had reached its lowest point in public esteem.

Such broad brush observations, however, like most generalizations, had major and significant exceptions. Small-town America, largely in the South and Midwest, never forgot their reverence for the country's heroes. National holidays such as Independence Day and World War I Armistice Day still drew spirited and heartfelt community celebrations. Everyone turned out to parade, picnic and wave flags. Military veterans, who marched to the cheers of their neighbors, proudly wore their old ill-fitting uniforms and held their chests out as their war medals sparkled in the sun. Small-town America, no matter the desperate state of the domestic economy, never lost its pride and affection for those who had served the country honorably in the common defense of the Union.

Ronald Reagan grew up in just such a mid-American town and was steeped in his country's adventurous history and its custom of honoring its national heroes. In Dixon, like most small towns, there was none of the growing "sophistication" of the larger urban centers that found flag waving and hero worship abhorrent. Over the years, the closed political society of Washington and the major news media centered in the larger cities made no attempt to understand mid-America in this regard.

Since the smaller communities in the country have always been very stable, changing little in population or moral standards over the years, it was probably inevitable that differing national perceptions would evolve. To these heartland communities, those past heroes were real people. Everyone in town knew or was related to most of those who were memorialized in bronze or lent their names to parks and main streets, and they were never forgotten. In the larger cities, with fluid populations, no one knew who that guy was who had his name on the plaque in the neighborhood park. In Washington, itself, which really should be the heart of the heartland, precious few of its residents can tell you who those heroic bronze figures all over town really represent! In the small town in which I grew up, our neighbor across the street, Bobby Washington, was related to George Washington, memorialized in bronze on Washington Avenue just a few blocks from the grave of Mary, the mother of George. You'd better believe that our country's heroes were real to us! Dixon was the same kind of community in which the army defenders against the warring Indians were still remembered, and a recent Mayor was the direct descendant of "Father" Dixon, the pioneer who founded the community over 150 years earlier!

Love for his country and a natural inborn patriotism led Ronald Reagan to join the Army Reserve in the mid 1930's. At that time, the U.S. Military was at one of its lowest points in history. With the devastating depression still in full bloom, the Federal Government had turned all its attention to a revolutionary *new* wave of social spending programs. The country's defense establishment had been relegated to the lowest point on the list of spending priorities. Despite the crippling low esteem of the Army at that time, Ronald Reagan still had a driving urge to serve his country in the military.

During the dreary years prior to World War II, while President Roosevelt recognized the danger to the United States posed by the growing turmoil in Europe, the Congress became more hardened in its anti-military stance. Like the latter-day anti-nuke protestors, Congress turned a deaf ear to the reality of world affairs and insisted Europe was none of the country's business. By sheer force of his dominant personality, along with liberal doses of political blackmail, Roosevelt forced a reluctant Congress to go along with rebuilding the nation's defense structure. With Roosevelt's guidance and support, serving one's country in the armed forces began to become respectable again.

Ronald Reagan, having maintained his ready reserve status in the Army, was well-prepared and anxious to serve his country in the looming crisis. Unfortunately, his poor eyesight killed his request for the active service he wanted, and he was limited to a public relations role for the U.S. Army. Had he not had that physical impairment, there is every reason to believe that Ronald Reagan would have gone on to a distinguished military career somewhat different from his later service as the country's Commander-in-Chief!

Emerging from World War II, the United States was on a patriotic high. The country could not do enough for its homecoming heroes. For several years after hostilities ended, American soldiers were enjoying joyous welcome home parades and parties. Military leaders were the toast of the nation. The supreme commander in the defeat of the European Axis, General Dwight Eisenhower, became a two-term President, virtually by acclamation. This was to be the last fling the United States would have with its military heroes.

Ostensibly to halt the spread of Communism, the United

States soon plunged into another war, this time on the side of a small South Korea stemming the aggression of a militant North Korea. When World War II hero, General Douglas MacArthur, moved to bring the killing of American soldiers to an end by crushing the opposition, President Harry Truman withdrew him from command of the U.S. Forces, relegating the American troops to a deadly stalemate. The United States military had become the instrument of a muddled political policy with no hope of victory in the field. Later, the armed forces were to be further degraded in Vietnam, as the Washington politicians, unwilling to back out of a stupid commitment, allowed young men to die needlessly in a jungle far from home.

The Vietnam War, if such a fiasco could really be called a war, was the ultimate killer of morale and pride in the United States armed forces. Even the news media did their part in the degradation, as they constantly depicted the U.S. military as cold and heartless aggressors, and the Communist opposing armies as simple, patriotic defenders of the soil!

Vietnam and the stridently anti-military Congress, almost overnight, turned the United States into a less-than-second-rate world power which was now even more vulnerable to outside attack than it had been in the War of 1812! The situation rapidly slid downhill as President Jimmy Carter and his cheerleaders in Congress mouthed praise for the "rights" of everyone else in the world. Carter, seemingly unable to curb his contempt for those who had served their country honorably in Vietnam, issued a full Presidential pardon to all the quivering U.S. draft dodgers who were hiding outside the borders of their homeland. Carter was showered with acclaim by the national news media for his "courage" in honoring those who fled their country. Suddenly, defectors were heroes, and the courageous soldiers who had died for their country were bums!

Carter's Presidency was to reach its lowest point of ineptitude when he tried to call upon the very defense forces to which he had shown such contempt. A military rescue effort, designed to free the civilian hostages being held in Iran broke down in the desert many miles from its intended goal. The military that he and the Congress had reduced to a disorganized shell of its former efficiency could not muster the leadership or the material and trained manpower to accomplish the mission. The once-proud American forces which had liberated enslaved Europe were now completely disgraced in the eyes of the rest of the world and unable to navigate even a small military unit across an undefended desert!

Ronald Reagan, after World War II and even before entering national politics, had been publicly preaching the theme of national preparedness and a strong, efficient military. The deplorable state of the country's defenses in the face of an ever-expanding and militaristic Soviet Union was a major factor propelling him into the electoral race for the Presidency.

In the Reagan campaign of 1980 against President Jimmy Carter, Reagan pulled no punches in his advocacy of a strong U.S. military. At a time when it was common for politicians and the main line news media to bash the military and label its supporters as "war mongers", he held firm in his insistence that the country be brought back to its former position of international strength. Few Presidential candidates have had to endure the kind of personal attacks launched against Ronald Reagan, who supposedly had his finger poised to punch the button starting a nuclear war.

Ronald Reagan, as a political campaigner, articulated with unequaled clarity his deep-rooted, patriotic love of country.

Despite the derision of supposedly-more-aware political experts, his message struck a resounding chord with mainstream Americans. America's latent patriotism and love for their country drew them to Ronald Reagan like a magnet. He was able to wipe away the deep distrust they held for politicians and government in general, for above all else, Reagan came through without guile. As to a kindly grandpa, the country gave him their hearts and, more importantly, their trust. Overnight, he made it fashionable again to salute the flag and openly express pride in the United States. There was nothing President Jimmy Carter could do. He didn't have a chance!

President Reagan wasted no time in getting to the task he had outlined during the election campaign. Much to the surprise of those who still were unable to understand the commitment and drive of Ronald Reagan, he entered office with a complete team ready to go from day one, as I have previously stated. Even those Presidents who have started off well with quick appointments to the high profile Cabinet jobs usually bogged down when it came to the several hundred key, mid-level positions. All too frequently, the incoming President is forced to turn over the mid-level executive staffing to his cabinet leaders, as he gets consumed by the day-to-day executive decisions. When the Cabinet officers are left with their own agendas, such administrations grow with a lack of central guidance and purpose.

Reagan's Cabinet, although made up of strong individual thinkers, had one commonality: they were all totally dedicated to Reagan's principles, knew his agenda, and, from the start, marched in unison. This should not have come as a surprise to seasoned political observers, as even his most severe critics in California had to grudgingly admit to the uniform quality and loyalty of his top advisers while he was Governor. The mid-level staff positions, always the hardest to fill with real talent as political hangers-on press for the Washington appointments, were virtually fully staffed when Reagan took office. Those key positions, in which most of the work is done and political theory is turned into working programs, were staffed with Reagan loyalists assembled by his California team. Most importantly, besides being politically loyal, they were administratively experienced. The Ronald Reagan Presidency was hitting on all cylinders from day one!

The overwhelming election victory and the swift assumption of Presidential power put the fear of God in an otherwise antagonistic Congress and entrenched bureaucracy. Not since Lyndon Johnson had there been a President who was so literally feared by the usually arrogant and independent Congress. In Johnson's case, it was the fear of what he knew and what he could do to them personally. Johnson, a long time member of that legislative body and a ruthless political fighter, knew where all the bodies were buried. As a result, he got just about anything he wanted from Congress under the implied threat of political blackmail. Reagan's hold on that body was different and, in some ways, more powerful. The Congress was in a state of shock at his demonstrated, astounding ability to relate to the American public. They could see that the country fell in line with his initiatives almost before he announced them. To the always political Congress, anyone who could sway home district voters the way Ronald Reagan did struck a primal note of fear in their breasts!

Speaking of the condition of the U.S. Military when he took office, Reagan said, "The day I took office, our armed forces were in a shocking state of neglect. I was surprised, even though I thought I had known something about it. We had shortages of skilled manpower, faulty equipment, lack of spare parts, and insufficient fuel and ammunition for proper training. We had planes that couldn't fly for lack of spare parts, ships that couldn't leave port and helicopters that could not stay aloft. I believe it's immoral to ask the sons and daughters of America to protect this land with second rate equipment and bargain basement weapons. If they can put their lives on the line to protect our way of life ... we can give them the weapons, the training, and the money they need to do the job right!"

Priority number one in that first Reagan Administration was to restore the country's ability to defend and protect its national interests. He did not hesitate to take the political battle to the floor of the same Congress that had gleefully decimated the country's defenses ever since the defeat in Vietnam. More importantly, he did what he was a real master at — going over the heads of pompous Congressional leaders and appealing directly to the people.

His campaign to restore faith and pride in the country worked so well it surprised even his most dedicated supporters. His evangelical zeal and unabashed patriotic call to the flag brought some unexpected results. Almost overnight, military recruiting offices were overwhelmed with applicants wanting to enlist in the armed services. When the military draft was abandoned after the Vietnam disaster, the armed forces had become an all-volunteer service. With the country's leaders and the prime time talking heads on television constantly degrading America's military, it was not to be unexpected that the quality and number of enlistments had fallen. Ronald Reagan's call to arms changed that. The armed forces now had more volunteers than they could handle and, for the first time, could enjoy the luxury of choosing only the best to serve in the defense of their country!

Reagan's emphasis on and success at rebuilding the nation's defenses and restoring pride and enthusiasm to the military forces brought forth even louder cries of "war mongering" from his critics. His counter to those charges further rallied the American people behind his crusade.

Speaking to a grudging Congress, he said, "In the last decade, while we sought the moderation of Soviet power through a process of restraint and accommodation, the Soviets engaged in an unrelenting buildup of their military forces."

To the country he stated, "As President, I can't close my eyes, cross my fingers and simply hope the Soviets will behave themselves ... It's morally important that we take steps to protect America's safety and preserve the peace."

To the strident antiwar protestors he said, "A truly successful army is one which, because of its strength, ability and dedication, will not be called upon to fight, for no one will dare provoke it. The more effective our forces are, the less likely it is that we will have to use them."

This last statement, repeated in many forms by Ronald Reagan, could well become a symbol of his Presidency, since it proved to have been a brilliantly enlightened prophecy.

Ronald Reagan's gift for transmitting his ideas clearly has been jealously acknowledged by his most severe critics. Hence the bestowing of the title, "Great Communicator". His detractors, however, tended to leave the impression that his message was flawed, even though the delivery was impeccable. His supporters saw it in a much different light.

Most Americans enthusiastically accepted his ideas because they recognized them as simple, straightforward and, most importantly, as right for them and the country. Not only did Reagan get his overall theme of defending and protecting America's ideals and way of life across to his countrymen, but also he snapped the Kremlin leaders in the Soviet Union to full attention.

"History doesn't offer many crystal clear lessons for those who manage our nation's affairs, but there are a few... One of them surely is a lesson that weakness on the part of those who cherish freedom inevitably brings a threat to the freedom. Tyrants are tempted. With the best of intentions we have tried turning our swords into plowshares, hoping that others will follow. Well, our days of weakness are over. Our military forces are back on their feet and standing tall!"

The new Commander-in-Chief had taken over with determination. The message was clear and forcefully delivered. The United States was no longer a "paper tiger". The United States suddenly had a real-life — by gosh — patriotic hero, and the country was ready to march to his beat. The Dixon drum major once again had the baton twirling and the flags waving!

CHAPTER 28

THE EVIL EMPIRE

In attempting to label blocks of the world's history, it is tempting to seek simplistic descriptions to explain complex human progress or lack thereof. As school students, we learned of the agricultural age, the industrial period and now, the electronic revolution. Similarly, in mankind's attempt to live with each other, we have seen varying periods and styles of government, some successful, most not, as we have tried to balance individual freedom with the common good. Significantly, the phenomenal periods of economic and technical growth arose during those periods of greatest individual freedom, while progress and peaceful advancement have been stymied during oppressive governing regimes.

313

So, after dazzling you with those words of historic wisdom, how come during the current century we have seen simultaneous expansion of political freedom and history's cruelest tyranny coupled with unprecedented economic and technological expansion? Our learned response to that query: "Who ever said mankind was either logical or predictable in it's approach to governance?"

In 1918, World War I came to a glorious end for the good guys and a total defeat for the bad guys. The victors and learned human relations experts were unanimous in their assessment that this had been the war to end all wars. Now mankind could live together in eternal peace and prosperity! OK, what was the "oops!" factor that brought on World War II, which was also touted by the same kind of experts as another war to end all wars? We might conclude that maybe man's great desire for freedom and independence just kept having losing encounters with humankind's natural stupidity in dealing with each other.

Germany, after its total defeat in that first "last war", was left in ruin and despair by the victors. After diddling with a republic that they could not make work, the Germans reverted to what they knew best, a totalitarian military government. Understandable, the apologists exclaimed. What could you expect from a totally beaten and humiliated, once-proud nation? If we grant the underlying causes that brought forth Adolph Hitler and his historically short, but vicious, reign of terror, how then do we explain the violent course change by one of the triumphant victors in that conflict?

The Russian revolution against the oppressive rule of the Czars appeared to be another great move towards individual freedom at the time. Unfortunately, the budding tyrants in that bedeviled country, while creating a vision of paradise, actually created a hell on earth in the form of Communism. It might be well to note, at this point in our guise as Monday morning quarterbacks that the slick salesmanship embodied in the spread of Communism must be compared to the other totalitarian forms of government. When Hitler promoted his "Third Reich", and we read of the Imperial Empire of Japan, somehow we knew they were bad at their core. Using the equivalent of modern sales promotion, the killer regime of Russia became the "Union of Soviet Socialist Republics" (USSR). Surely, with such a fine, humanitarian sounding label, the product must really be excellent! Unfortunately, too much of the world ignored what Communism really did, while worshiping what it promised. In the United States during the 1930's, as the USSR expanded, many misguided public figures were buying its phony evangelism.

For many reasons better explained by a textbook on psychology, the sales pitch for Communism was gaining the most vocal following from those who had the most to lose. In the exciting fantasyland of Hollywood, as motion pictures exploded into the world's favorite entertainment, those involved in the industry enjoyed seemingly unlimited prosperity, while the rest of the country languished near poverty. This unlikely isle of plenty produced in the United States the most fertile patch of Communist cells outside the Soviet Union. That the Hollywood benefactors of economic opulence beyond even what the deposed Czars had once enjoyed should embrace the doctrines of Karl Marx is a paradox that will provide long employment for future historians. Of importance to us is that these individuals, wanting nothing in the way of physical pleasures and tangible property, did embrace a doctrine so contrary to their own experience. Communism exceeded all other forms of socialism in its demands that government confiscate all forms of individual production for redistribution to the non-producers in society. Like most fanatical cults, Communism created intolerance for those who questioned their doctrines. Woe be unto anyone who did not bow down to the pronouncements of their deity, Karl Marx, or the edicts of their current preacher, Joseph Stalin!

Ronald Reagan, arriving in Hollywood from his early life in the nearly rural areas of Illinois and Iowa, was probably looked upon as a country hick by the self-styled sophisticates of movieland. His family and cultural background would have to undergo a radical change to fit into this new society. To Ronald's credit and the world's benefit, the radical socialists of that California environment did not change his values. To the contrary, his basic Mid-American personal values seemed to be reinforced by the pressures. It is significant that, upon his arrival in Hollywood, he found a small conservative church of his old denomination from Dixon, the Disciples of Christ. Also, as soon as he acquired the financial ability, he moved his mother and father to a new home he acquired near Hollywood. With Jack and Nelle nearby and quickly involved locally, you can be sure the radical, Communist fringe in his industry was facing a nearly impossible task to win over this budding new star!

During those difficult domestic years of the thirties, Communism and its adherents in the United States were looked upon with a fair degree of tolerance. The Soviet Union was a completely closed society, with the life of its citizens unknown to most Americans. The Red Cells in this country were viewed

316

as weird social clubs advocating immoral living. With the advent of WW II, Communism, as an oppressive force dedicated to world dominance, began to emerge to general view. The first indication of its real aims came when Joseph Stalin joined with Adolph Hitler to crush Poland and subjugate its people. Awareness was growing of this other force in the world (besides Germany) dedicated to destroying any vestige of freedom in the rest of civilization.

The vocal anti-Communist voices in the United States were publicly muted when the Germans and Soviets turned on each other. Following the old dictum that "the enemy of my enemy is my friend," the United States and its allies welcomed the USSR into the battle against Germany and Japan. Home front American propaganda depicted the Soviets as simple peasants defending their homes and families against the Axis beasts! Although the official government line decreed our two nations' love for each other, there were many who could not forget what those simple peasants had done to Poland!

Despite the official U.S. Government line of solidarity with the Communist Soviet Union, there were many, particularly among the U.S. Military leadership, who looked upon Joseph Stalin's visions of world conquest as an even greater threat than the over-extended Adolph Hitler!

Ronald Reagan, like many of his fellow veterans returning home after the victory in Europe, was convinced that the United States needed to keep its guard up against the Red menace. Becoming a gifted and knowledgeable speaker on world affairs, he engaged in a regular circuit of appearances before veterans' groups and preached American vigilance against this godless outside threat to our way of life.

When he made his strong public appeal on behalf of the Goldwater campaign, his strong anti-Communist position propelled him into the conservative political leadership of the country. From the very start, Ronald Reagan's fervent opposition to communism arose not so much from governing ideology as from his strong conviction that its anti-God, anti-Christian base struck at the very core of Americanism.

From the start, when he entered the Presidential electoral race, Reagan was depicted as a trigger happy cowboy who couldn't wait to get into a shooting war with the Soviet Union. So strong was the campaign on the part of the general news media to portray him as an unstable war hawk, they ignored the real source of his concern over the Red Menace.

The American public has always been far ahead of the national news media, which are more intent on selling their own philosophy than in reporting public concerns. In this case, America understood and related to Reagan's deep concerns for the country before the news media figured out what it was all about.

In March of 1983, speaking before a Christian Church group in Florida, Ronald Reagan made forever clear the deep root causes for his determination to halt the spread of Communism. As always, the clearest and most concise understanding of Ronald Reagan is found in his own eloquent words.

In that Florida address, he referred to public positions taken by the country's founding fathers. From William Penn he quoted, "If we will not be governed by God, we must be governed by tyrants." From Thomas Jefferson, he repeated, "The God who gave life gave us liberty at the same time." And from George Washington, he quoted, "Of all the dispositions and habits which lead to political prosperity, religion and morality are indispensable supports." And finally from that great observer of early America, Alexis de Tocqueville, he stated, "America is good. And if America ever ceases to be good, America will cease to be great."

Reagan then went on to say what became one of the most-discussed statements of his Presidential administration: "Soviet leaders have openly and publicly declared that the only morality they recognize is that which will further their cause, which is world revolution. I think I should point out I was only quoting Lenin, their guiding spirit, who said in 1920 that they repudiate all morality that proceeds from supernatural ideas — that's their name for religion — or ideas that are outside class conceptions. Morality is entirely subordinate to the interests of class war. And everything is moral that is necessary for the annihilation of the old, exploiting social order and for uniting the proletariat."

He continued on America's relations with the Soviet Union, "... They must be made to understand we will never compromise our principles and standards. We will never give away our freedom. We will never abandon our belief in God. And we will never stop searching for a genuine peace."

Later in his address, speaking of his hope that someday the Soviet leaders and their oppressed subjects would discover the joy of knowing God, Reagan ignored the usual system of diplomatic doublespeak popular in Washington and pointed an accusing finger directly at the Soviet empire. "... but until they do, let us be aware that while they preach the supremacy of the state, declare its omnipotence over individual man, and predict its eventual domination of all peoples on the earth, they are the focus of all evil in the modern world."

This 1983 speech of Ronald Reagan would normally have been largely ignored by the main stream news media because it was given before a gathering of Christian Church leaders, hardly a politically correct group in the minds of those opinion molders. One reporter, however, turned it into the political event of the year, as Reagan was reported to have called the Soviet Union an "Evil Empire"! The media and Reagan's political adversaries, always happy to find an area of attack to reinforce their inane "trigger-happy" label, ran with this one like they were headed for the winning touchdown!

Sensing pay dirt, syndicated columnists and blow-dried TV commentators solemnly grieved that Reagan had deeply insulted the sensitive, peace-loving Soviet leaders and pushed us ever closer to a devastating war!

The American public, however, loved it! The average citizen, with little faith in Washington's pompous politicians or media that always seemed to find more fault with U.S. leaders than those of Communism, cheered their Commander-in-Chief for calling a spade a spade!

Ronald Reagan later was to reflect on the reaction to that speech. "For too long, our leaders were unable to describe the Soviet Union as it actually was. I've always believed, however, that it is important to define differences, because there are choices and decisions to be made in life and history. The Soviet Union, over the years, has purposely starved, murdered and brutalized its own people. Then why shouldn't we say so?"

Ignored in all the bombast and pious shock expressed by the country's news media over Reagan's aggressive attitude was the internal reaction of the Soviets' own leadership towards the U.S. President. During the ten years prior to Reagan's Presidency,

South Vietnam, Laos, Cambodia, South Yemen, Mozambique, Ethiopia, Angola, Afghanistan, Nicaragua and Grenada had come under Soviet Communist domination. During the eight years of Reagan's two administrations, no new countries had fallen to Communist control! Surely, Ronald Reagan was doing something right, unless you happen to be a paid-up member of your local Communist cell!

Andrei Gromyko was, for many years, Foreign Minister of the Soviet Union. The wily old Communist outlasted a number of Premiers who generally had short terms in that rough environment. In the 1980's, during Reagan's leadership, Gromyko, in a little noticed interview, revealed the Soviet analysis of the outspoken U.S. President. Inside the Kremlin, housing the super secret and paranoid top management of that nation, Ronald Reagan was referred to as the "Crusader". Gromyko indicated the real fear they had of the American leader when he indicated that all their allies had been cautioned to exercise care and flexibility with the United States and to soften their public positions so as to reduce United States concern.

That their internal assessment of the "Crusader" was accurate received early confirmation from Ronald Reagan. The tiny island nation of Grenada, for some years dominated by Communist Cuba, a long-time Soviet showcase, became an example. Fidel Castro, Soviet puppet dictator of Cuba, ignoring the Kremlin's warnings, proceeded to turn Grenada into a Cuban military air base. Without prior warning or the usual useless diplomatic palaver, President Reagan launched a military invasion of the captive island nation. He sent the Cubans packing for home and shut down the Communist outpost. The "Crusader", true to Gromyko's assessment, showed that he meant what he said concerning Communist expansion and domination!

Ronald Reagan, the "Crusader", had gotten the full attention of the "Evil Empire", and world history was about to find a whole new track!

CHAPTER 29

ARMAGEDDON

From the Book of Revelation.

"Then I saw three evil spirits... they are spirits of demons... and they go out to the Kings of the whole world, to gather them for the battle of the great day of God Almighty... they gathered the Kings together to the place that in Hebrew is called Armageddon . . . out of the temple came a loud voice from the throne, saying, it is done! Then there came flashes of lightning, rumblings, peals of thunder and a severe earthquake. No earthquake like it has ever occurred since man has been on earth, so tremendous was the quake... the cities of the nations collapsed... every island fled away, and the mountains could not be found. From the sky huge hailstones... fell upon men... and they cursed God on account of the plague of hail, because the plague was so terrible."

Except for those who attempt to rewrite history to fit the political fashion of the day, there is little argument concerning the Christian emphasis behind the formation of the United States. Even in a perfunctory reading of the Founding Fathers' own words, you cannot help being struck by the conviction that God and their deep Christian Faith were the primary forces behind their actions. Washington, Jefferson, Madison and Monroe left little doubt, in their subsequent writings and statements, that they were guided by prayer and continuous reference to the bible in formulating our government.

During most of the first two hundred years of governing under the United States Constitution, Congress, the Executive and the Courts functioned with this deep faith as an integral part of every deliberation and official act. In recent history, there has been a concerted drive to secularize the United States and draw it away from the spiritual faith that has been the nation's past hallmark. In this major change in attitude, the proponents of a spiritually neuter society have made effective use of the Constitutional judiciary system. The Federal Courts, by broadening the Constitutional ban on a state-mandated religion, have leaned heavily towards a de facto ban on religion, most especially the Christian Faith of our founders.

The voices of those advocating the politically correct, non-religious approach to life became so effective that, for many years, the country's traditional religious denominations were pulling into their shells, and their congregations appeared to be in a precipitous decline.

As the major organs of communication and entertainment happily climbed aboard the secular bandwagon, it seemed all the country's old morality and social standards were fading from life. First, Christian prayer, then all prayer was banned from public schools so as to not contaminate the formative minds of our youngsters. It took awhile for the general public to begin to understand that, in the guise of non-religion, the country was actually adopting a new religion of agnosticism or even atheism!

As in many seemingly popular movements in this country, what is preached from the throne of power and the halls of public information does not, in fact, represent the heartfelt beliefs of the majority of Americans. That our political leaders are somewhat uncomfortable over the direction in which they are pushing the country shows up in a number of ways. While vociferously advocating the ban on prayer in public schools, our heroic Congress continues to open every session with a solemn prayer to the very God they wish to hide from our kids! Our pompous Supreme Court, in their priestly robes, is not above frequent pleading to that same God for guidance, while snarling at parents who would like the schools to seek similar help in molding their children!

I know of no major political leader who would dare make public claim to agnosticism. To the contrary, on any Sunday morning in Washington, those political types most in the eye of the news media will always be found dutifully marching off to church. Even those Congressional leaders who most vehemently orate against any public evidence of Godly faith are careful to maintain the personal appearance of piety for the benefit of their constituents. The simple fact is that they all know the heart of the country has not lost its traditional faith and standards. "They may have been badly bent, but they ain't broken!"

The first indication of a simmering revolt against the trend to total secularism in public life came during the election campaign of Jimmy Carter. Carter, with deep roots in the conservative Southern Baptist Church, was the first Presidential candidate in modern times to openly display his fundamental Christian faith. Moving well beyond the typical politician's symbolic church-going and head-bowing in public, he openly and proudly portrayed himself as a "born again" Christian. The general news media and entertainment industry quickly jumped on this revelation and used their considerable talent at satire and ridicule to put Carter down.

Jimmy Carter's public profession of Christian faith and the loud snorts of derision from the politically correct aroused the American heartland to an awareness of their government leadership not seen for many years. Carter's subsequent election as President can be directly attributed to the outpouring of support from the Christian community that had long been indifferent toward politics.

President Carter, unfortunately, lost this great edge of support as he was perceived to have been captured by the secular politicians of Washington. Although they turned away from a leader they perceived to have let them down, the newly awakened Christian voters did not turn their backs on the electoral system.

Ronald Reagan was the right man, at the right time and in the right place. Himself a conservative fundamental Christian, he had very much in common with Jimmy Carter, who had suddenly risen from obscurity in Georgia to the Presidency of the United States. Unlike Carter, however, Reagan had no affinity for the existing political structure in Washington and

326

was strong enough in his conservative moral standards to prevail in the inevitable clash of wills.

The conservative Christians in the country quickly recognized Ronald Reagan as one of their own and a carrier of the faith not likely to be subverted by the alien Washington system. On his part, Reagan realized that the media were particularly prone to using personal ridicule to destroy those they disliked, as they had done with Carter. The term "born again" is an overly simplistic label used by many Christians to depict one who has accepted their faith. Most non-Christians, as well as many believers, cringe at the term as not being sufficiently meaningful, while appearing smug to outsiders. The general news media pounced on the term and quite effectively portrayed Carter, who persisted in using it, as somewhat simple-minded in his religious faith. Ronald Reagan, already under attack from news hounds and political commentators as being overly simple in his approach to everything, deftly avoided all their efforts to "Carterize" him and his Christian beliefs and cruised to an easy electoral victory.

President Reagan's media and political opponents thought they had found a chink in his armor when he made his first reference to the possibility of a battle of "Armageddon" with the enemy. Columnists and usually expert commentators, caught flat-footed, quickly scrambled for long-unused bibles to look up Reagan's battle of Armageddon. Although they didn't have to look long, for there is only one reference to this awesome battleground in the bible, the passage in the Book of Revelations proved obscure to most of them.

The biblical forecast of the end of civilization as we know it, culminating in the epochal battle at Armageddon, follows a pattern common throughout that book of revelation and doctrine. In all of God's prophecies, the message runs true. It is up to man to make his own free decision in setting the course of his fate. He must personally choose between good and bad, and then must live or die with that decision. Even in His forecast of the end of the world, God leaves man with the ability to make the guiding decisions and final choices. Mankind can bring on its own ultimate end tomorrow if man so chooses, or he can put it off through wise and moral decisions. Thus, the last battle at Armageddon, while accepted by believers as an accurate prophecy, is given no fixed timetable in the bible. The Book of Revelation gives many signs that point toward the final destructive battle, but most Christians believe an enlightened leadership can postpone the final confrontation. Ronald Reagan's strong Christian faith was such that he could not, in good conscience, wait placidly for Armageddon. His mission in life was to do his utmost to stop mankind's headlong race toward that final destructive encounter. How he went about it is the key to his Presidency and resulted in the lasting mark he left on history.

In 1947, a group of nuclear scientists, deeply troubled by the destruction wrought on the Japanese cities of Hiroshima and Nagasaki which ended World War II, instituted a "Doomsday Clock" as a graphic symbol of mankind's proximity to the final nuclear war. Through their journal, "The Bulletin of The Atomic Scientists", they have kept the world alerted to the nuclear danger. The hands of their symbolic clock move closer or farther away from doomsday at midnight according to their assessment of world tensions. While political commentators generally ridicule the prophesy of Armageddon, they uniformly give great credence to the scientists' Doomsday Clock. While these two predictors of the last unthinkable clash of man are in many ways similar, they do have one major difference, one which keeps their mutual adherents at odds with each other.

The secular view of the world seems to find that all human difficulties are the result of physical things other than man himself. In that approach to solving the world's problems, all crime can be stopped by eliminating guns, illegitimacy of birth can be eliminated by free abortions and banning the bomb will stop wars. That philosophy would seem to indicate that the Nazi atrocities in Germany could have been prevented if all furnaces had been outlawed!

On the other side, those who place their faith in the Deity of God believe that man, not things, is the source of evil. In this view, the banning of cavemen's clubs, Napoleon's swords or today's bombs would have had little effect toward eliminating senseless wars. It is interesting to note, then, the critical difference between the Armageddon and Doomsday scenarios. In God's prophecy, there is no reference to any form of wartime weapon. Man's own immorality is the causative factor, and a turn to morality the ultimate answer. For Doomsday adherents, the big bomb is the problem. Ban the bomb, and who cares how evil the empire is. War will be averted!

While Ronald Reagan realized he must curb his public comments on Armageddon to still the critics, he never wavered from his core belief that God was showing us the way in His prophecy recorded in the Book of Revelation. The end of the world would be postponed only by forcing man to back away from his warlike aggressiveness. A basic character change, rather than removing hardware, was the answer.

Ronald Reagan was on a crusade to preserve the world and deter man from marching towards Armageddon!

CHAPTER 30

CRUSADE

From his first public appearance back in the 1950's until his campaign for the Presidency in 1980, Ronald Reagan made quite clear what he saw as the greatest danger facing the United States and the rest of the free world. Communism, with its subversion of all human initiative and independence, was a scourge which needed the forceful attention of all people who cherished the free pursuit of life, liberty and happiness. The Soviet Union, having given birth to Communism during the Russian Revolution, represented a tangible danger to all the world in the eyes of Ronald Reagan and a substantial majority

331

of his fellow Americans. That the country and the rest of the free world were not adequately facing up to this threat was the cornerstone of his 1980 campaign.

Let's set the stage or, as your favorite prime time talking head would put it, "First, a little background."

No one would seriously argue that the Allies' decisive victory in World War II could not have been accomplished without the United States. This country not only provided the productive and economic power to turn the tide against the Germany/Japan axis, but also it showed a level of leadership and personal military courage never before witnessed on the world stage. Coming out of that conflict, the United States, with its character and economic strength largely undented by the prolonged war, was clearly the world's most powerful nation by any measure. Had it not been for one key element in that war, introduced, ironically, by the United States, the world would have continued apace with little, if any, challenge to continuing American leadership. But that disrupting element was a doozy, as the United States brought an abrupt end to hostilities by introducing mankind to the age of the atom. Although scientists around the world had been moving ever closer to unleashing the power of the atom, fate decreed that it would be the brilliant minds in an obscure laboratory near Chicago who would present the country with the ultimate war weapon.

Even though the United States, largely untouched by the ravages of war, would have held its world leadership position in any event, possession of the atomic bomb added an indisputable guarantee to that dominance. Always a compassionate and peace-loving nation, the United States used those immediate, post war years to rebuild and revitalize the rest of the world, winners and losers alike. During those years, as the country got back to a prosperous peace time economy, not much sympathy or attention was wasted on those who were so desperately warning of the danger from the rapidly-spreading Communist menace.

While the normally democratic nations were busy rebuilding home economies with generous American help, the Soviet Union was busily preaching and enforcing its brand of suppression throughout the rest of the world. When they had moved as far west in Europe as they could, after the manner of a schoolyard roughneck, a hostile line was drawn in the charred soil of Eastern Europe and a dare issued to all outsiders to just try to cross it. Labeled by that master of language, Winston Churchill, the uncrossable barrier was called the "Iron Curtain". American leaders and their shrinking European allies did little more than grumble over the increasing tensions developing along that curtain.

Again, the rapidly advancing science of the atom was to effect a real change in world relations. Almost overnight, it seemed that everybody knew how to make a nuclear bomb, and the Soviet Union, particularly, geared up to turn them out in great numbers. The clear superiority of America's military power was gone. Now the Soviet Union, China and other international bullies could openly spit in Yankee's faces with impunity!

The Soviet arrival as a nuclear power drastically changed the world ballgame and rekindled old concerns about the desire of Communism to dominate the world. While the free world had been pushing the nuclear age forward in the pursuit of such things as electric power and advanced scientific exploration, the

Soviets concentrated on bombs and ballistic missiles capable of being delivered by them anywhere in the world. To make sure everyone got the message, in a masterful display of applied psychology, the Soviets delighted in huge Moscow parades of their gigantic missiles passing before wildly cheering crowds. Even Adolph Hitler, with his awesome Bundesgarten rallies, looked a piker, compared to the Soviet Red Mayday rallies of sheer force!

An inherent facet of the Soviet strategy was to discredit and humiliate the United States and its allies at every opportunity. When they shut off access to the allied sector of occupied Berlin, Germany, in the fifties, their drive for world dominance became a palpable threat. As American and west European leaders became paralyzed before the Soviet bear, the free world's humiliation was advertised through the costly airlift used to feed the hostage city of Berlin. The Soviet Union and its "superior" system of Communism had forced the free world to back down! From that point forward, it was clear to many, including Ronald Reagan, that we were in a real war, not the so-called cold war as depicted by the news media.

The total ineffectiveness of the United States in combating the aggressive spread of Communism was brought home unpleasantly by the failed efforts in Korea and Vietnam. The Soviet Union apologists and the "anti-nuke" hand-wringers in the United States did much to contribute to the low international esteem towards our country. A clear sense of defeatism appeared to be sweeping the country, particularly in its political leadership.

Fortunately the malaise did not get a total grip on the country, as a few brave souls expressed their belief that we were allowing the schoolyard bully to bluff us out. Senator Barry Goldwater sensed that feeling and attempted to rally the nation into a general spine stiffening. Although he failed, due mostly to vicious political and news media attacks on him personally, he did open the door for Ronald Reagan to take the anti-Communism lead in the country.

When President Richard Nixon took office, the first attempts were made to seriously address the threat of nuclear war presented by the Soviet Union in particular, while holding a jaundiced eye on Communist China. Talks aimed at creating non-nuclear war treaties between the two nations were instigated with Moscow leaders. These talks, and the much-heralded agreements to follow, were an exercise in futility from the start. The Soviets had amassed an inventory of nuclear weapons so far outnumbering anything in the West that there was no way of meeting on an equal footing. All talks were based upon halting weapon proliferation or reducing arms on a tit-for-tat basis. This, of course, always left the Soviets in a dominant position and had no effect on the overall imbalance of nuclear power, which was clearly weighted in their favor.

Since the nuclear treaty talks were popular with the news media, they quickly became a rite of passage for every President. As the television prime time talking heads cooed and the politicians preened, the United States and the Soviet Union instituted a permanent nuclear soap opera. With much pontificating over trading this missile for that warhead, or your "throw-weight" against mine, the properly somber negotiators came up with tentative agreements. Then the two nations leaders, in a suitably plush location readily accessible to the TV cameras, would sign a "precedent-setting" agreement and go back home to plan the next final treaty meeting!

During this continuing charade in international peace negotiations, there was a nagging, underlying perception that nothing was really being accomplished. To counter this worry, the ever-nimble word twisters in Washington came up with yet another of their brilliant obfuscations. Tacitly admitting that the Soviet Union would always dominate the United States in total nuclear fire power, while still refusing to acknowledge the futility of the treaty talks, the new concept of MAD was introduced. In typical Washington love of the acronym, MAD stood for "Mutual Assured Destruction". This theory pronounces that, although the Soviets had an overwhelming superiority in the number of missiles they could launch at us in an attack, we still had enough that our retaliation would destroy them, even as we were disappearing into dust! In the peculiar sort of logical reasoning that takes place in the murky confines of Washington, the concept of MAD became the cornerstone of United States/Soviet relations!

Ronald Reagan found little logic in the MAD concept of potential mutual obliteration of the two countries and its probability of ending civilization itself. He made no bones about his contempt for this defeatist philosophy espoused by many government insiders. He, instead, held firm to the view that all nuclear missiles must be eliminated or made ineffective to insure a meaningful coexistence with the rest of the world. Needless to say, President Reagan was considered a naive dreamer by those who firmly believed MAD was the answer. We all just had to learn to live with the tensions it produced!

Ronald Reagan's crusade was not to be deterred, however, as he stubbornly pressed ahead with his master plan. One key to that plan we've already touched upon, as his national defense moves were rapidly turning the United States military into the finest in the world. His bulldog insistence on upgrading the nation's defense hardware was vitally important, but the quantum leap in quality and morale of the all-volunteer services was the most significant. The new Commander-In-Chief was rallying the cream of the country's young men and women into the armed services. The always-vigilant and considerably paranoid leaders of the Soviet Union in Moscow were well aware and secretly apprehensive over this Reagan crusade.

The Reagan restitution of America's military was not accomplished at the expense of individual prosperity and well-being. His domestic economic moves launched the country on one of its longest sustained periods of growth and prosperity, more than compensating for the increased defense expenditures. Generally ignored by media and political critics was the fact that Reagan's major in college was economics, and he never strayed from his awareness of the importance of the country's economic strength. It would take another book to adequately expound upon those domestic initiatives. For now, we'll only address its effect on the international situation.

Despite increasingly strong reports emanating from the Soviet Union concerning the low morale and efficiency of their armed forces, that situation was not the result of any lack of trying on their part. Even while spending ten times the proportionate share of their national budget on the military compared to the United States, they were still plagued with debilitating organizational problems in their widespread forces.

In Afghanistan, they were bogged down in the same "no win" and high casualty situation that the United States had suffered in Vietnam. In their occupied territories, euphemistically called "Republics of the Soviet Union", Soviet soldiers were despised and shunned by the local populace.

Ronald Reagan lost few opportunities to point out the Soviet Union's problems in managing their colossus. He stated, "The Soviet Union is a huge empire ruled by an elite that holds all power and privilege. They hold it tightly because, as we have seen in Poland, they fear what might happen if even the smallest amount of control slips from their grasp. But in the midst of social and economic problems, the Soviet dictatorship has forged the largest armed force in the world. It has done so by preempting the human needs of its people and in the end, this course will undermine the foundations of the Soviet system."

The Soviet Union was maintaining an economically insupportable spending rate on its military, giving a tangible lie to their professed desire for international peace and accord. Again, Reagan took note of this and the danger it posed. "As the Soviets have increased their military power, they have been emboldened to extend that power. They are spreading their military influence in ways that can directly challenge our vital interests and those of our allies. The final fact is that the Soviet Union is acquiring what can only be considered as an offensive military force. They have continued to build far more intercontinental ballistic missiles than they could possibly need to deter an attack. Their conventional forces are trained and equipped not so much to defend against an attack as to permit sudden, surprise offensives of their own."

Ronald Reagan saw and repeatedly warned against the clear and present danger posed by the Communist Soviet Union. No amount of reliance on MAD or the meaningless parade of new summit agreements was going to stop this menace.

There was, however, another new factor about to be entered into the equation, and the Reagan Crusade was to gain new impetus in its drive to change the course of history!

Norman Wymbs

CHAPTER 31

THE SDI FACTOR

In March 1983, Ronald Reagan addressed the nation and introduced an initiative that was to ultimately bring about the postponement of Armageddon and cause the concerned scientists to turn back their Doomsday Clock!

"My predecessors in the Oval Office have appeared before you on other occasions to describe the threat posed by Soviet power and have proposed steps to address that threat. But since the advent of nuclear weapons, those steps have been directed toward deterrence of aggression through the promise of retaliation, the basis being that no rational nation would launch an attack that would inevitably result in unacceptable losses to themselves. This approach to stability has worked. We and our allies have succeeded in preventing nuclear war for three decades. In recent months, however, my advisors, including the Joint Chiefs of Staff, have underscored the bleakness of the future before us.

Over the course of these discussions, I have become more and more deeply convinced that the human spirit must be capable of rising above dealing with other nations and human beings by threatening their existence. Are we not capable of demonstrating our peaceful intentions by applying all our abilities and our ingenuity to achieving a truly lasting stability? I think we are — indeed, we must!

Let me share with you a vision of the future that offers hope. It is that we embark on a program to counter the awesome Soviet missile threat with measures that are defensive. Let us turn to the very strengths in technology that spawned our great industrial base and that have given us the quality of life we enjoy today. Until now, we have increasingly based our strategy of deterrence upon the threat of retaliation. But what if free people could live securely in the knowledge that their security did not rest upon the threat of instant retaliation to deter a Soviet attack. We could intercept and destroy strategic ballistic missiles before they reached our own soil or that of our allies.

I know this is a formidable task. Current technology has attained a level of sophistication at which it is reasonable for us to begin the effort. Is it not worth every investment necessary to free the world from the threat of nuclear war? We know it is!"

Reagan went on in that address to the American people to reveal the most important proposal of his eight years as President. "I call upon the scientific community, who gave us nuclear weapons, to turn their great talents to the cause of mankind and world peace — to give us the means of rendering those nuclear weapons impotent and obsolete. Tonight, ... I am taking an important first step. I am directing that a comprehensive and intensive program begin, to achieve our ultimate goal of eliminating the threat posed by strategic nuclear missiles. This could pave the way for arms control measures to eliminate the weapons themselves. We sell neither military superiority nor political advantage. Our only purpose — one all people share — is to search for ways to reduce the danger of nuclear war."

The reaction to President Reagan's speech on the development of a "Strategic Defense Initiative" (SDI) to neutralize the danger of nuclear warfare was immediate and, based upon past experience, predictable. The major news media commentators and syndicated print columnists dismissed the whole prospect as a figment of misguided imagination. One reporter labeled the proposal "Star Wars", after a comic strip depiction of the future in a current popular movie of that name. Prime time TV was flooded with "experts", most of whom had no background in the sophisticated sciences behind the research, who flatly declared the SDI impossible. Political experts almost frothed at the mouth as they vilified Ronald Reagan for the obstacle he had placed in the way of the still-continuing TV extravaganzas, called nuclear treaty talks, with the Soviets.

Ronald Reagan adamantly stuck to his guns, and SDI became a major research project of the United States. In light of subsequent history, we need to take a closer look at the real impact of this major Presidential initiative, while ignoring the media and political smokescreens designed to squelch the project.

While a young man studying for an eventual college degree in Aeronautical Engineering, I did an in-depth research paper on the ultimate top speed of aircraft. Using what I thought was brilliant engineering perception, my thesis proved that aircraft could never be designed to exceed the speed of sound (just under 700 mph). At the time, my already substantial ego got a boost, as the head of the school's aeronautic engineering department gave the paper an "A", propelling me well along toward my degree. The details of that learned effort rest heavy in my memory, as only a few short years later intrepid pilots were zipping through the skies at more than 2000 mph in craft built without the benefit of my astute engineering. That episode in my youth probably had a great deal to do with why I did not make a career out of aeronautical research!

I cite that personal experience as a friendly warning to those who maintain that Ronald Reagan's SDI is only a dream. There are too many sharp minds and dogged researchers out there to ever say "can't" to any new technical proposal. Aside from the scientific probability of eventual success in the effort to stop nuclear missiles, we need to take careful note of how the major players took the announcement.

The American public, usually far more astute than the learned TV critics give them credit for, took to the idea, and Reagan's initiative ranked high in all the opinion polls. Most people, aware of such startling achievements as the bouncing of a tiny laser beam off the moon and catching it back on Earth, saw nothing far-fetched in such beams zapping an incoming nuclear missile. After all, these fantastic light beams had already proven their capability in such delicate areas as eye surgery and tough jobs like slicing heavy steel plates. Why couldn't they stop a missile?

Besides the see-saw arguments in the press and on TV, there was a far more important reaction. The Soviet Union immediately objected to any continued research on such a defensive system. They were so quickly alarmed, to the extent of threatening to break off any future talks with the United States, that they must have felt there was substance in the project. The Soviet Union itself had not been a slouch in the science department. Not only did they beat the United States into space, but also they had reached a sophistication in which their astronauts were left working in space for months at a time. Later events were to reveal that they were also hard at work on their own SDI, but economics and basic research capabilities were lacking, and they were far behind the United States.

The American news media seemed unable to cope with the root cause of the Soviet's open fear of SDI, turning instead to an attack on Ronald Reagan for having upset the Communist leaders. Much of that attitude stemmed from the ongoing love affair that the news media was having with the Soviet Union's leader of the moment. One declining news magazine even gushed over the final Red dictator as their "Man of the Decade".

During the period of most opposition to SDI, the recently elevated Mikhail Gorbachev was popping up all over the airwaves, offering veiled threats about what Reagan's ill-advised attitude would do for hopes of world peace. The campaign that continued against President Reagan's SDI program had little effect against his ongoing crusade!

During Reagan's period in office, the "summit" meetings between the two giant powers had continued. Following what had become a tradition for U.S. Presidents and Soviet Dictators, these meetings usually produced, besides meaningless little concessions on military hardware, much smiling and toasting before the cameras. Between the summits, political posturing and sniping between the countries' leaders continued. The continuing antagonistic reaction of the Soviets to Reagan's SDI strained tempers to the point where any further summits were problematical.

It was finally agreed between the two increasingly frosty leaders that they would have a meeting with no specific agenda or treaty on the table. The media immediately picked up on the offbeat approach and labeled the coming confrontation a "non-summit" summit! The non-discussions were to take place in Reykjavik, Iceland, in October 1986 — certainly a time of year and location conducive to a cool meeting between the two strongly opinionated leaders!

Gorbachev approached that meeting with firm pronouncements that not only would the Soviets refuse any further armament agreements if the U.S. proceeded with SDI, but also, he hinted darkly, that all their prior agreements stood in jeopardy over the issue. Reagan, on the other hand, cheerfully approached the non-summit, insisting the United States' SDI development was not negotiable.

The Iceland meeting began much like it had been planned, as a friendly social affair between the two world leaders. The Soviet Dictator, who had been making many brownie points with the United States press with his affable declarations in support of world peace, continued to play for the cameras at Reykjavik. So confident were the Soviets that world opinion was flowing with them, they took the unprecedented, for that Communist empire, move of opening all of their meetings to the news media. In this apparently open and democratic setting, the heads of the two major world nuclear powers got into a discussion in which both sides would consider the eventual total elimination of nuclear weapons!

Just when it appeared that this non-summit would turn into the first meaningful meeting of the two powers, Gorbachev played his final card. No agreement of any kind would be made unless the United States agreed to immediate and total abandonment of the Strategic Defense Initiative. The Soviets had not only gone for the bait but they had also swallowed the hook, and Reagan skillfully proceeded to land the catch!

President Reagan advised Gorbachev that he had nothing to fear from the purely defensive initiative. In fact, he promised to make all the technology available to the Soviets as soon as it was operational. Reagan reasoned that, with both sides having a solid defense against nuclear missiles, there would no longer be any need for the awesome weapons. That open-handed approach by the United States President exposed the Soviet peace offensive for the sham it really was, and Gorbachev, caught unprepared, responded, "I don't believe you."

Having had his last card trumped by the still-affable U.S. leader, Gorbachev and his Communist entourage broke off the meeting!

Addressing the country after that Iceland confrontation, President Reagan put the meeting in perspective. "I told him

(Gorbachev) that I had pledged to the American people that I would not trade away SDI. There was no way I could tell our people that their government would not protect them against nuclear destruction. Some Americans may be asking tonight why not accept Gorbachev's demand? Why not give up SDI for this agreement?

Well, the answer, my friends, is simple. SDI is America's insurance policy that the Soviet Union would keep the commitments made at Reykjavik. SDI is America's security guarantee if the Soviets should — as they have done too often in the past — fail to comply with their solemn commitments. SDI is what brought the Soviets back to arms control talks at Geneva and Iceland. SDI is the key to a world without nuclear weapons .

The American people should reflect on these critical questions. How does a defense of the United States threaten the Soviet Union or anyone else? Why are the Soviets so adamant that America remain forever vulnerable to Soviet rocket attack? As of today, all free nations are utterly defenseless against Soviet missiles fired either by accident or design. Why does the Soviet Union insist that we remain so forever?

So, if there's one impression I carry away with me from these October talks, it is that, unlike the past, we are dealing now from a position of strength... so, there's reason, good reason, for hope."

The United States news media almost unanimously declared Reagan's performance in Iceland a "disaster". Even some of his usually staunch policy supporters expressed public disappointment over his blowing the opportunity for further agreements with the Communist Soviet Union. There were, as always, however, strong signs of solid support from the American people. Major public opinion polls conducted by openly antagonistic news organizations showed the general public's supporting Ronald Reagan's position by factors of 70% to more than 80%! But, even more important than the muttering talking heads and the pollsters' findings was the reaction where it counted most.

The Soviet Union, as Reagan had surmised, was smack up against a major national economic crisis. Their massive spending on a top-heavy military structure had all but destroyed their already weak domestic economy. It was becoming increasingly difficult to keep the citizens in their far-flung empire from open rebellion over their personal plight. For years, the Communist leaders had quelled complaints over domestic hardships with public assurances that personal sacrifice was paying off in keeping the hated Yankee imperialists at bay! Increasingly, however, the Soviet public was becoming aware of failures of their government's control over the rest of the world. News and evidence of the unprecedented prosperity and good life in the supposedly oppressed United States were causing them to openly question their own leader's preaching of Yankee danger. When Gorbachev returned to Moscow, having to admit he failed to get President Reagan to back down on his Strategic Defense Initiative, the Soviet empire began to unravel. A victim of his own masterful job of convincing the Soviet people (as well as the American press) that SDI was the world's greatest threat to peace, he could not cope with the personal antagonism when he had to admit he could not stop it!

The unraveling of the broad Soviet empire was already under way as they were engaged in a Vietnam-like retreat in Afghanistan. Poland had thumbed its nose at the Communist masters and was headed toward full autonomy. Communist East Germany, once a showplace of Communist shtick, was literally pleading to be rejoined with the prosperous ally-supported West Germany. The Balkan nations, always a fractious bunch, were starting their first rumblings toward breaking from the Soviet yoke.

Gorbachev's personal popularity in his own country was plummeting, as the anticommunist movement spread throughout the Evil Empire. Unaccountably, the American news media continued to fawn over the failed dictator, while signs were growing all over the world that his day was past.

Ronald Reagan, through all this Soviet upheaval, was jaunty and in good spirits. He was satisfied that his efforts to rebuild the United States defense capabilities, the much strengthened national economy and the visibly upbeat national morale had won the day. This attitude showed when the two leaders met again in December, 1987. Without more demands to drop SDI or overt threats of force, that meeting was all happy talk! Reagan was gracious and confident of the growing United States victory in the Cold War, while Gorbachev, a consummate politician, was laying the groundwork for his eminent retirement from power.

Reagan's confidence was most evident when the two leaders held their last meeting in Moscow in June, 1988. The United States President gave public speeches in that founding city of Communism on the superiority of the American capitalistic system. Indicating the tidal change that had been wrought, his speeches were received enthusiastically by the Soviets, and the meeting turned into a love fest!

Ronald Reagan's Crusade had been successful beyond even his fondest dreams! The Evil Empire was no more, and Armageddon was fading farther into the future. Even the Doomsday Clock was turned back farther away from the end time than it had been since World War II!

Although the American news media found it almost impossible to give Ronald Reagan any credit for bringing on the rapid deterioration of the Soviet Empire, that nation's leaders were not so blind. In a report made public years after President Reagan retired, top former Soviet officials admitted to Reagan's major role in history. They insisted that the Reagan Strategic Defense Initiative had played the major role in Gorbachev's decision to halt the U.S./Soviet competition. Just as Reagan had reasoned, any attempt by the Soviets to match SDI would have wrecked their already tottering economy.

Ronald Reagan's masterful use of the real potential of the Strategic Defense Initiative in his-face-to-face encounters with the Soviet leaders won the day for the West! It will probably take a few years, but history will eventually show that President Ronald Reagan of the United States pulled off the coup of the century in his crusade against Communism!

Norman Wymbs

CHAPTER 32

AND IN CONCLUSION

In a country that generally grows tired of its heroes, actually turning on them in many cases, Ronald Reagan left office still high in the esteem of his countrymen. Prohibited from seeking a third term as President due to a Constitutional limit of two terms (the Roosevelt Amendment), his departure triggered many calls to change the law so that he could remain in the Oval Office. Unable to vote again for the Gipper, the American voters turned to his apparent protege and eight-year Vice President, George Bush.

While riding his mentor's coattails into office, George Bush never generated the personal affection and deep support that Ronald Reagan had enjoyed. Lacking the leadership ability or ideological vision of his predecessor, his administration started with two strikes already against it. His lack of any specific agenda of his own was best illustrated by the fact he had no second tier of officials ready to come on board when he entered the White House. To get under way, he retained most of the Reagan team, and they ran the administration for that first year. In the second year, Bush systematically purged his administration of the Reagan carry-overs, and from then on, his term in office was marked by its lack of direction and purpose. George Bush had still not been able to understand and cope with what he called "that vision thing".

In 1992, the voters, now well aware that Ronald Reagan was irretrievably gone, with Bush unable to fill the bill, elected William Clinton as President. Clinton entered office with no more clear-cut vision than had Bush and appeared to be a throwback to President Jimmy Carter, who never learned when to stop campaigning and start to be President! Clearly, there would be no extension of the Ronald Reagan crusade.

During those ensuing years after President Reagan retired to his California ranch, the tangible results of his hard-fought crusade were becoming more and more evident. The Soviet Union was dissolving faster than anyone could have predicted, as each of its formerly submissive country members defiantly declared its independence. The Evil Empire had been totally destroyed by the Reagan initiatives. Reagan had won the war without a bomb ever having been dropped or a gun fired in anger!

The one bright spot in a generally drab Bush Administration was yet another vindication of Reagan's sure and correct vision. When the United States (ostensibly in the name of the United Nations) launched a preemptive war against the small nation of Iraq, the whole world got a demonstration of Reagan's rebuilt military. Recalling the ignominious failure of the United States in a minor military action launched by Reagan's predecessor, Jimmy Carter, the Iraq campaign became even more remarkable. Just as everything that possibly could go wrong in the Carter attempt to rescue hostages in Iran did, so everything in Iraq went perfectly. Carter's expedition in the same desert had displayed abysmal military leadership, poorly trained personnel and failing equipment in a small operation. The Iraq War, on a much larger scale, showed excellent military leadership, highly efficient personnel and military equipment so technically advanced and accurate in operation as to startle even the experts. That the Iraq expedition was so quickly consummated in complete victory with virtually no loss of life was a final and clear vindication of Ronald Reagan's eight-year campaign to bolster the country's defense capabilities.

At a small dinner meeting with Ronald Reagan two years after his retirement, we had another of those rare opportunities to penetrate beneath his surface reserve. Harriet, sitting next to him that evening and never one to hold back on issues dear to her heart, drew the President into a warm discussion of his past crusade and the future outlook.

When asked of his opinion on the breakup of the Soviet Union and what it portended for the future, he was unusually open and philosophical. He admitted that he no longer considered the Soviet Union to be the Evil Empire of biblical prophesy, but felt, rather, that they now had much of a positive nature to contribute to the rest of the world. While never assuming personal credit for the result, he did admit, "Armageddon has been postponed."

During the conversation, his strong Christian faith was quite evident as he displayed a deep knowledge of the bible and its prophesies concerning end times. At one point he asked, "Do you know the English translation for Chernobyl?" A few years earlier, Chernobyl had been the scene of a disastrous meltdown in a Soviet nuclear power plant. The resulting radiation leaks caused hundreds of deaths, doomed thousands more and left miles of devastated and uninhabitable territory. Continuing, he answered his own question, "Chernobyl means wormwood in English."

In the bible, wormwood signified decay from within. Wormwood devoured everything, leaving behind corruption and death. Reagan went on, "Until the nuclear age, we had no way to explain the devastation created by wormwood. When the final battle of Armageddon is fought, the hordes from the North will be destroyed by nuclear power (wormwood), and the dead, as predicted in the bible, will be counted in the millions." As the conversation continued, the rest of the small party seemingly forgotten, Harriet and the President warmed to their subject as she asked, "Since the Soviets have been effectively eliminated, who do you see as the possible evil nation in the prophesy?" His quick reply was, "China".

He went on to further explain, indicating that he still felt the world was near the biblical end of times and that Armageddon was still in view. In his opinion, many of the preliminary

356

prophecies were being fulfilled, save for Israel's rebuilding the Temple in Jerusalem. He also pointed out that the drawing together of the European free nations into a cooperative quasi-empire bore an uncanny resemblance to the biblical prophecy of the ten kings banding together to be led by the ultimate evil nation in the guise of humanitarianism. During the course of the discussion, Reagan revealed that he had frequent discussions with the Reverend Dr. Billy Graham concerning the matter of biblical prophecy.

In the midst of the serious discussion, Reagan suddenly turned pensive saying, "I'm too old now to live to see the events of the end times. I hope the 'Rapture' is near, but none of us can know God's timetable."

Ronald Reagan, that evening, displayed the supreme contentment of an individual who had successfully clung to the heart of his deep Christian faith in an unsympathetic world. Even among those supporters who were not aware of his deep spiritual motivation, all knew he had accomplished something good for all mankind in his crusade.

In November of 1991, the Ronald Reagan Presidential Library was dedicated in Simi Valley, California. In a history-making gathering, five United States Presidents presided at the dedication. Honoring President Reagan were Presidents George Bush, Jimmy Carter, Gerald Ford and Richard Nixon. As they each took turns lauding Ronald Reagan, the words of President Richard Nixon, as always concise and to the point, best summed it up.

"This magnificent library is a splendid tribute to a great President of the United States. But, Ronald Reagan does not need a building to remind us of his legacy. He will always be remembered as the President who built up the military power, which President Bush used so brilliantly in winning our spectacular victory in the Persian Gulf.

He will be remembered even more for another reason. Throughout his career, Ronald Reagan has been a leader who had profound beliefs, the courage to fight for those beliefs and the eloquence to inspire his countrymen to support those beliefs.

He believed in the American dream.

He believed in freedom and democracy.

He believed America was on the right side of history, standing for what was good against the forces of evil in the world.

Some dismissed him as an ideologue. But history has proved he was right.

Permit me to put it in personal terms. Thirty-two years ago in Moscow, Soviet Premier Nikita Khrushchev jabbed his finger into my chest and said, 'Your grandchildren will live under Communism.' I replied, 'Your grandchildren will live in freedom.'

At that time, I was sure he was wrong. I was not sure I was right. Now we know.

Thanks in great part to the strong and idealistic leadership of President Ronald Reagan, Krushchev's grandchildren now live in freedom."

No more fitting or deserved accolades have been given any man!

END

EPILOGUE

"ONE MORE FOR THE GIPPER"

When the preceding chapter was written, it seemed like a fitting close to this narrative about Ronald Reagan and his impact upon the hearts and minds of his countrymen. After many years of involvement in the volatile world of politics, this author should have known that the crusade of Ronald Reagan would encounter fierce opposition as it attempted to surge onward after his retirement from active duty.

The presidential election of 1988, which elevated perpetual supporting player George Bush to the lead billing, appeared to be a final affirmation of Ronald Reagan's eight years of world leadership. There can be little argument that Bush rode into the Presidency on the broad shoulders of Ronald Reagan, with U.S. voters showing a strong desire to continue his legacy. There was little argument, apparently, except with George Bush himself. Political egos being what they are, President Bush saw the election as a personal mandate and quickly began to divorce himself from Reagan's policies while purging the carry-over Reagan team from his administration.

Bush's self-centered conviction of his own leadership qualities played right into the hands of the political opposition in the Democrat party. The Democrats, taking dead aim at the next Presidential election four years ahead, knew they had to destroy the Reagan legacy to have any hope of reoccupying the White House. Ronald Reagan hardly had time to settle into the saddle of his favorite horse at his California ranch before the vilification of the "Reagan Years" began. Not since the nonstop trashing of former President Herbert Hoover during the 1930's and 40's by the "New Deal" Democrats had there been such an unremitting attack on a former national leader. The generally whole-hearted support of the war against Reagan by the mostly liberal national news media was to be expected. What was unexpected and distressing to the American public was George Bush's unwillingness to come to the defense of Ronald Reagan against the highly personal attacks.

As bad as Bush's non-support of his political mentor was his almost total abandonment of Reagan's policies. George Bush, who freely admitted puzzlement over the "vision thing" as he put it, never established a clearness of purpose or a cohesive direction for the country. Instead of following the clearly-delineated path established by Reagan or forging his own vision, he sought accommodation with the opposition Democrats. Such a policy, really a lack of policy, led to the Bush Administration's becoming a poor echo of the very programs he had been elected to oppose. It would seem that George Bush was forever destined to be a "second banana"!

Unable, or unwilling, to mount a counterattack to the persistent Reagan bashing by the Democrats and their supporting news media, and with no cohesive vision of his own, Bush was a sitting duck for the opposition in 1992. Democrat William Clinton doggedly campaigned against the "selfish" Reagan years, while Bush gave him tacit support with a feeble promise to do better in the future. Clinton won the Presidency, as devoted Reagan supporters deserted Bush in electoral disgust.

The Democrats, blindly supported by the national news media, were seemingly no better at analyzing the American mood than had been the hapless Bush. Having won the election while mercilessly bashing Reagan, they concluded that more of the same would produce even greater results. Thus, the country endured the first two years of the Clinton Presidency with the incumbent spending more time continuing the campaign against Ronald Reagan than in running his administration.

With the 1994 national elections approaching, the leadership of the Democrat Party chose to continue along the 1992 path, misinterpreting the clear signs of an incipient voter revolt. The rumblings sounded to them as though the public was angry at opposition to their liberal agenda and ready to obliterate any vestige of the Reagan legacy still remaining. The Republican

Congress, however, rightly saw the discontent arising from the national agenda to erase Ronald Reagan from history. The Republican Congressional campaign, with a nationwide plan they labeled, a "Contract With America", came right out of the Gipper's playbook!

Apparently unheard by the general news media and the Democrat Party were the growing grass-roots-expressed desire to "bring Ron back". This longing for a return to the positive, upbeat leadership embodied in Ronald Reagan was not being helped by Reagan himself. The former President, unswervingly patriotic and with deep respect for the office of the Presidency, had, for six years, refrained from any public criticism or second guessing of his successors in office. The persistent quiet from the Reagan retirement office in California left his legion of supporters rudderless in the opposition storm. A very personal communication from Ronald Reagan hit the news wires in early November, 1994! In a personal, handwritten letter to the American public Ronald Reagan announced:

My Fellow Americans,

I have recently been told that I am one of the millions of Americans who will be afflicted with Alzheimer's Disease.

Upon learning this news, Nancy and I had to decide whether, as private citizens, we would keep this a private matter, or whether we would make this news known in a public way. In the past, Nancy suffered from breast cancer, and I had my cancer surgeries. We found that, through our open disclosures, we were able to raise public awareness. We were happy that, as a result, many more people underwent testing.

They were treated in early stages and were able to return to normal healthy lives.

So now, we feel it is important to share it with you. In opening our hearts, we hope this might promote greater awareness of this condition. Perhaps it will encourage a clearer understanding of the individuals and families who are affected by it.

At the moment, I feel just fine. I intend to live the remainder of the years God gives me on this earth doing the things I have always done. I will continue to share life's journey with my beloved Nancy and my family. I plan to enjoy the great outdoors and stay in touch with my friends and supporters.

Unfortunately, as Alzheimer's Disease progresses, the family often bears a heavy burden. I only wish that there was some way I could spare Nancy from this painful experience. When the time comes, I am confident that, with your help, she will face it with faith and courage.

In closing let me thank you, the American people, for giving me the great honor of allowing me to serve as your President. When the Lord calls me home, whenever that *may be, I will leave with the greatest love for this country of ours and eternal optimism for its future.*

I now begin the journey that will lead me into the sunset of my life. I know that, for America, there will always be a bright dawn ahead.

Thank you, my friends. May God always bless you.

Sincerely,
Ronald Reagan."

It is important to understand the circumstances and atmosphere in the country on the eve of that election in November, 1994. Ronald Reagan's well-remembered grace and morality stood out starkly in contrast to the devious nature and low personal standards of President Clinton. Although the Administration and liberal news media were giving lip service to restoring the country's higher moral purpose, their actions belied the words. The national memory of those Reagan years and the high respect for their moral direction were not fading.

The grace and godly faith of Ronald Reagan, as it always has, glowed like a beacon from his letter announcing the fatal illness. Here was none of the victimization or self-pity that had become the prevailing standard for the American opinion shapers.

The contrast was sharply outlined, as Democrats were actively campaigning against the Republican "Contract With America" as an attempt to return the country to those horrible "Reagan Years".

Well, as Ron would say, the opposition had hit the nail right on the head! A longing for a return to those "Reagan Years" was exactly what had the American public stirring in discontent!

With the election coming up less than a week after Reagan's letter, the Democrats were comfortable with opinion polls showing that they would surely retain control of the U.S. House of Representatives and, most probably, the U.S. Senate as well. Since there was insufficient time to assess any voter mood swings since Reagan's letter, the Democrats and their supporting liberal media were sure they had dodged another electoral bullet!

As was their regular habit, the liberal pundits had no inkling of the mood in America or the tremendous moral uplift that the Reagan letter had given to the voters. He had brought back their collective memories of the pride and optimism they had in their country during his Presidency. If these new Republicans really wanted to contract for a return to those upbeat Reagan years, the country was with them.

While not a single incumbent Republican in Congress was turned out, the American voters kicked out Democrats with abandon. Not only did control of the U.S. Congress fall to the GOP, but governorships and state legislatures nationwide also went strongly Republican!

The American public had expressed itself in no uncertain terms. They were ready to go back to the "Reagan Years". They had answered Ronald Reagan's letter in the best way they knew how. They had won —

"One More for the Gipper".

Honoring Our Nation's 40th President

Ronald Wilson Reagan, born on February 5, 1911, has strong roots in small-town, middle America.

Working his way through Eureka College and earning a Bachelor of Arts Degree in 1932, his commitment to leadership and following grounded values has set an example of patriotism, a legacy full of integrity and faith in the American spirit and way of life.

Ronald Wilson Reagan is without question America's most influential leader of modern times and is the pre-eminent historical figure of recent years. In honor of Reagan's contributions to America, *The Norman and harriet Wymbs Foundation* has commissioned the design and creation of an extraordinary work of art.

The pose for this sculpture, the President astride a standing Palomino, originates from a Reagan visit to the estate of Mr. Charles Walgreen during one of "Dutch's" trips to his boyhood home-town, Dixon, Illinois.

The Reagan Bronze embodies not only a hint of his greatness, it captures for posterity Reagan's unshakable faith in the American spirit. His charismatic, avuncular persona is eloquently portrayed in this piece of valuable art.

The sculptor, D.L. Reed is a fourth generation foundry man. He has studied and trained both in America and France. His work is collected at home and abroad by corporate leaders, industrialists, political dignitaries, and social and cultural luminaries too numerous to mention.

The Reagan Bronze will be produced in D.L. Reed's own foundry in the United States. As both the artist and foundry man, Reed will maintain artistic control and supervision of the molding and casting process. This will insure a level of care and quality, rarely found in the production of collectable, fine art.

THE REAGAN BRONZE STATUE

Perpetuating a legacy is traditional in the United States. Weighing fifty pounds, this seventeen inch high, by six inch wide, by eighteen inch long Reagan Bronze is a statement of the Reagan Legacy and is a fitting tribute to a great American and honored Commander-in-Chief.

Your tax deductible purchase of $6,800 for this beautiful table-size original will contribute to the completion of the life-size version.

The eight and one half foot tall life-size bronze will grace the Central Hall of the Dixon Historic Center. This center, located at South Central School, celebrates Ronald Reagan's years in Dixon and his attendance there as a young student.

Ronald Reagan Bronze Statue - Order Form

Please place my order immediately so that I may be assigned the next edition number.

Confirmation of your order will be made to your address or phone. Thank you.

Payment Schedule: $3,400 deposit
           Balance: $3,400 (due prior to shipment)
      Full Price: $6,800 (Plus shipping and handling)

Name: _____

Street Address: _____

City:_____ State ____ Zip _____

ORDERING INFORMATION

RONALD REAGAN'S CRUSADE
(HARDCOVER)

PLEASE CALL, WRITE OR FAX TO:

VYTIS Press, Inc.
5100 North Federal Highway
Ft. Lauderdale, FL 33308
PHONE: (954) 772-1236
FAX: (954) 772-8707

PRICE (EACH) $25.00 USD
NUMBER OF BOOKS   _____
TOTAL   _____
SALES TAX - FL RESIDENTS (6%)   _____
S / H ($1.50 PER BOOK)   _____

                              TOTAL   _____

WE ACCEPT

CHECK
MONEY ORDER (U.S.D.)